myBook 2

Authors and Advisors

Alma Flor Ada • Kylene Beers • F. Isabel Campoy
Joyce Armstrong Carroll • Nathan Clemens
Anne Cunningham • Martha C. Hougen
Elena Izquierdo • Carol Jago • Erik Palmer
Robert E. Probst • Shane Templeton • Julie Washington

Contributing Consultants

David Dockterman • Mindset Works®
Jill Eggleton

Printed in the U.S.A.

ISBN 978-1-328-76047-0

5 6 7 8 9 10 2536 27 26 25 24 23 22 21 20 19

4500770643 B C D E F G

myBook 2

Welcome to myBook!

Do you like to read different kinds of texts for all kinds of reasons? Do you have a favorite genre or author? What can you learn from a video? Do you think carefully about what you read and view?

Here are some tips to get the MOST out of what you read and view:

Set a Purpose. What is the title? What is the genre? What do you want to learn from this text or video? What about it looks interesting to you?

Read and Annotate. As you read, underline and highlight important words and ideas. Make notes about things you want to figure out or remember. What questions do you have? What are your favorite parts? Write them down!

Make Connections. How does the text or video connect to what you already know? To other texts or videos? To your own life or community? Talk to others about your ideas. Listen to their ideas, too.

Wrap It Up! Look back at your questions and annotations. What did you like best? What did you learn? What do you still want to know? How will you find out?

As you read the texts and watch the videos in this book, make sure you get the MOST out of them by using the tips above.

But, don't stop there… Decide what makes you curious, find out more about it, have fun, and never stop learning!

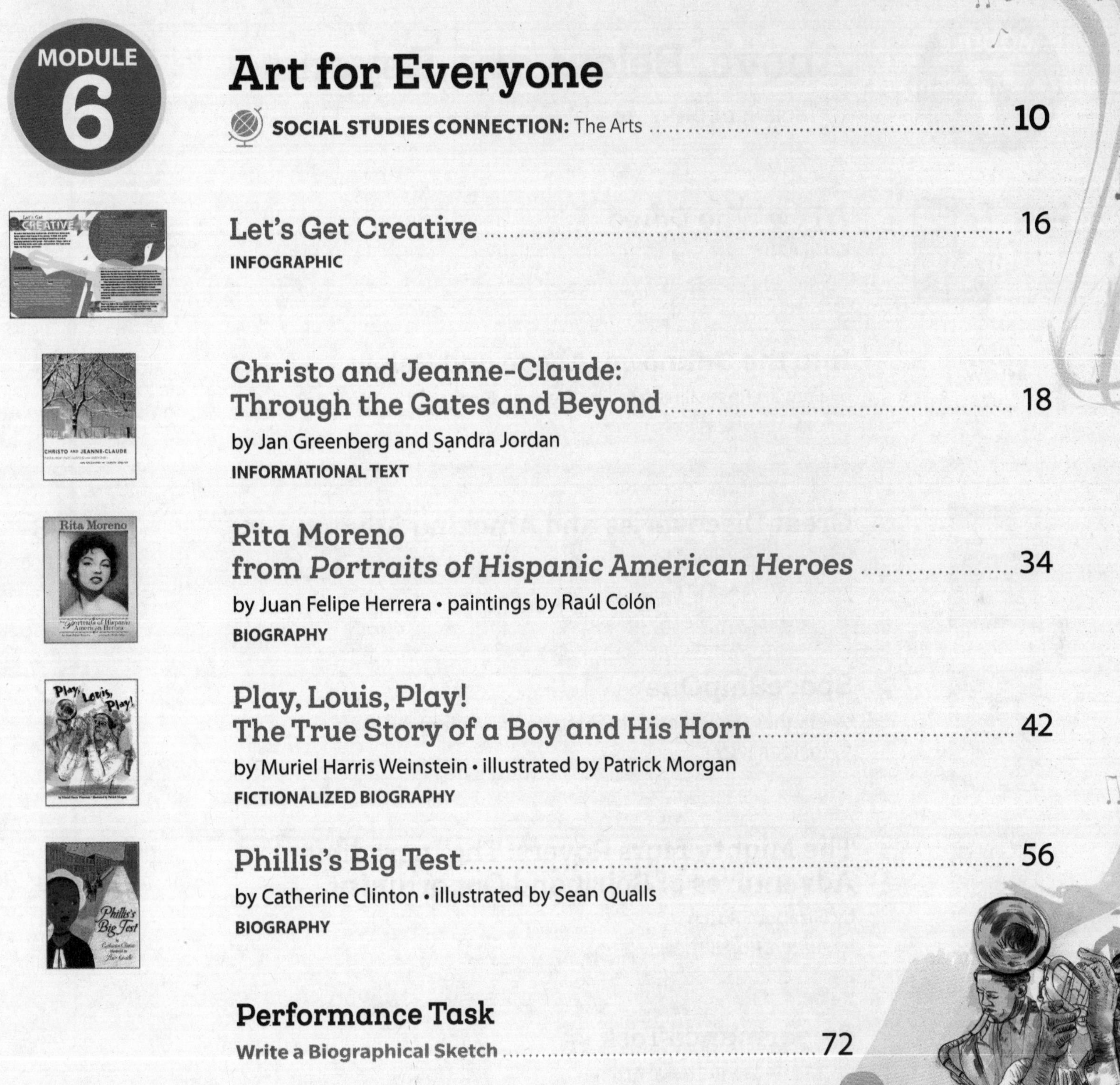

MODULE 6

Art for Everyone

MODULE 7

Above, Below, and Beyond

MODULE 8

A New Home

MODULE 9

Unexpected, Unexplained

MODULE 10

The Lives of Animals

MODULE 6

Art for Everyone

"The world is but canvas to our imaginations."

—Henry David Thoreau

Essential Question

How do different art forms impact people in different ways?

Big Idea Words

Words About the Arts

The words in the chart will help you talk and write about the selections in this module. Which words about the arts have you seen before? Which words are new to you?

Add to the Vocabulary Network on page 13 by writing synonyms, antonyms, and related words and phrases for each word about the arts.

After you read each selection in this module, come back to the Vocabulary Network and keep building it. Add more boxes if you need to.

WORD	MEANING	CONTEXT SENTENCE
classic (adjective)	A classic piece of art, music, or literature is one that people appreciate for many years. Its popularity is not just temporary.	*Mona Lisa* is a classic painting that people have been admiring for hundreds of years.
tribute (noun)	A tribute is something that is said or done to show respect for someone's work or actions.	The ceremony included a tribute to the respected woman.
striking (adjective)	If you describe something as "striking" you mean it's very impressive or noticeable.	The huge, colorful mural on the side of the school building is very striking.
provoking (adjective)	Something that is provoking causes a reaction, such as a thought-provoking book.	The thought-provoking story made me wonder how it feels to be an immigrant.

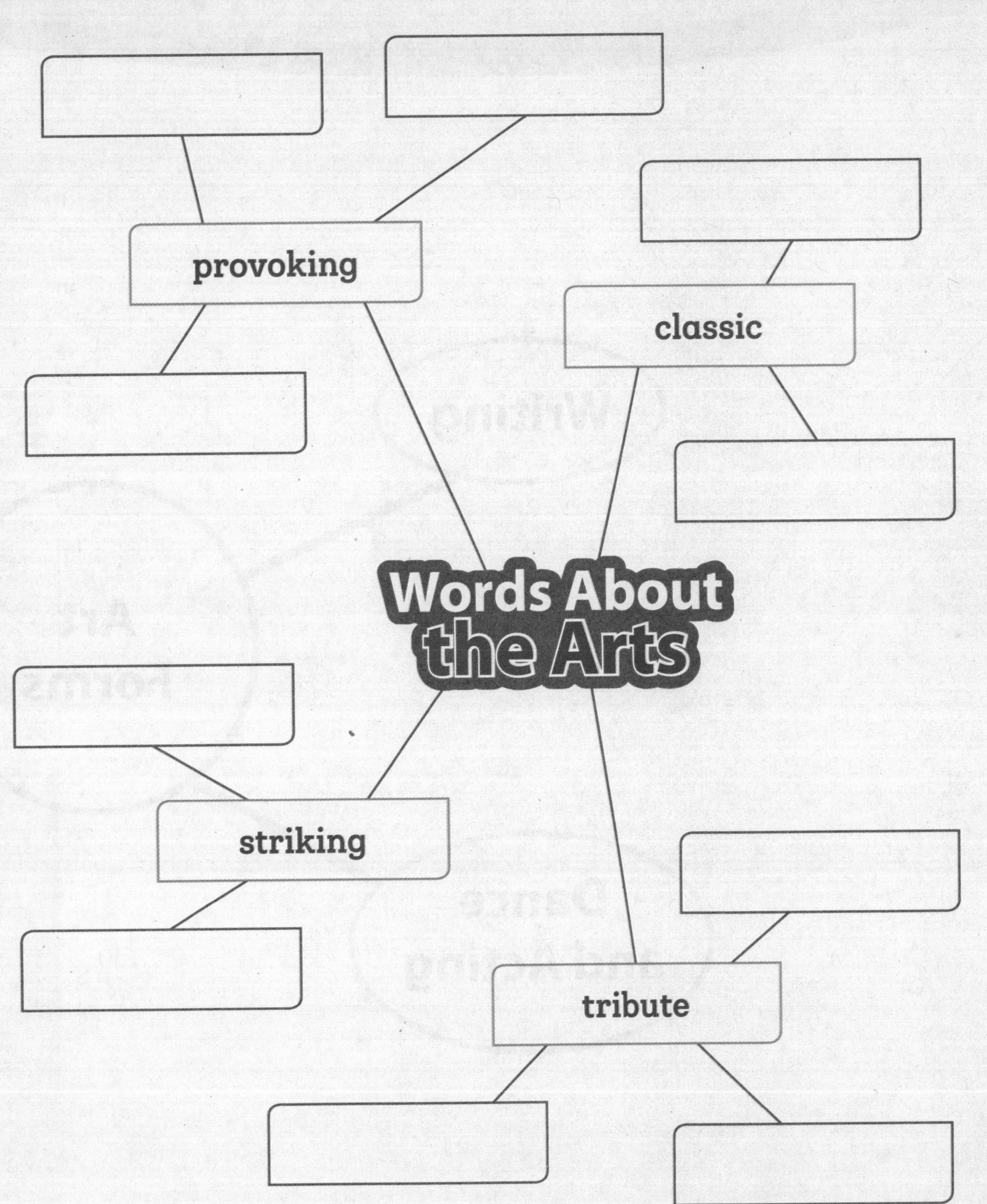
Words About the Arts
provoking
classic
striking
tribute

Knowledge Map

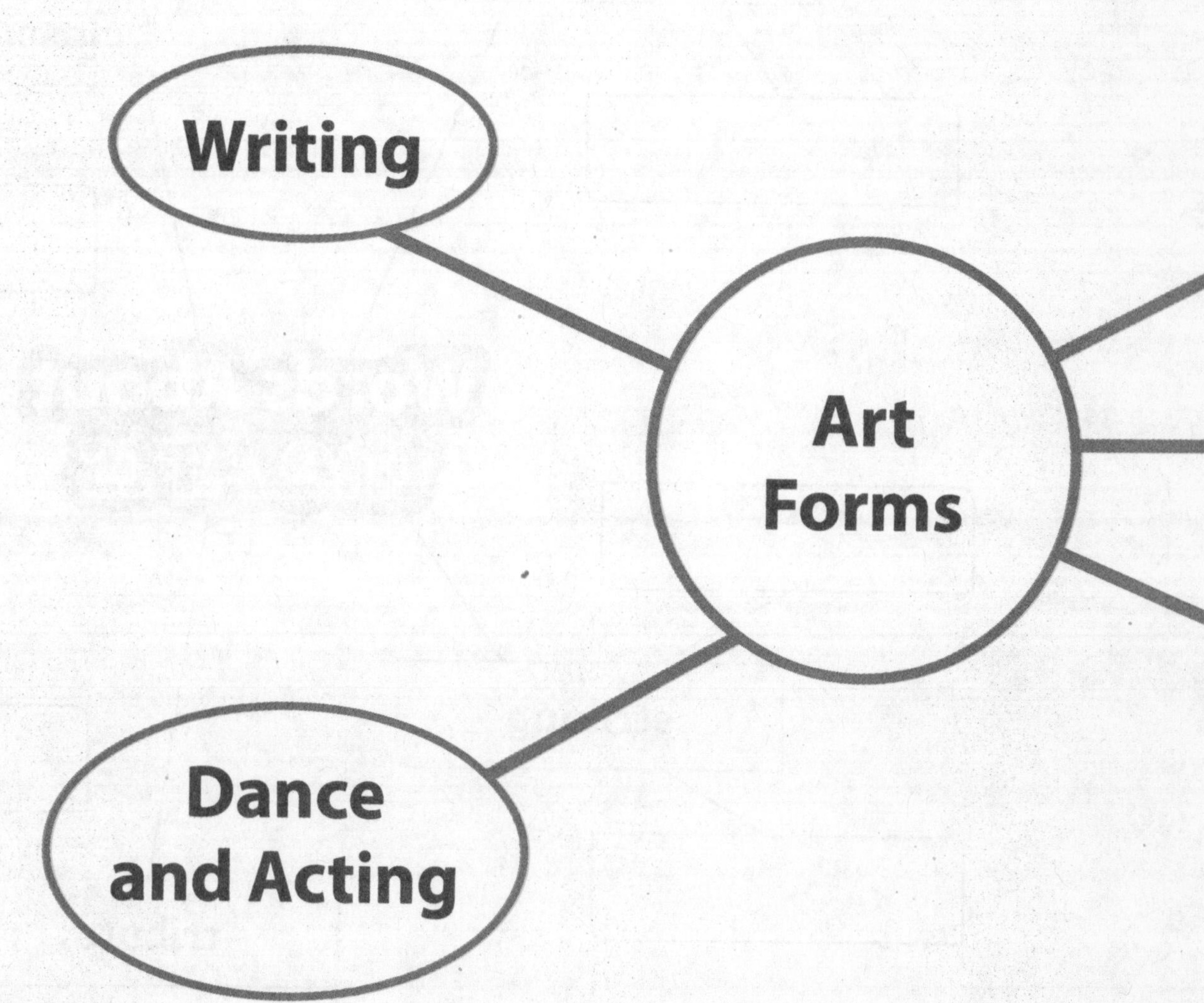

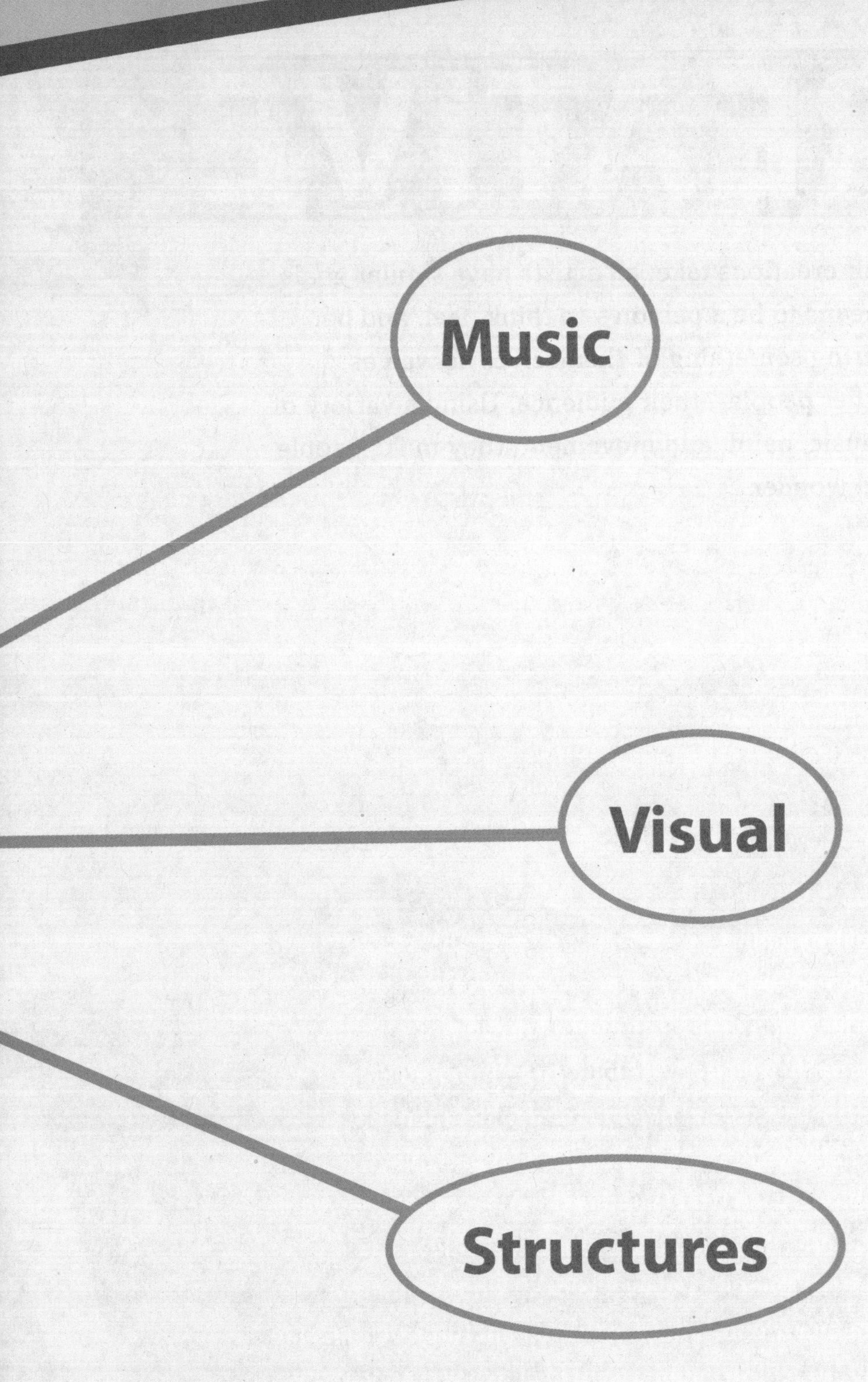
Music
Visual
Structures

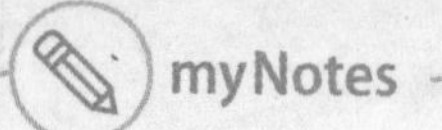
myNotes

Short Read

Let's Get CREATIVE

1 No matter what form their creations take, all artists have similar goals. Artists explore what it means to be a person—to think, feel, and be. They're interested in sharing something of themselves as well as provoking emotions in other people—their audience. Using a variety of tools, including words, music, paint, and movement, they make people laugh, cry, fear, hope, and wonder.

Storytelling

2 People have been using words creatively for many thousands of years. Storytelling began long before people invented writing. Back then, people passed stories along orally. The oldest known written story is a classic tale, ***The Epic of Gilgamesh***, which pays tribute to an honored king. It was first written on clay tablets in the late second or early third millennium B.C.E.

3 Today's storytellers have many ways to share their work: books, plays, screenplays, magazines, and blogs. Even tweets and text messages can be creative. Writers can use words, letters, and even emojis to communicate ideas.

4 Writers' stories describe places, people, and events of all kinds. Some are fantastic, such as an interplanetary friendship set in the distant future. Others are more realistic, such as a lonely student struggling to fit in at a new school. Writers often use dialogue to help readers understand characters' relationships, moods, and motives.

Visual Art

5 Carved stone and shell beads from Africa are the oldest known examples of visual art. Some experts think that some of these objects of art were created about 75,000 years ago. In Europe, people made stone carvings and simple yet **striking** cave drawings more than 35,000 years ago. Over the centuries, ancient artists used a variety of media, from clay and cloth to bone and wood, to make objects that were beautiful and often useful as well. These ancient artifacts tell us stories about what it was like to live long ago.

6 Modern visual artists tell stories and provoke emotion by painting with oils, acrylics, and watercolors. They carve in wood and stone and sculpt in clay. They work with metal, plaster, cloth, and many other materials. They take photographs. Digital tools, from cameras to computers and cell phones, enable artists to collect, duplicate, and alter images to create art. Digital art can reach audiences all over the world.

Music and Movement

7 Music has been around since ancient times. The first musical instrument was the human voice. The oldest known crafted instruments, flutes made from bone and ivory and discovered in Europe, are about 40,000 years old! Since that time, humans have used many other instruments, from animal-skin drums to synthesizers, to make music.

8 Today's musicians may perform before thousands of fans and many share recorded music digitally with millions of fans. Yet these artists have the same goal as the earliest music makers. They want to connect with others through the power of sound.

9 In the art of dance, movement expresses emotion. The first dances were probably performed in religious ceremonies. Later, people began to dance as a way to socialize and have fun. Ballet and modern dance use music and movement to tell stories or evoke moods.

10 There's no limit to the ways humans can express themselves. Maybe the future will bring new, unimaginable art forms. One thing is for certain, though: the human urge to create will always enrich our world.

Notice & Note
Quoted Words

Prepare to Read

GENRE STUDY **Informational texts** give facts and examples about a topic.

- Authors of informational texts may organize their ideas using main ideas with key details, including facts and quotations.
- Informational texts may include visuals, such as photographs.
- Informational texts include text features, such as headings and captions. Some information may be shown in bulleted lists.

SET A PURPOSE **Think about** the title and genre of this text. What do you know about visual artists? What do you want to learn? Write your ideas below.

CRITICAL VOCABULARY

- gracing
- controversy
- skeptical
- manufactured
- incorporated
- persistence
- ambitious
- ingenious
- opinion
- traversed

Meet the Authors:
Jan Greenberg and Sandra Jordan

CHRISTO AND JEANNE-CLAUDE

THROUGH THE GATES AND BEYOND

JAN GREENBERG AND SANDRA JORDAN

myNotes

THE GATES

CENTRAL PARK, NEW YORK CITY 1979–2005

"We have never done a sad work."
Christo

"Most human beings are afraid of what is new. It is our work to convince them that they will enjoy it, and even if they don't, to allow us just for sixteen days to create a work of art."
Jeanne-Claude

1 In the winter of 2005, Christo and Jeanne-Claude became two of the most visible artists in the world, gracing the covers of magazines from New York to Japan. What had riveted the world's attention? *The Gates, Central Park, New York City, 1979–2005*, the largest work of art ever created for the largest of all American cities, was about to be completed with great fanfare. Seventy-five hundred and three shimmering saffron panels would be unfurled in New York's Central Park. Would *The Gates* cause celebration or controversy?

2 BACK IN 1979 what were the chances of Christo and Jeanne-Claude constructing a giant artwork stretching 23 miles through Central Park? After all, Central Park is New Yorkers' big backyard, the place where they run, bike, walk dogs, play ball, skate, and even take rides in horse-drawn carriages. It has acres of green grass. Thousands of stately trees. Long curving paths, a lake, ponds, fountains, a castle, a zoo, sculptures, and a merry-go-round. The mayor was skeptical of the artists' proposal. Some environmentalists worried about it damaging the park's trees, plants, and wildlife. In 1981, the Parks Commissioner published a 185-page book saying "no."

gracing If a photo is gracing the cover of a magazine, it is making the cover attractive.
controversy If something is a controversy, people have strong feelings and disagreements about it.
skeptical If you are skeptical about something, you have doubts about it.

CHRISTO: *The Gates Project for Central Park, New York City. Drawing in two parts.* (top)

Jeanne-Claude and Christo (left)

Steel for the bases was manufactured at ISG steel mill in Pennsylvania. *(left)*

Special saffron nylon fabric was woven at the Schilgen plant in Germany, then sewn and cut into panels. *(center, right)*

3 But Christo and Jeanne-Claude never give up easily. All of their grand-scale outdoor works of art are the result of countless meetings with countless people over long periods of time. Talking to the public about their concerns is part of the artistic process, and issues—from the environment to safety and the use of the site—are incorporated into the work. Getting a "yes" took energy, persistence, and 26 years. Finally, in 2003, the artists signed a 43-page contract with the city allowing *The Gates* to go forward. The long wait was over. On February 12, 2005, Christo and Jeanne-Claude would transform Central Park into one huge work of art.

4 Who would pay for such an ambitious undertaking? The artists accept neither sponsors nor public money. All outdoor projects are financed by the sale of Christo's "indoor" artworks—including collages, drawings, scale models, and some early works.

manufactured Something that is manufactured was made in a factory.

incorporated If items are incorporated into something bigger, they are included in it.

persistence A person who has persistence keeps doing something even when it is hard and takes a long time.

ambitious If a project is ambitious, it is large and requires a lot of work.

myNotes 

5 For months Christo holed up in his studio, often spending 15 hours a day making preparatory drawings. Downstairs, Jeanne-Claude fielded telephone calls and organized thousands of details. As creative partners, the artists worked together in a whirlwind of activity.

6 Usually an artist labors in the studio and exhibits a finished artwork in a museum or gallery. But *The Gates* would be erected in Central Park while the whole world watched.

7 In January of 2005, 15,006 mysterious looking black steel boxes were spaced roughly every 12 feet along the miles of paths in the park. These boxes were actually solid bases, an ingenious solution to the problem of supporting the posts without digging holes in the grass or walkways.

8 On February 6, six days before *The Gates* was scheduled to open, 600 workers, paid by Christo and Jeanne-Claude, fanned out across the park in teams of eight. They confirmed that the black boxes were level. On the bases they put up tall, saffron-colored poles made in a factory for that project. Tightly wrapped banners extended across the tops, ready to be unfurled.

ingenious If an idea is ingenious, it is very clever or has not been tried before.

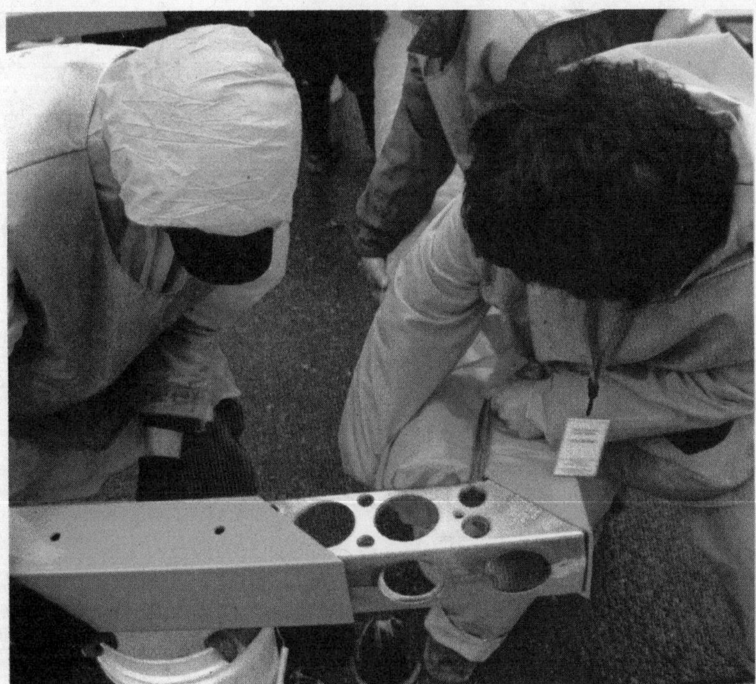

Aluminum corner sleeves are inserted into the tops of the vertical poles and bolted in place.

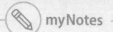

The gates are elevated and bolted onto the bases.

9 **The public became more and more curious.**

10 Television and newspaper commentators argued back and forth. It seemed as if everyone had an opinion. Why would these two artists spend millions of dollars to create a gigantic artwork that would remain for only two weeks?

11 **Was it art?**
What did it mean?
Why did they do it?

12 When questioned, the artists always insist that they make their art to please themselves. Jeanne-Claude says, "Artists paint apples because they have the urge to paint apples. And if people like the art, that's a bonus."

13 Now *The Gates* would snake through Central Park, offering a fiery burst of color on a bleak winter landscape. It was Christo and Jeanne-Claude's 21 million-dollar gift to their adopted city.

14 You had to be there to see it.
You couldn't wait.
Because in 16 days it would all disappear.
The stage was set for opening day.

opinion Your opinion is what you think or believe about something.

ENTER THE GATES

"Nobody can buy these projects. Nobody can own these projects. Nobody can charge tickets for these projects. Even we do not own these projects."

Christo and Jeanne-Claude

FIVE, FOUR, THREE, TWO, ONE! As crews unfurl each saffron fabric panel into the freezing February morning, the crowd cheers. Thousands of people are gathered to watch teams of workers, dressed in gray uniforms with "The Gates" emblazoned in bright orange, spread out across Central Park and set the panels free. Surrounded by Mayor Bloomberg, officials of New York, and other well-wishers, Christo and Jeanne-Claude laugh with joy. Like fluted columns, the nylon fabric panels seem to stand in silence for a moment . . . then, with a gust of wind, they float back and forth in swaying rhythms.

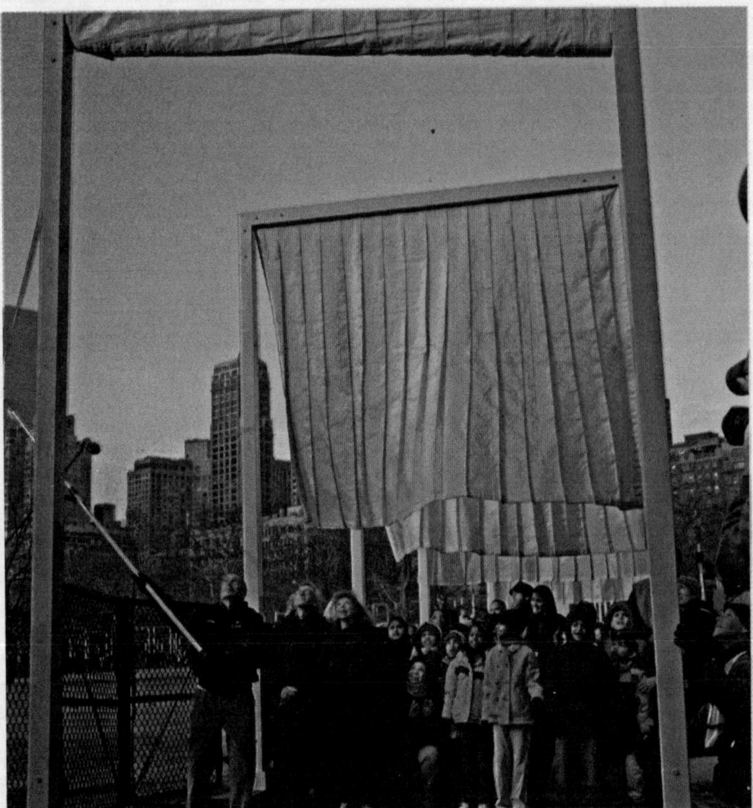

New York City mayor Michael R. Bloomberg opens one of the first gates with Christo and Jeanne-Claude beside him.

16 "Look at the colors, the light," says Christo. "It's like a painting." A painting with nature as its canvas!

17 *The Gates* follows the 23 miles of walkways, from 59th Street across from the fabled Plaza Hotel up to 110th Street in Harlem. It spreads in ripples of brilliant saffron, weaving, circling through the footpaths of the great park . . . in and out . . . up and down, crisscrossing and rising. Old linden, oak, and maple trees hover, their bare branches forming skeletal patterns against the blue sky. The New York City skyline rises beyond the park. From grand brick and limestone buildings and hotels on Central Park South, spectators can get a bird's-eye view of the saffron canopies. The artists say, "They [are] like a golden river appearing and disappearing through the bare branches."

18 "People enter Central Park in a ceremonial way. It is surrounded by a stone wall," says Christo. "There are many entrances, each called a gate by the landscape architects, Frederick Law Olmsted and Calvert Vaux, who designed the park. *The Gates* is a very ceremonial project, a festive project." Once the gates are completely unfurled, a parade of people march through them from one end of the park to the other.

19 "The fabric has a dynamic quality," says Christo. "All our projects are like living objects. They are in continuous motion all the time, moving with the wind."

20 The weather affects the way we experience *The Gates*. On some days the sky is flat and gray and the fabric panels hang solidly against the dark sky. On other days the sky is blue and the wind is blowing—the panels flap and wave, and seem to glitter in the bright light. Rain, snow, sunshine, each change in the weather gives us a new view of the work.

Aerial view of part of *The Gates*. *(left)*

21 People fly in from all over the globe. Hotels in Manhattan are filled, the restaurants booked. For 16 days, it seems as if everyone in New York is trying to find the words to describe what they saw and felt. But young or old, rich or poor, New Yorker or tourist, art lover or skeptic, they all have something to say about the artwork in the park!

22 "It touches people. And it makes people happy."

"*The Gates* reminds me of Samurai warriors, their orange banners raised, marching through the park."

"I come every day. My favorite was the day it snowed. My dog liked it, too."

23 "THE GREATEST SURPRISE of a project," says Jeanne-Claude, "is that when it is completed it is a million times more beautiful than our wildest dreams." Those who use the park all the time and take it for granted find themselves noticing the details with a fresh eye—the stone arched bridge, the copper beech trees, the reflection of the gates in a half-frozen pond, the birds, gray rock formations.

24 Jeanne-Claude asserts again and again, **"It has no purpose. It is not a symbol. It is not a message."** During their many trips to the park, when fans surround the artists, asking them to pose for photographs, Jeanne-Claude in her direct way instructs them to look at *The Gates*, not at her and Christo.

25 Then suddenly it's over. After 16 stunning days, workers begin to remove the artwork. By the middle of March, as promised by the artists, the materials are hauled away, the steel bases melted down to be recycled, the aluminum used for cans of soda, the fabric shredded and made into carpet padding. The vinyl poles are also recycled. The artists do not sell any part of *The Gates* to private collectors or museums. When spring arrives a few weeks later, and flowering trees blossom in the park, no trace of *The Gates* remains, except in our memories, the photographs, books, a film, and countless articles.

26 Christo likes the expression "once upon a time." He has said, "Once upon a time, *The Gates* were in Central Park." Jeanne-Claude has something else on her mind: "As soon as *The Gates* come down, we will continue working on our next project."

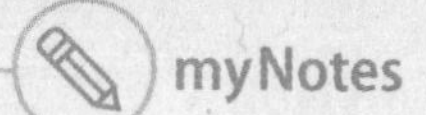

THE GATES

SOME STATISTICS

27 **CHRISTO AND JEANNE-CLAUDE** became familiar with every inch of the 23 miles of paths their gates traversed. Most of the gates were sited and then spaced 12 feet apart, but sometimes an overhanging branch or low-growing tree made an adjustment necessary. Not even one branch was trimmed, tree roots were avoided, and rock formations were respected. All proceeds from the sale of posters, mugs, T-shirts, sweatshirts, and other memorabilia went to support nature protection foundations.

28 **CHIEF ENGINEER AND DIRECTOR OF CONSTRUCTION:** Vince Davenport
PROJECT DIRECTOR: Jonita Davenport

29 To put up **7,503** gates took the following materials, which were manufactured to Christo and Jeanne-Claude's exacting specifications: 7,503 gates, 16 feet high. The width varies from 5 feet 6 inches to 18 feet, depending on the width of the path.

- **315,491 LINEAR FEET** of recyclable saffron-colored vinyl tubing, to make the five-inch square vertical and horizontal poles
- **5,290 TONS** of steel to make 15,006 steel bases that weigh 600 to 800 pounds each, to make certain that each gate was stable
- **15,006** cast-aluminum corner reinforcements
- **165,000** bolts and self-locking nuts
- **116,389 MILES** of saffron nylon thread to make 46 miles of hems
- **7,503** panels made of woven nylon, a highly reflective synthetic fabric

traversed A gate that traversed a path extended across it.

Respond to the Text

Collaborative Discussion

CHRISTO AND JEANNE-CLAUDE
THROUGH THE GATES AND BEYOND

Look back at what you wrote on page 18. Tell a partner two things you learned from the text. Then work with a group to discuss the questions below. Look for details in *Christo and Jeanne-Claude* to support your ideas. In your discussion, cite specific details from the text and summarize key points.

1. Review pages 20–23. Why did it take 26 years for *The Gates* to be approved? What challenges did the artists have to overcome?

2. Reread page 29. What happened to *The Gates* after the project ended? What does it show about the artists' motives?

3. What does the text tell you about the two artists and their reasons for making *The Gates?*

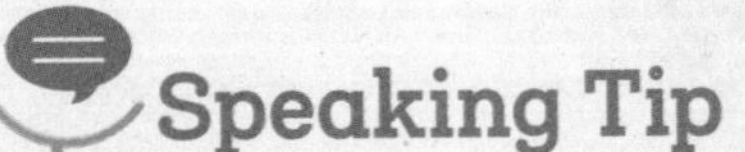

Listening Tip

Listen to each speaker's ideas and think about how they connect to important points in the text.

Speaking Tip

Build on other speakers' ideas by quoting or summarizing related points from the text.

Write an Editorial

PROMPT

In *Christo and Jeanne-Claude*, you read about two artists and their idea to create a giant work of art called *The Gates*. The authors wrote that "it seemed as if everyone had an opinion" about *The Gates*.

Imagine that you live in New York before *The Gates* was created. Write an editorial for your school or local newspaper arguing either for or against the creation of *The Gates*. Use facts and details from the text to explain why you think *The Gates* will either enhance or disrupt the use of the park. Don't forget to use some of the Critical Vocabulary words in your writing.

PLAN

Make notes based on the text's central ideas and supporting details. Then write your opinion.

WRITE

Now write your editorial arguing for or against *The Gates*.

Make sure your editorial

- ☐ states your opinion clearly.
- ☐ provides reasons for your opinion.
- ☐ uses evidence from the text to support your reasons.
- ☐ is organized in an order that makes sense.
- ☐ ends with a concluding sentence.

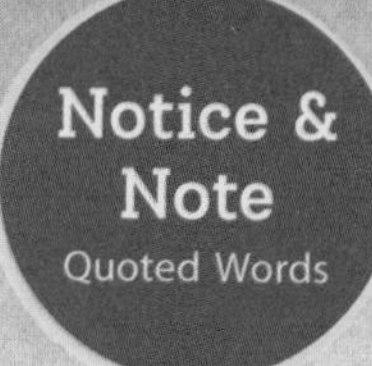

Prepare to Read

GENRE STUDY A **biography** is the story of a real person's life written by someone other than that person.

- Authors of biographies present events and details about a person in ways that help readers better understand him or her.
- Authors of biographies use literary language and devices, such as idioms, to describe major events in a person's life.
- Biographies often include the subject's own words.

SET A PURPOSE **Think about** the title and genre of this text. What do you know about Rita Moreno? What do you want to learn? Write your ideas below.

CRITICAL VOCABULARY

- exposure
- willful
- stereotypical
- authentic
- discriminatory

Meet the Author and Illustrator: Juan Felipe Herrera and Raúl Colón

Rita Moreno

from Portraits of Hispanic American Heroes

by Juan Felipe Herrera · *paintings by* Raúl Colón

BORN: DECEMBER 11, 1931, IN HUMACAO, PUERTO RICO

1 **"I finally got a chance . . .** to play a real Hispanic person, . . . someone with character and strength!" said Rita Moreno about her 1962 Oscar-winning role in *West Side Story*. By then she had been in over twenty films. Rita held that Oscar up high, like the Statue of Liberty grasping the torch.

2 Rosa Dolores Alverio came from a family of *jíbaros*, small independent rural farmers in Puerto Rico. During the Great Depression, Rosa's mother left for New York City to work in the garment industry and took her daughter, known as Rosita, along. Rosita missed her little brother and father, and her homeland, and she didn't speak any English. There wasn't any extra money, but her mother enrolled her in dance classes because Rosita really wanted to learn to dance.

3 When Rosita was seven, she made her first public appearance, dancing at a nightclub in Greenwich Village. During the day she would struggle to learn English at school, and at night she took acting and dance classes and went to auditions. At the age of thirteen, Rosita landed her first role on Broadway.

4 Soon enough Rosita caught the attention of Hollywood talent scouts. This led to more professional song and dance shows and her first film, *So Young, So Bad*. Still a teenager, she shortened her first name, changed her last name, and became Rita Moreno.

5 Even though she was getting public exposure, Rita was not happy with the casting roles where she had to dance barefoot, make pouty and sulky faces, and act sultry. Then the big break came—a chance to audition for *West Side Story*. She tried out for the role of Anita, the strong, willful older sister who is the head of the family. There was not one but three auditions—in acting, singing, and dancing. "The thing that scared me the most was dancing, because I hadn't danced at that time for at least ten years!" Rita registered for dance classes before the audition. Trying to get her groove back, she rehearsed jazz dance eight hours a day until the audition. Rita won the role, and then she won the Oscar. She had come a long way.

> **"There were no role models. I was my own role model—myself."**

6 "Once I had that little gold man [the Oscar] in my grasp, I thought, okay, that's it—no more of those stereotypical Conchita-Lolitas." But Rita was not offered a serious role and did not make a major film for the next seven years. "I just couldn't believe that I wasn't getting any offers," she said.

exposure If someone gets a lot of exposure, he or she becomes well known by performing in many places.
willful A person who is willful is very determined to get what he or she wants.
stereotypical A stereotypical idea is one that is false about a particular group, even though many people believe it.

myNotes

7 So she turned to acting onstage and performed in London and New York. It was one place where people of color could reach for the stars and just maybe catch one. Television was another option—*The Muppets*, *The George Lopez Show*. In the seventies she focused her talents on children's shows, appearing on *Sesame Street* and *The Electric Company*. Rita's mission was to inspire Hispanic children. When interviewed at the time, she mentioned how alone she had felt as a child because she was different, and she wanted the new generations of children to feel positive about their identities. Rita told the media proudly that she was Latina and knew what it felt like to be different.

8 By the end of the '70s Rita Moreno's dream came true. Measuring five feet and two and half inches, she became one of the all-time great Puerto Rican entertainers—the only female artist to win the four major entertainment awards: an Oscar, a Tony, a Grammy, and two Emmys. When her star was unveiled on the Hollywood Walk of Fame, Rita fell on it, weeping. "I had been dreaming of this day since I was six."

9 Rita Moreno's life and career were not merely lists of outstanding work and dazzling awards in the performing arts. Rita continued to cross boundaries and to break borders—not for herself but for others, young people in particular. For Latino children and youth, she became a new positive figure, a multitalented, authentic model of creative action.

10 In June of 2004, President George W. Bush awarded Rita Moreno the Presidential Medal of Freedom. She was acknowledged as a great artist and a pioneer in her ability to go beyond the early discriminatory practices of Hollywood.

authentic A person who is authentic is real and true to himself or herself, not fake or phony.

discriminatory Rules, laws, or practices are discriminatory if they leave out a group of people or treat that group unfairly.

Respond to the Text

Collaborative Discussion

Look back at what you wrote on page 34. Talk with a partner about what you learned during reading. Then work with a group to discuss the questions below. Make your answers stronger by including details from *Rita Moreno*. Show respect for others' ideas by following your class's rules for a good discussion.

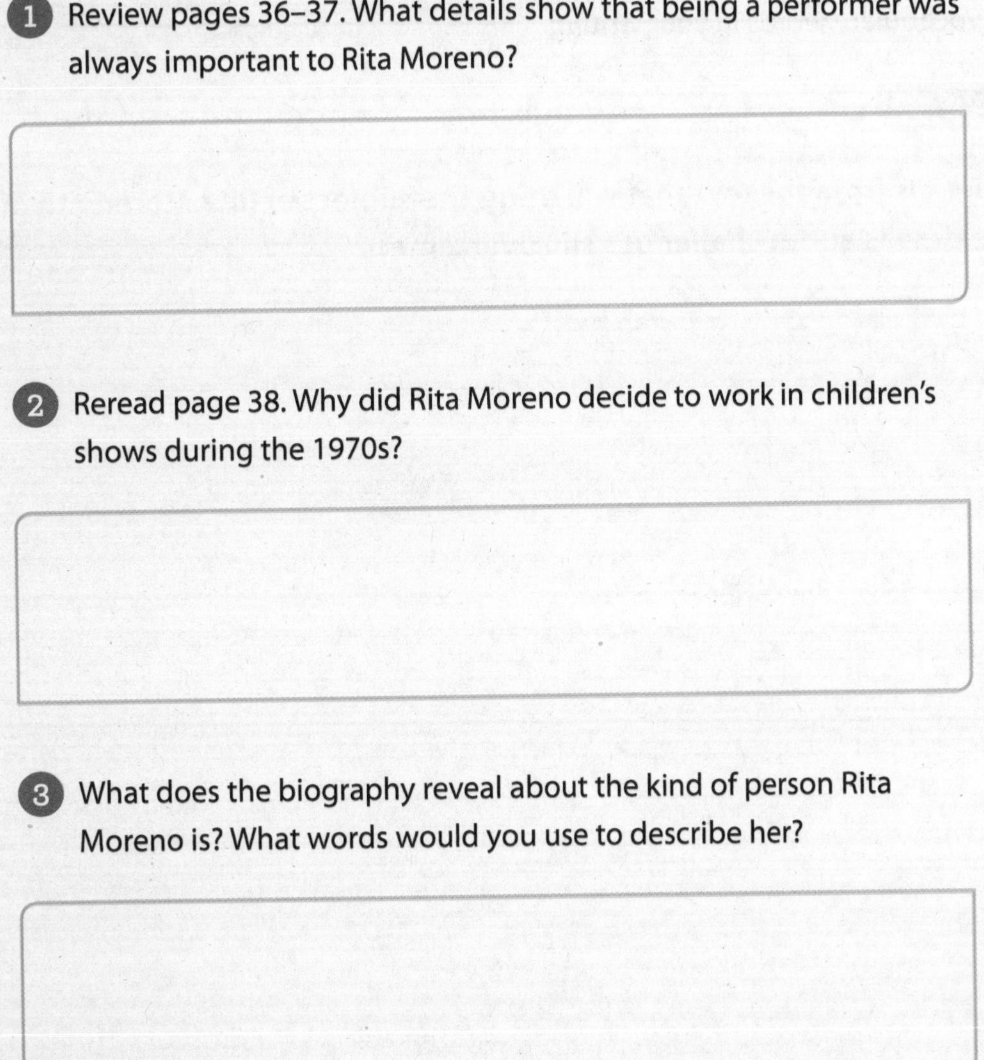

1. Review pages 36–37. What details show that being a performer was always important to Rita Moreno?

2. Reread page 38. Why did Rita Moreno decide to work in children's shows during the 1970s?

3. What does the biography reveal about the kind of person Rita Moreno is? What words would you use to describe her?

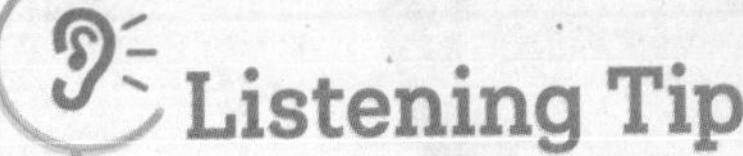

Listening Tip

Show that you are paying attention by looking toward each classmate while he or she is speaking.

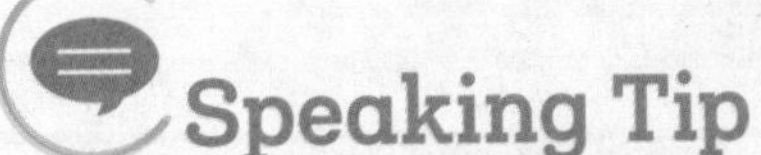

Speaking Tip

Wait for your turn to speak. If you disagree with someone, do so politely and use details from the text to explain your thinking.

Cite Text Evidence

Write a Speech

PROMPT

In the biography *Rita Moreno*, you read about the challenges Rita Moreno encountered as she achieved success.

Imagine that you have been asked to introduce Rita Moreno at an awards ceremony held in her honor. Write a speech that you will present at the awards ceremony telling about the challenges she overcame in her career. Don't forget to use some of the Critical Vocabulary words in your writing.

PLAN

Write details from the text that will bring the subject of Rita Moreno to life. Include details about challenges she overcame.

WRITE

Now write your speech about the challenges Rita Moreno overcame in her career.

Make sure your speech

- ☐ begins with a clear, focused introduction.
- ☐ identifies challenges Rita Moreno overcame in her career.
- ☐ uses facts and details from the text.
- ☐ presents information in an order that makes sense.
- ☐ includes a closing statement.

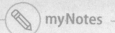

Notice & Note
Words of the Wiser

Prepare to Read

GENRE STUDY A **fictionalized biography** is the story of a real person's life that includes some made-up events or characters.

- Biographies present events in sequential, or chronological, order to help readers understand what happened and when.
- Fictionalized biographies can include literary language and devices, and they often read like a story.
- A fictionalized biography may be told from the point of view of a fictional character.

SET A PURPOSE **Think about** the title and genre of this text. What do you know about Louis Armstrong? What do you want to learn? Write your ideas below.

Meet the Author: Muriel Harris Weinstein

CRITICAL VOCABULARY

- bars
- contagious
- fever
- duets
- solos

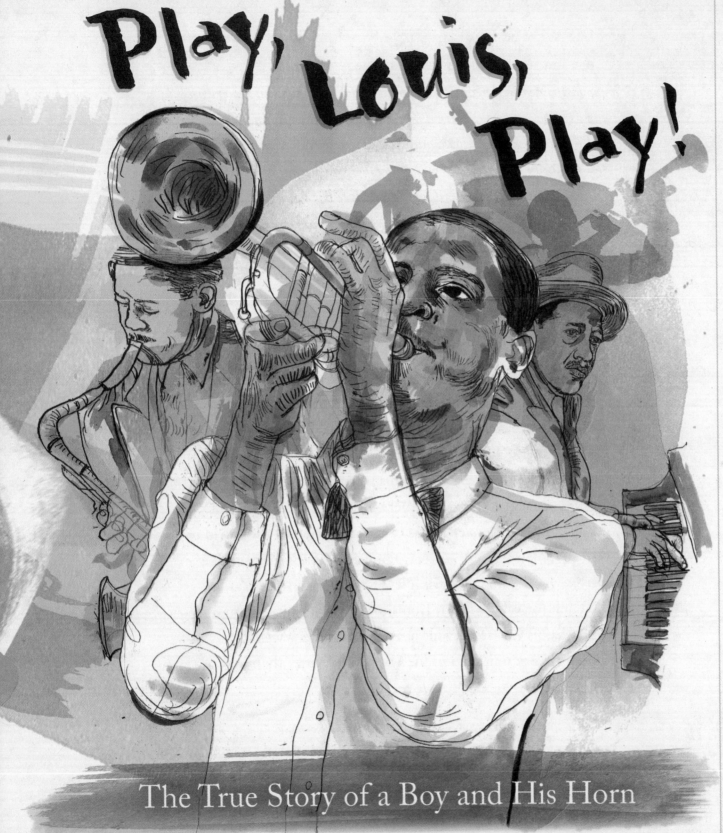

Play, Louis, Play!

The True Story of a Boy and His Horn

by Muriel Harris Weinstein • illustrated by Patrick Morgan

1 *Louis Armstrong, also known as "Satchmo," was an American jazz singer and trumpeter who came to be known as one of the most influential figures in jazz music. Armstrong started out playing in local brass band parades, looking to older musicians for inspiration. His hero, cornet player and jazz great Joe "King" Oliver, eventually became Armstrong's mentor and gave him what may have been his biggest break. Armstrong's story is one of talent, passion, and commitment, and who better to tell it than his truest companion, his very own trumpet.*

2 One day Joe Oliver, *the* Joe Oliver, Louis' hero, asked Louis to stop by and play a few bars of music. The best part was that Louis brought me along—me, his hock-shop horn. I wanted to impress Joe Oliver too.

3 Joe thought Louis was a natural. He took a real interest in him. Not like the other musicians who were too busy rushing around or had no time to bother with a kid. Joe gave him tips on playing. He even let Louis carry his cornet. In the world of honky-tonk musicians, *that* was one cool honor. You see, Joe Oliver was the main man in New Orleans jazz.

4 Then Joe Oliver asked Louis to sit in with his combo one night. Louis was as nervous as a fly in a spider's web. He thought every musician in Joe's band was better than he was.

bars Bars are short sections of a longer piece of music.

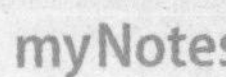

5 Louis walked to the front of the stage. They had no mics then. Louis tilted his head back and blew a new kind of blues, blowing notes higher than anyone had ever heard, holding them longer than anyone else—notes that moaned, then turned sugar sweet and soared so high they touched the moon. One by one each note turned colors: first blue, then lazy purple, then spinning round like pink molasses and cotton candy, then into swirls of rainbow-colored ribbons. All floated down as soft as velvet, turning in the air, curling into your ears.

myNotes

6 Louis blew with such a passion, he swung with such rhythm that his music made you snap your fingers or swing your hips.

7 More bandleaders started noticing Louis. They liked his style. They thought he was so darn good, they invited him to sit in with their bands. Sitting in was a way to try out—if the bandleader liked you, he might offer you a spot. Before you could sing "Potato Head Blues," Louis was swinging away, trying out each night. When Louis played, he felt he was *home.*

8 Night after night after night, he experimented with music. He tested his ideas, wanting to make music no one else tried and no one else heard, trying to find that music he heard in his head.

His music flew free and his rhythm was so contagious that every musician, even the cats in Joe Oliver's band, wanted to follow his style. It was as if I was part of Louis' n' he was part of me. My sound was his voice. I, me, the horn, was Louis. Sound crazy? No, that's why we weren't just buddies. We were brothers.

9 His music set everyone in a fever. And Joe Oliver's ears grew as large as an elephant's as he listened to Louis play his cornet.

10 It wasn't long before Joe Oliver said, "You're in, Louis. I'll give you a dollar a night."

contagious If a feeling is contagious, it spreads quickly among people.
fever A fever is a feeling of great excitement.

11 Louis was so excited! He didn't sleep for the next thirty nights. Louis shoveled coal all day for the Andrews Coal Company. In spite of aching muscles, he played his music every night, all night. Nothing was going to keep him from Joe Oliver's band.

12 Louis was the best cornet player in the band. He was so good, Joe and Louis started playing duets. They'd get up to the front of the stage and take turns playing solos. It was as if the horns were talking to each other, telling secrets, laughing and teasing, chasing one another around corners. But they mostly played together. Joe Oliver would take the lead and Louis would follow with clever harmony underneath Joe's melody. What Louis did was not an easy-breezy thing to do. He had to be good, yet he couldn't suddenly burst out in a wild melody, strutting his stuff, because Oliver was the leader of the band and the lead horn player.

13 About that time, Chicago, the jazz center of the world, offered Joe Oliver a job at the famous Lincoln Gardens. It was what Joe Oliver dreamed of. He had to go, but he was worried about leaving Louis. He knew Louis never wanted to leave New Orleans. Louis always told Joe that the New Orleans mud was in his shoes.

14 One night Joe invited Louis home for supper.

15 Of course they talked only about music. But Joe also tried to make Louis see that it was important to move forward, not only in music but also to other parts of the country. Joe told Louis, "You gotta grow. You can't stay in the same place playin' the same music. I know you love tryin' new ideas. You belong in Chicago."

duets Duets are pieces of music that two people sing or play together.
solos Solos are pieces of music that one person sings or plays alone.

16 Louis didn't want to lose Joe. He was family to Louis—really, more like a father than anyone else had been.

17 Louis listened, but he didn't say anything about being willing to move to Chicago or any other place.

18 Then Joe did something that made Little Louis cry.

19 "Louis," he said, "your talent is so special that every musician wants to imitate your style. There's no one like you. Your horn's full of miracles. So, I'm givin' you a present. It's *my cornet*. It's time I bought me a new one. Now, take my cornet, little brother."

20 Louis hugged his hero and his eyes grew watery. Then Louis did something that surprised me and Joe.

21 Louis kissed *me*, the old hock-shop horn, and said, "No one was more reliable, more dependable than you. You helped me play my kind of music. You're part of me. So I can't leave you. When I'm out on the stage playin' Joe's horn, you'll be waitin' for me in my dressin' room. *Where I go, you go*."

◆ ◆ ◆

22 And that's how Louis rose to fame and I went with him. It wasn't long before Joe Oliver, now called King Oliver, left for Chicago. And it wasn't long after that when he called Louis from Chicago and said, "C'mon up. I need you here."

23 Louis, who had never left New Orleans, was nervous about going so far. He didn't count the riverboats 'cause they were a short distance away. But when Joe Oliver called, Louis *had* to go.

24 He heard Chicago was c-c-cold, with a big wind blowing in from the huge lake and the wide sky over Lake Michigan, so Louis bought the longest, warmest underwear he could find. Then, with a trout sandwich wrapped in a brown paper bag, his underwear folded in another one, and Joe Oliver's cornet under his arm, he boarded the train for Chicago, the Windy City. Of course, I was there too.

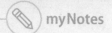

25 Wow! Was he a success. He performed for overflowing crowds, playing his heart out. Every city, every country, every continent wanted him. He was like an eagle soaring toward the sky, into the height of fame. He never slowed down and never stopped playing.

26 That's the story, the true story of how Louis Armstrong, the great Satchmo, became the world's greatest horn player. Jazz poured from his soul like a river. He loved sharing the music that haunted his heart, that bounced around in his head. When he picked me up to play a solo, I was so proud! I felt there wasn't a cornet around as happy as I was. And there wasn't a horn player as happy as Louis.

27 He sure loved his music, and he loved the world. And the wonderful thing was, the world loved him back.

Respond to the Text

Collaborative Discussion

Look back at what you wrote on page 42. Tell a partner two things you learned during reading. Then work with a group to discuss the questions below. Strengthen your answers with details from *Play, Louis, Play!* During the discussion, listen carefully so you do not repeat others' ideas.

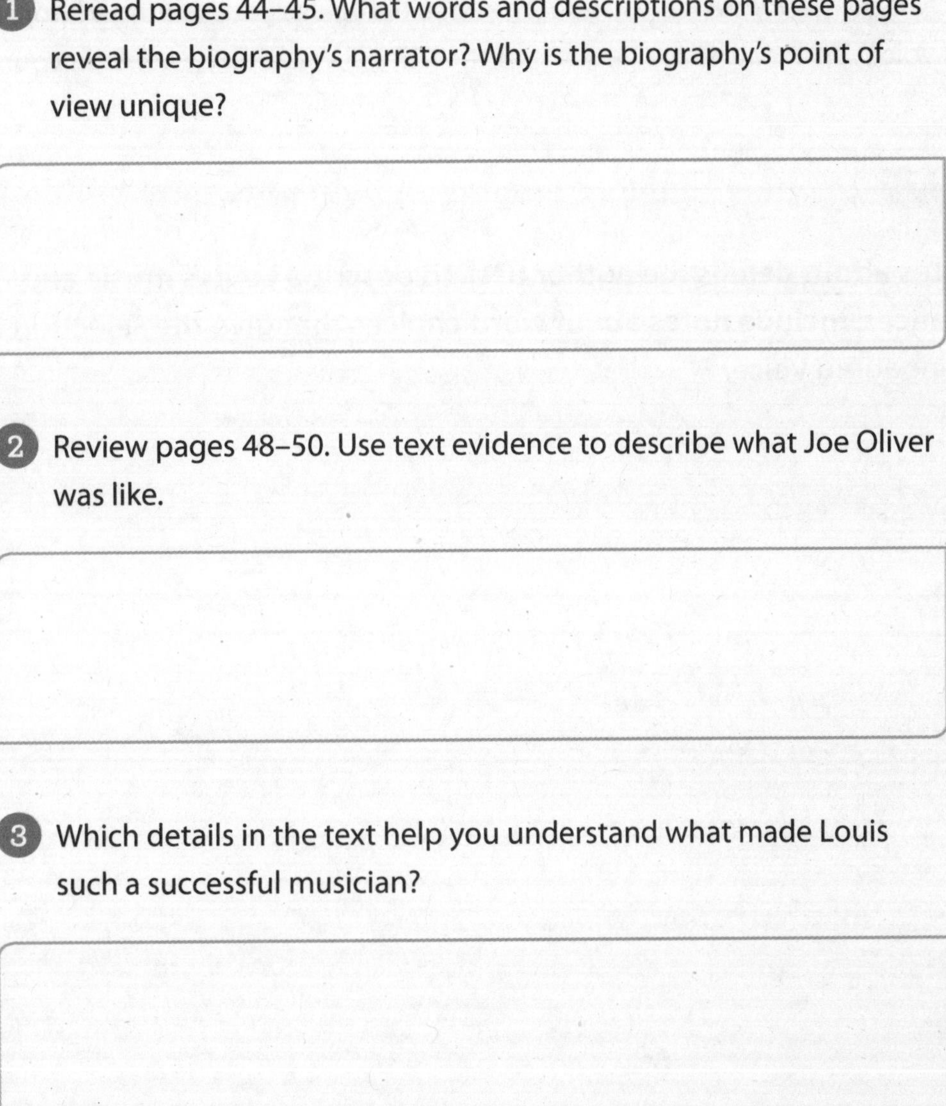

1. Reread pages 44–45. What words and descriptions on these pages reveal the biography's narrator? Why is the biography's point of view unique?

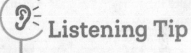

2. Review pages 48–50. Use text evidence to describe what Joe Oliver was like.

3. Which details in the text help you understand what made Louis such a successful musician?

Listening Tip

As you listen to the comments of others, think about how they relate to specific parts of the text. What information can you add to build on them?

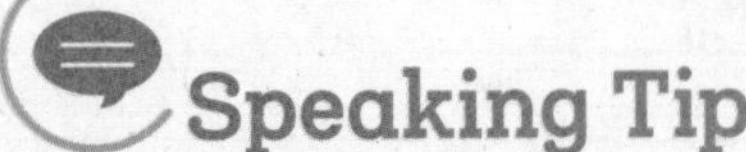

Speaking Tip

Add comments of your own to build on what other speakers say. Refer to specific words in the text to support your ideas.

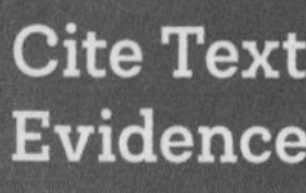

Write a Review

PROMPT

In *Play, Louis, Play!*, you read that Louis Armstrong played for "overflowing crowds" in places all around the world.

Imagine that you are a music critic assigned to review one of Louis Armstrong's concerts. Using information from *Play, Louis, Play!*, write a review that describes the experience of the performance. Include language that gives your writing a strong, engaging voice. Don't forget to use some of the Critical Vocabulary words in your writing.

PLAN

Make notes about details the author uses to describe Louis's music and performances. Include notes about word choices that give the selection a strong, engaging voice.

WRITE

Now write your review describing Louis's performance.

Make sure your review

- ☐ states an opinion about Louis's performance.
- ☐ gives reasons for the opinions in an order that makes sense.
- ☐ uses text evidence to support reasons.
- ☐ includes language that gives your writing a strong voice.
- ☐ includes a concluding statement.

Notice & Note

Words of the Wiser

Prepare to Read

GENRE STUDY A **biography** is the story of a real person's life.

- Biographies usually present events in sequential, or chronological, order.
- Biographies can include literary language and devices, including flashbacks and figurative language.
- Biographies include third-person pronouns such as *he, she,* and *they.*

SET A PURPOSE **Think about** the title and genre of this text. What do you know about Phillis Wheatley? What do you want to learn? Write your ideas below.

CRITICAL VOCABULARY

- consented
- sheaf
- outcome
- homeland
- advised
- content
- testifying

Meet the Author and Illustrator: Catherine Clinton and Sean Qualls

Phillis's Big Test

by
Catherine Clinton
Illustrated by
Sean Qualls

1 *In 1773, Phillis Wheatley became the first African American to publish a book of poetry. When she went to London to meet with literary admirers, she became the most famous black person on both sides of the Atlantic.*

2 *But in 1772, Wheatley's book almost didn't get published, because printers in colonial Boston could not believe that an African-born enslaved girl wrote such wonderful verses all by herself.*

3 *To prove the poems were her very own, the teenage poet consented to be cross-examined by eighteen of the most learned and powerful men of Massachusetts. Phillis's big test . . .*

4 One crisp early-autumn morning, Phillis Wheatley was crossing the Boston cobblestones with a sheaf of papers held tightly under her arm. When her master, John Wheatley, had offered her a ride to her examination, she said she would prefer to walk.

5 She would make her own way to the public hall where the most important men of the Massachusetts Bay Colony would examine her and settle the question once and for all: was she or was she not the author of her poems?

6 She had spent recent evenings copying and recopying her poetry in her own neat handwriting. She knew each poem inside out. What kind of questions would they ask? Why should she have to defend her own verse?

consented If you consented to something, you agreed to it.
sheaf A sheaf of papers is a bundle of sheets held together.

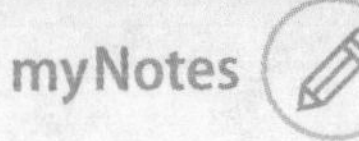
myNotes

7 As she turned the corner of Mackeral Lane, reading one of her poems, the wind gusted and blew it out of her hand. As the page danced in the wind, she gave chase, catching it before it disappeared.

8 Even if it had disappeared, would it matter? She knew every line, every syllable, by heart. She wrapped the pages tightly in a roll, pages of poems that had come from deep inside her—and could not be taken away, no matter the outcome of today.

9 Still, she had something to prove. Not just because she was young, not just because she was female, but because she was a slave and came from Africa. She paused as a billowing sail moving into the harbor caught her eye.

10 Was this like the boat she had arrived on one day in July more than eleven years before? A slave ship full of human cargo?

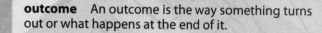

outcome An outcome is the way something turns out or what happens at the end of it.

11 She could remember little about crossing the Atlantic, and even less about her African homeland. She was just shedding her front teeth when John Wheatley bought her on the Boston docks as a servant for his wife, Susanna. They christened their new slave Phillis, the name of the ship on which she arrived.

12 She remembered the strangeness of the Boston house that became her home. Her first winter was so very cold and awful. She survived only by the kindness of her masters, especially the Wheatleys' twins, Nathaniel and Mary, who eagerly shared their lessons with the young slave girl. They taught her not just English but also Latin and Greek. Soon Phillis spent more time on her studies than on serving her mistress.

13 As she began to read poetry, glorious sonnets had inspired her to try her own hand at writing. And soon she was reciting her poems to the Wheatleys' friends.

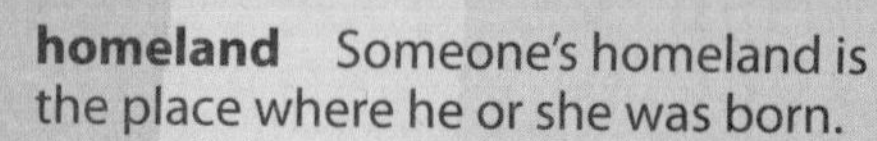

homeland Someone's homeland is the place where he or she was born.

14 She had been staying up late, night after night, preparing for what lay ahead. Was she ready? Would she ever be ready?

15 Last night, her mistress, Susanna, had taken away the candle at midnight and **advised**: "Tomorrow you will look them straight in the eye as you answer all their questions. Your talent will speak for itself. They will discover the poet we know you to be! And when your book is published, everyone will know!"

16 Phillis had hoped this might be true. Doubts danced in her head—but she had studied as hard as she could, and she would just have to have faith. As she said her prayers, her worries began to fade, and she drifted off to sleep, dreaming of her very own book.

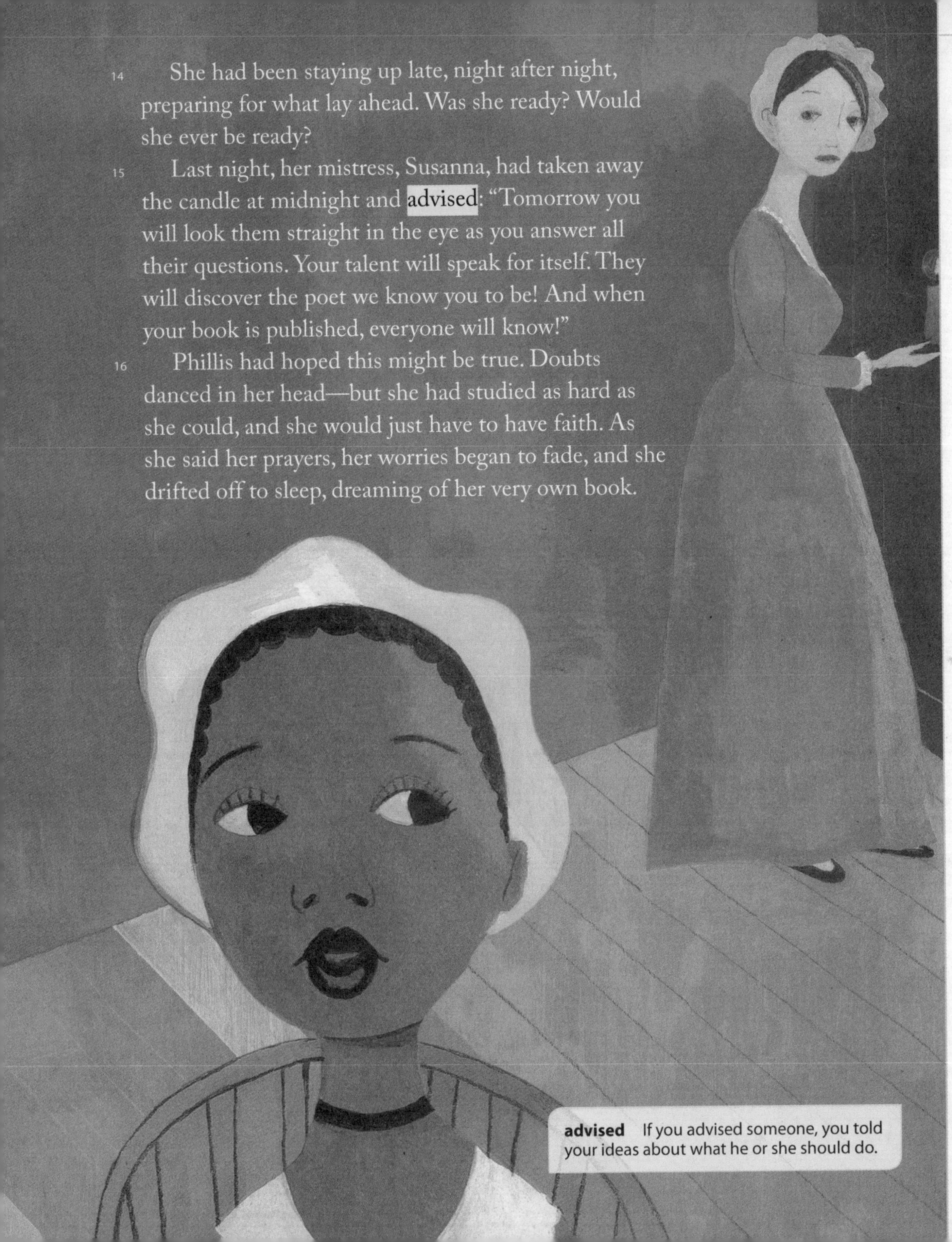

advised If you advised someone, you told your ideas about what he or she should do.

17 Books had opened up a whole new world to Phillis, as she was taught literature and geography, as she memorized the names of cities and countries, lists of kings and queens, and dates of discoveries.

18 Over time she had come to appreciate her own time and place, her very own role in the chain of events stretching from past to present.

19 She did not know why she had been brought from Africa to Boston, or why she had ended up in the Wheatley home. But she knew that she must now make the most of her opportunities. She must make her voice heard.

20 She was not content to recite her verse in drawing rooms or to read one of her poems from a newspaper. She wanted her own book because books would not last just a lifetime; they would be there for her children and her children's children.

content If you are content with something, you accept it or agree with it.

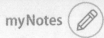

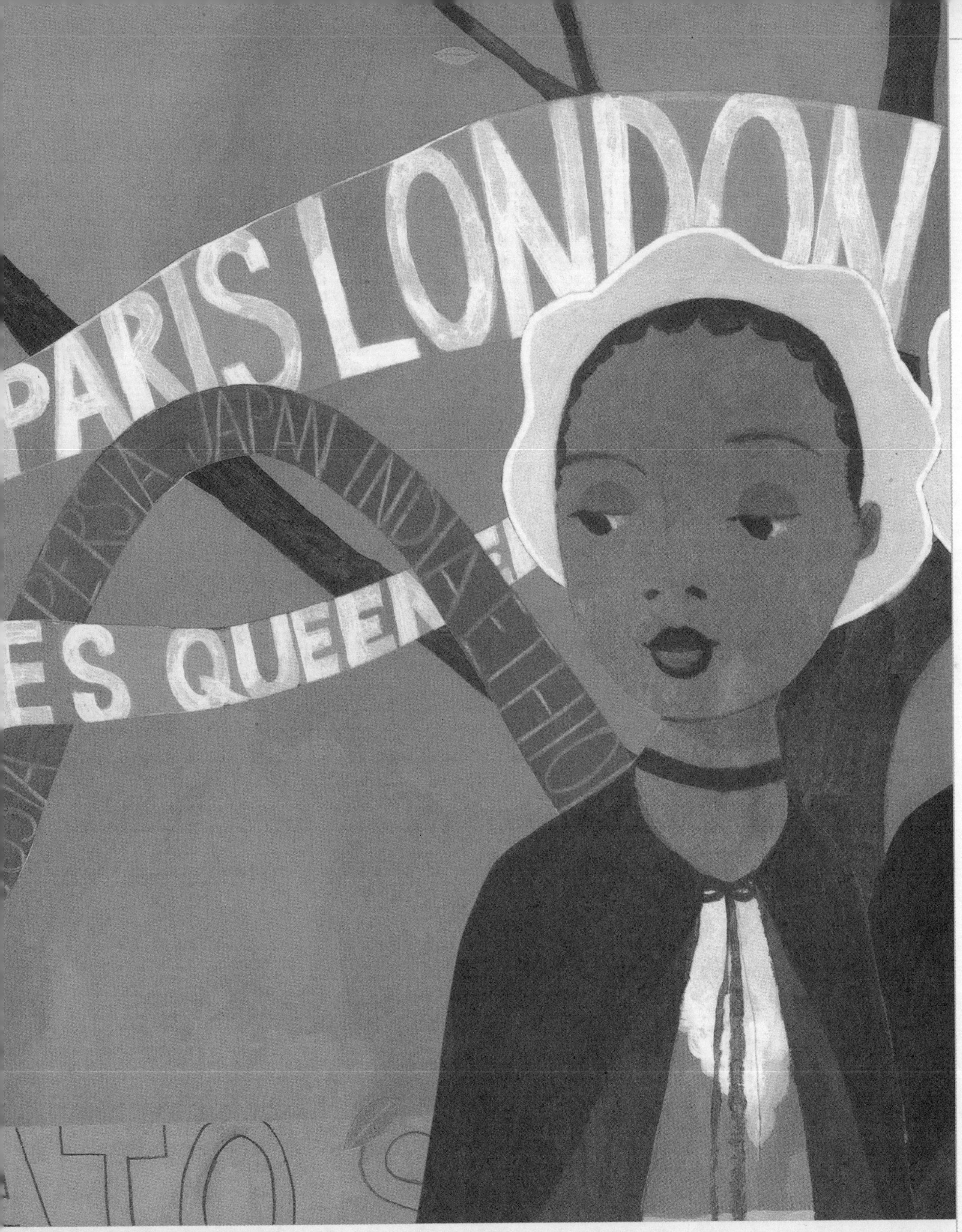
PARIS
JAPAN
PERSIA
INDIA
QUEEN

21 She hurried by the bookseller's shop that she visited weekly. Today, Phillis did not have time to step inside and smell the leather bindings. But maybe soon she would make a visit and find her own name on a volume.

22 But she must first pass this examination to make her dream come true! There would be only a dozen and a half gentlemen. She had often entertained as large a crowd in the Wheatley parlor.

23 This group, though, would include the governor, the lieutenant governor, famous ministers, and published poets . . . all learned men. Many had studied across the river at Harvard and knew so much more than she did. Phillis felt a chill as she approached the building.

24 She shuddered and started to turn away, but then Susanna Wheatley's words echoed in her head: *Your talent will speak for itself.*

25 Who knew her poems better than she did? She could not run away.

26 Phillis slowly mounted the steps. She would face her examiners—not just for herself or for the Wheatleys but for her family back in Africa, and for her new brothers and sisters in America, who deserved their own poet.

27 As she turned the handle on the large wooden door, the sunlight framed her entrance. She moved into the hall as all eyes turned toward her:

28 "Good day, gentlemen. I am the poet Phillis Wheatley."

Epilogue

29 No record exists of her examination, but we now know that Phillis passed her test with flying colors, as the eighteen men signed a document testifying to Wheatley's authorship, which appeared in the back of her volume of poems, published in 1773. She went abroad to England to meet with literary patrons, and after returning to America she was freed by her master. When both her master and mistress died, Wheatley married a Boston shopkeeper.

30 Phillis Wheatley wrote several patriotic poems during the American Revolution and was invited by George Washington to visit him at his headquarters, another journey the poet gladly made.

31 After America achieved independence, Phillis hoped to publish another volume of verse, but she died in December 1784 before this second collection could appear, and her unpublished poems disappeared.

testifying If you are testifying, you promise that what you say is true.

Respond to the Text

Collaborative Discussion

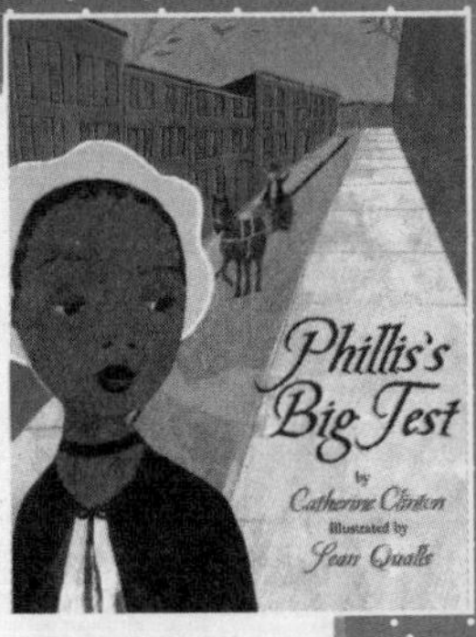

Look back at what you wrote on page 56. Tell a partner two things you learned from the text. Then work with a group to discuss the questions below. Look for details to support your answers in *Phillis's Big Test*. Follow class rules for having a good discussion.

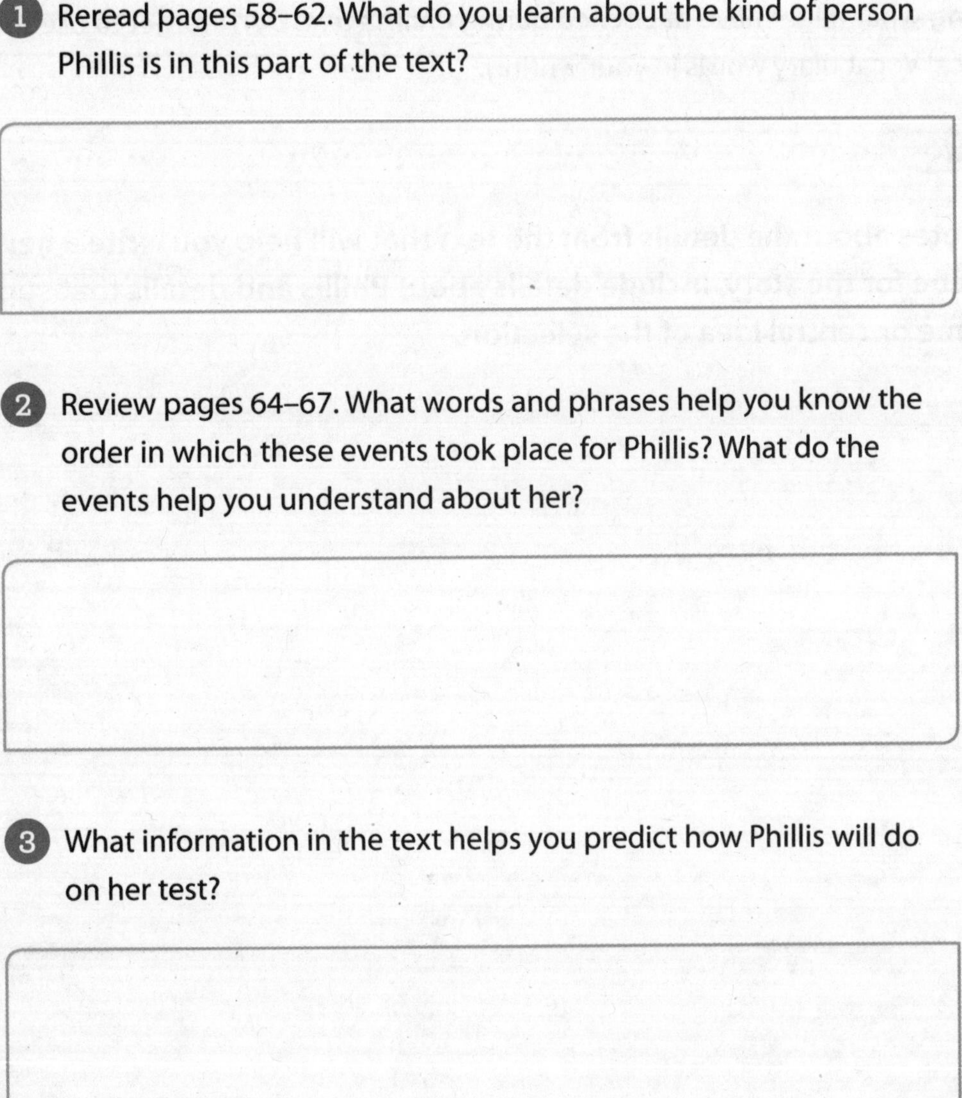

1 Reread pages 58–62. What do you learn about the kind of person Phillis is in this part of the text?

2 Review pages 64–67. What words and phrases help you know the order in which these events took place for Phillis? What do the events help you understand about her?

3 What information in the text helps you predict how Phillis will do on her test?

Listening Tip

Listen politely and pay careful attention to each speaker's ideas.

Speaking Tip

Wait your turn to speak. If you disagree with someone, do so calmly and support your ideas with details from the biography.

Cite Text Evidence

Write a Scene

PROMPT

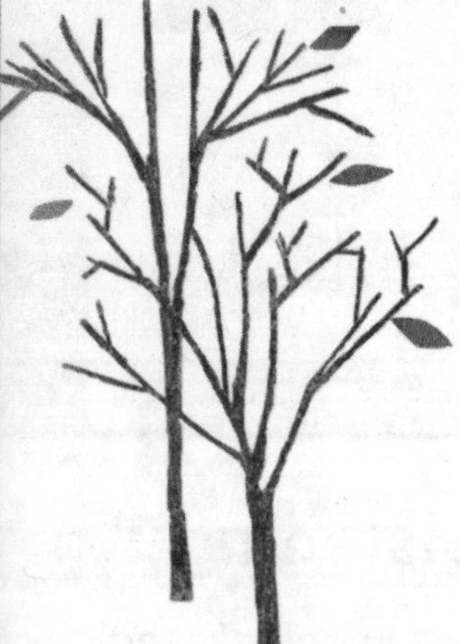

In *Phillis's Big Test*, you read about how Phillis Wheatley had to prove that she wrote her poems. The author tells the reader that Phillis "passed with flying colors," but does not tell what happened during the test.

Use what you learned from *Phillis's Big Test* and your imagination to write a scene describing what might have happened during Phillis's test. Don't forget to use some of the Critical Vocabulary words in your writing.

PLAN

Make notes about the details from the text that will help you write a new final scene for the story. Include details about Phillis and details that support the theme or central idea of the selection.

WRITE

Now write your scene about what might have happened during Phillis's test.

Make sure your scene

- ☐ tells what happened during the exam.
- ☐ presents events in an order that makes sense.
- ☐ makes sense based on text details about Phillis and her work.
- ☐ uses dialogue and description to tell the story.
- ☐ includes a conclusion.

Performance Task

Essential Question

How do different art forms impact people in different ways?

Write a Biographical Sketch

PROMPT Think about what you learned about artists and their art forms in this module.

Imagine that your school is having an arts festival. The festival program will include brief articles about the lives of artists whose work is featured. Choose an artist from one of the texts or another artist you are familiar with. Use evidence from the texts or other sources to write a biographical sketch of the person's life and work.

I will write about ______________________________.

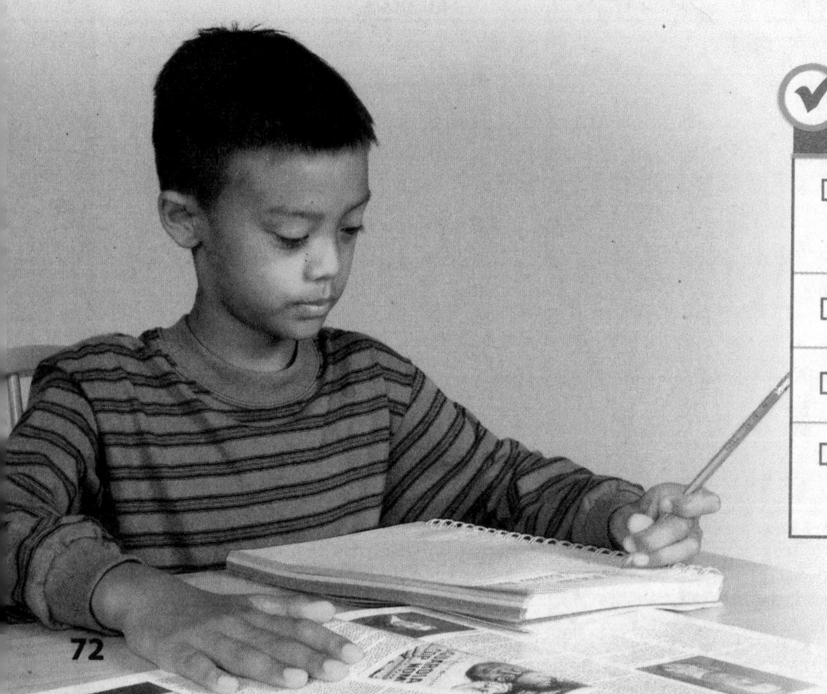

Make sure your biographical sketch

- ☐ introduces the artist and the art form he or she is known for, such as music or painting.
- ☐ includes facts and details about the person's life and work.
- ☐ uses precise language and vocabulary related to the art form.
- ☐ contains a conclusion that leaves readers with an understanding of the artist's contributions.

PLAN .... **Gather Information.**

What will you share about the artist's achievements and his or her life? Look back at your notes and revisit the texts and other sources for details.

Use the web below to plan your biographical sketch. Write the name of your artist in the center circle. Then write important facts about the artist in the surrounding circles. Add supporting details, such as examples and quotations, to the outer circles. Add more circles if you need them.

My Topic: ____

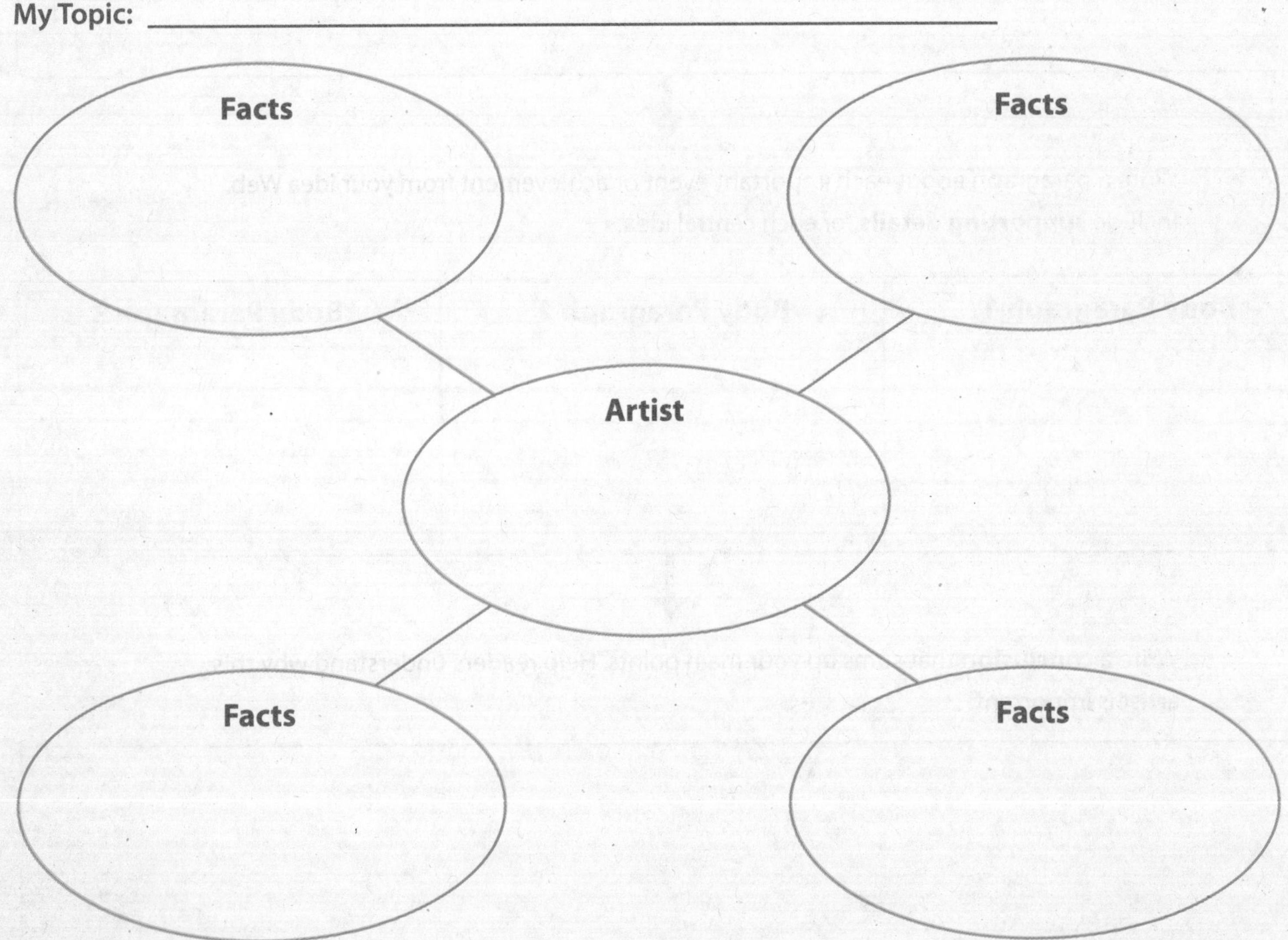

Performance Task

DRAFT ········ **Write your biographical sketch.**

Write an **introduction** that introduces your artist and gets readers interested in learning about him or her.

Write a paragraph about each important event or achievement from your Idea Web. Include **supporting details** for each central idea.

Body Paragraph 1	Body Paragraph 2	Body Paragraph 3

Write a **conclusion** that sums up your main points. Help readers understand why this artist is important.

REVISE AND EDIT ······ Review your draft.

Revising and editing is your chance to review your draft and decide how it can be improved. Work with a partner. Read each other's drafts and ask questions about any information that isn't clear. Also, use these questions to help you look for more ways to improve your biographical sketch.

PURPOSE/ FOCUS	ORGANIZATION	EVIDENCE	LANGUAGE/ VOCABULARY	CONVENTIONS
☐ Will my sketch get readers interested in learning about the artist? ☐ Does each paragraph focus on one aspect of the artist's life or work?	☐ Are the ideas presented in a logical order? ☐ Does the conclusion "fit" with the information that came before it?	☐ Did I include strong evidence, such as facts, examples, and quotations?	☐ Did I use precise language and vocabulary related to the art form? ☐ Did I use linking words to connect ideas?	☐ Have I spelled all words correctly? ☐ Did I correctly punctuate quotations and titles of works?

PUBLISH ······ Share your work.

Create a Finished Copy Make a final copy of your biographical sketch. You may want to include illustrations or photos to enhance your text. Consider these options for sharing your biographical sketch.

1. Combine your biographical sketch with those of your classmates to create an online "Encyclopedia of Artists" for the school library web site.
2. With classmates who wrote about different types of artists, conduct a panel discussion on the module's essential question: *How do different art forms impact people in different ways?* Discuss specific examples from your biographies.
3. Read your biographical sketch aloud to the class and share examples of the artist's work. Be prepared to respond to questions from your audience.

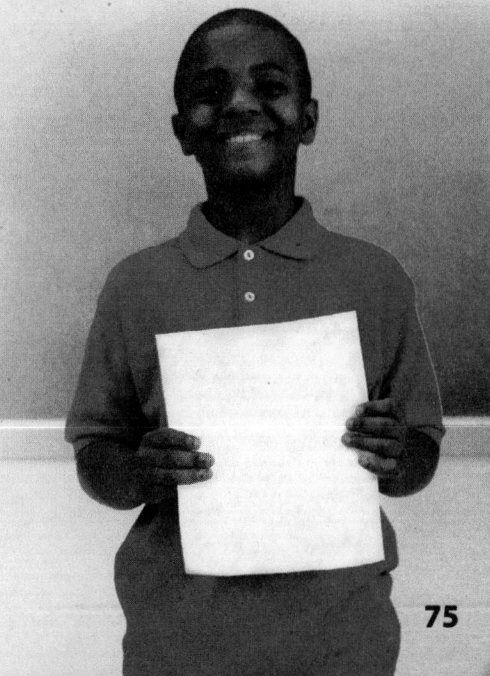

MODULE 7

Above, Below, and Beyond

"Man cannot discover new oceans unless he has the courage to lose sight of the shore."

—André Gide

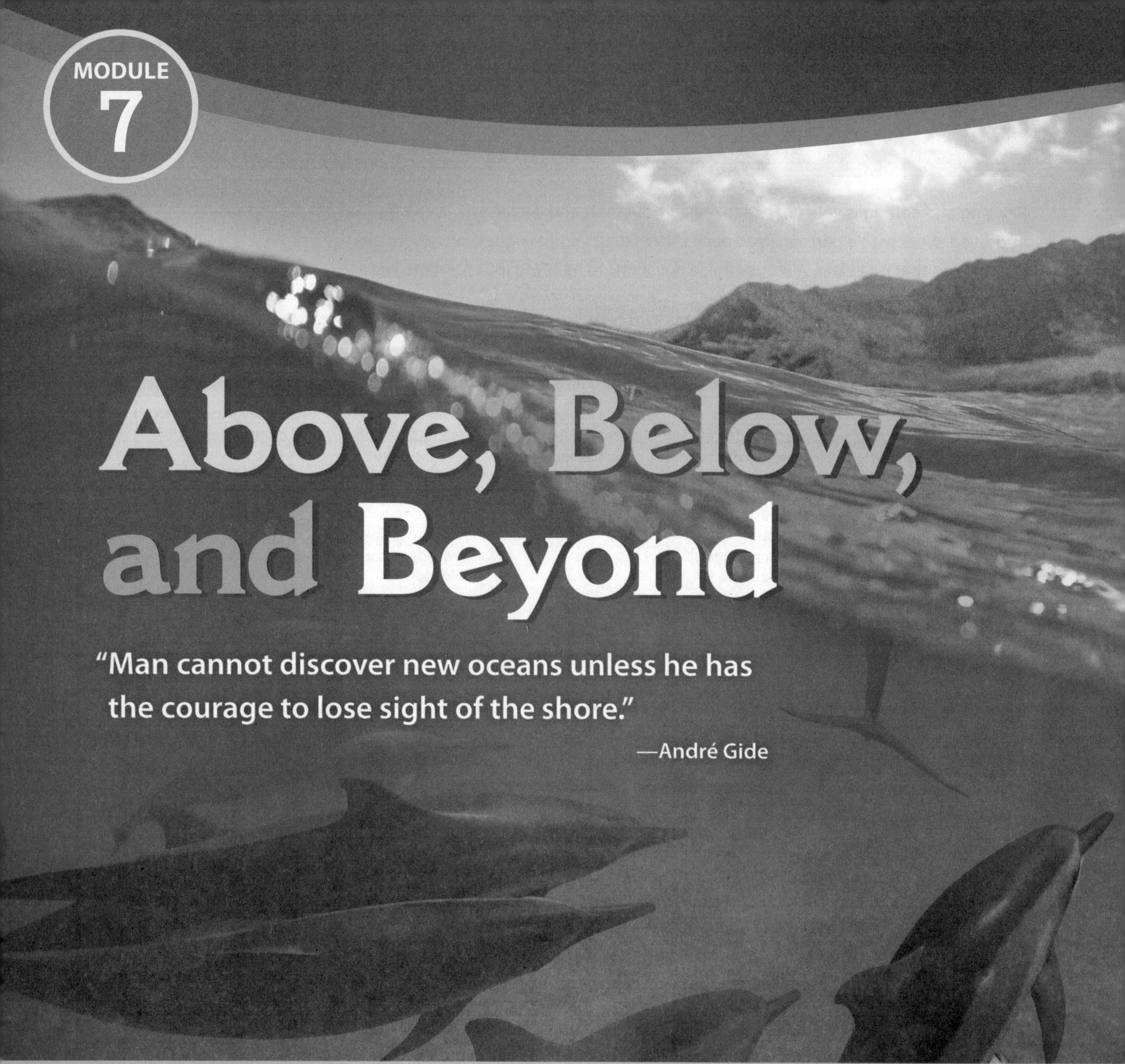

Essential Question

What role does curiosity play in exploration?

Get Curious
Video

Big Idea Words

Words About Exploration

The words in the chart will help you talk and write about the selections in this module. Which words about exploration have you seen before? Which words are new to you?

Add to the Vocabulary Network on page 79 by writing synonyms, antonyms, and related words and phrases for each word about exploration.

After you read each selection in this module, come back to the Vocabulary Network and keep building it. Add more boxes if you need to.

WORD	MEANING	CONTEXT SENTENCE
expedition (noun)	An expedition is a trip that has a purpose, such as exploration or research.	The goal of the expedition was to reach the South Pole.
incredible (adjective)	Something that is incredible is so amazing that it's hard to believe.	The hikers were amazed by the incredible lost city they found in the jungle.
progress (noun)	To make progress is to improve or to complete steps toward reaching a goal.	Today, the climbers made great progress toward reaching the top of the mountain.
chronology (noun)	A chronology records the time and order of a series of events.	The researcher wrote a chronology of the expedition in her digital journal.

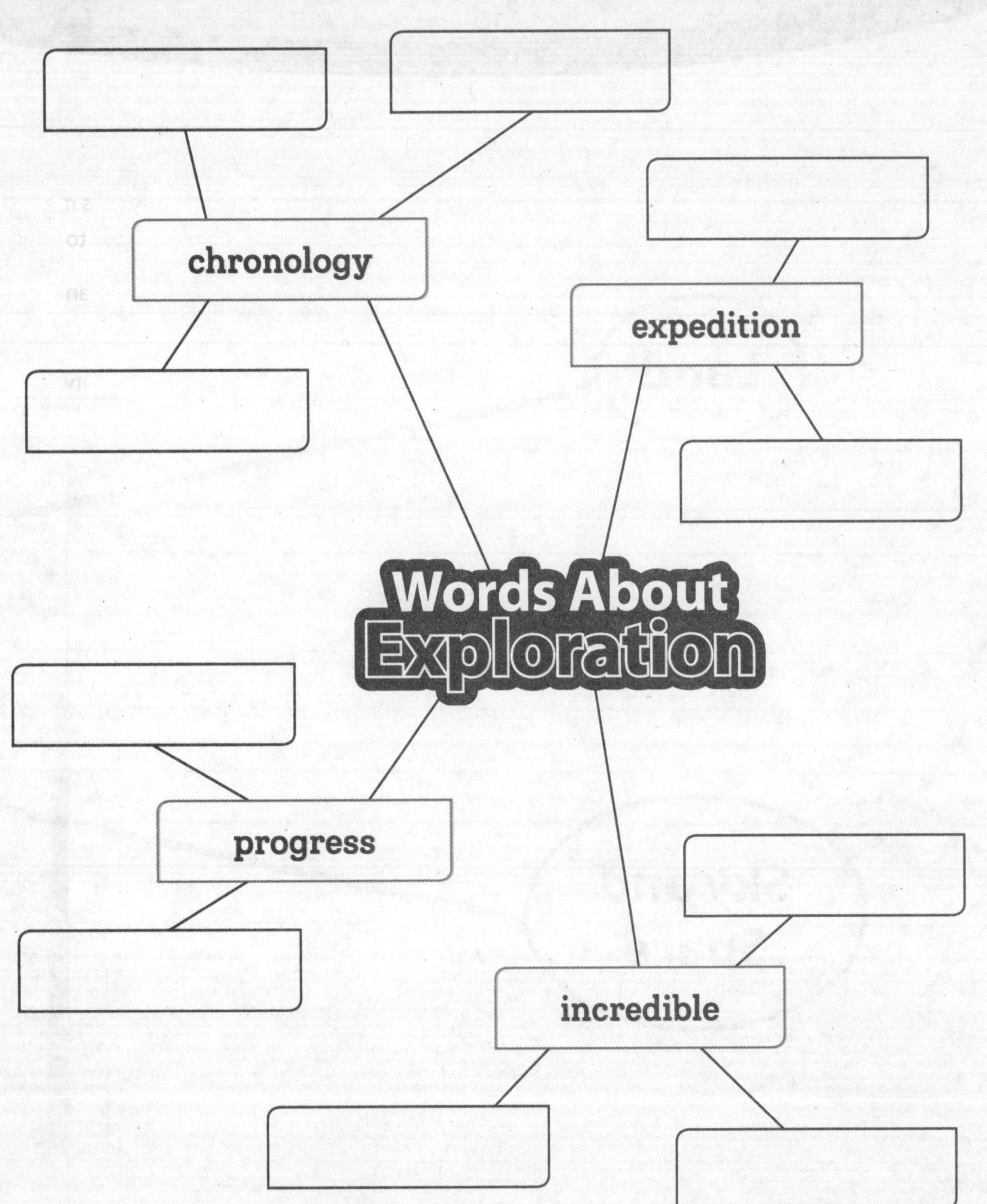
chronology
expedition
Words About Exploration
progress
incredible

Knowledge Map

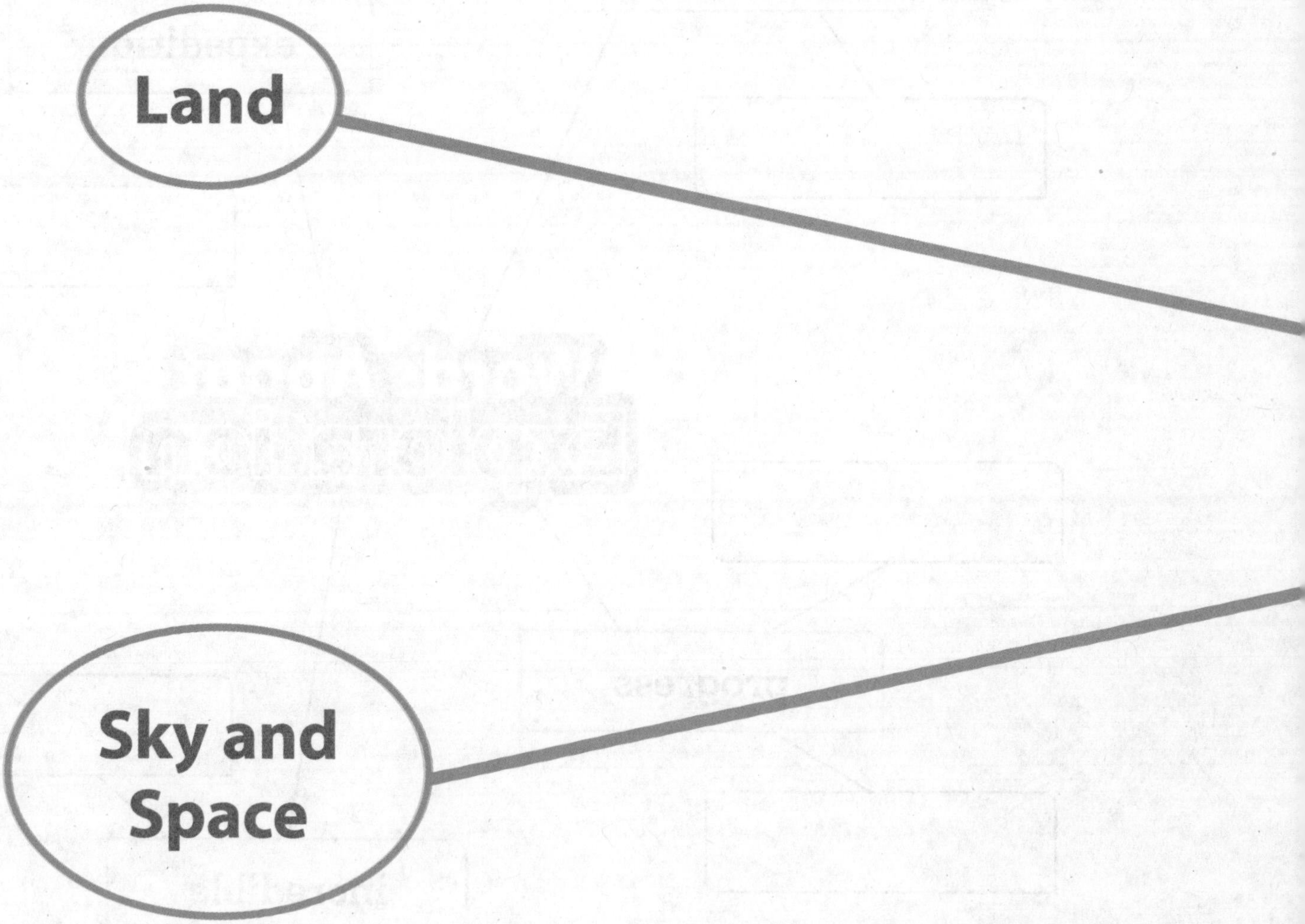

Land

Sky and Space

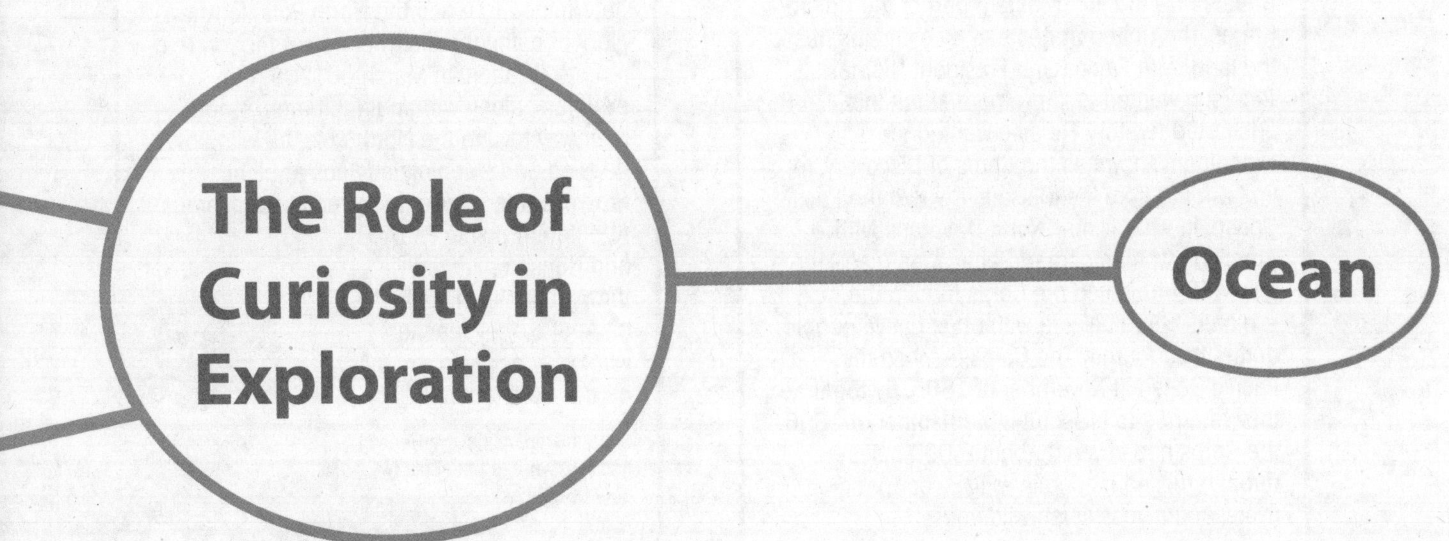
The Role of Curiosity in Exploration
Ocean

Short Read

A Few Who Dared

1 Throughout history, courageous men and women have boldly ventured into little-known—sometimes unknown—territory. Some explore to answer the call of curiosity. Others do so for glory or the chance to be first. Still others thirst for the chance to discover new lands or spaces. From the top of the world to the bottom of the sea to outer space, this timeline is a **chronology** of a few of history's daring explorers from the last two centuries.

1804

Meriwether Lewis, William Clark, and Sacagawea

What they explored: The northwestern United States

2 **Details:** In 1804 leaders Meriwether Lewis and William Clark and a team of more than thirty people embarked on a two-year exploration of what is now the northwestern part of the United States. The United States had recently purchased the land from France and President Thomas Jefferson wanted to know more about this uncharted territory. He also wanted the expedition, known as the Corps of Discovery, to find a route from the Missouri River to the Pacific Ocean. In what is now North Dakota, a Native American woman named Sacagawea (sah-kuh-guh-WEE-uh) joined the Corps to help the explorers communicate with other native people during their journey. The Corps reached the Pacific Ocean in November of 1805. By the time they returned to Missouri in September of 1806, the Corps had covered about 8,000 miles—through rugged mountain ranges, down raging rivers, and across harsh wilderness.

The name *Sacagawea* means "Bird Woman."

1909

Matthew Henson and Robert Peary

What they explored: The Arctic

3 **Details:** By 1909, Americans Matthew Henson and Robert Peary had already made several expeditions together to the Arctic. They were determined to reach the North Pole, for the glory of being the first men to set foot on that remote location. In March of 1909, the explorers, along with four Inuit men, made their way toward the North Pole, traveling by dogsled and sleeping in igloos at night. Progress was slow—and extremely dangerous. At different points Peary and Henson plunged through the ice. Finally, on April 6, they reached what they believed to be the North Pole.

Some historians believe Henson and Peary missed the Pole by about 60 miles.

1975

Jacques Cousteau

What he explored: The ocean

4 **Details:** Born and raised in France, Jacques Cousteau (koo-STOH) had a lifelong curiosity about the sea. He hungered for knowledge about the world's oceans and the life they contain. Cousteau was the co-inventor of the Aqua-Lung, the first automated scuba diving tank. Additionally, he and his team designed underwater laboratories where scientists could live and do research. Through his TV series *The Undersea World of Jacques Cousteau,* viewers were able to accompany Cousteau on his incredible ocean adventures. In 1975, off the coast of Greece, he located and explored the wreck of *Britannic—Titanic's* sister ship—which sank in 1916.

The word *scuba* is an acronym that stands for "**s**elf-**c**ontained **u**nderwater **b**reathing **a**pparatus."

1983

Sally Ride

What she explored: Outer space

5 **Details:** Sally Ride and Dr. Mae Jemison share the distinction of being two "firsts" in space exploration. In 1983, Ride became the first American woman to travel to outer space, aboard the space shuttle *Challenger.* During her historic flight, Ride operated a robotic arm to move satellites.

1992

Mae Jemison

What she explored: Outer space

6 **Details:** Dr. Jemison became the first African American woman in space, aboard the space shuttle *Endeavour.* Dr. Jemison, who was also a medical doctor, performed a number of experiments during her eight-day space flight.

A huge fan of the TV show *Star Trek,* Dr. Jemison appeared on an episode of *Star Trek: The Next Generation.*

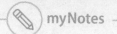

Notice & Note
Extreme/Absolute Language

Prepare to Read

GENRE STUDY **Informational texts** give facts and examples about a topic.

- Authors of informational texts may present their ideas in sequential, or chronological, order to help readers understand what happened and when.
- Content-area words that are specific to the topic may be used.
- Informational texts include visuals, such as charts, diagrams, graphs, timelines, and maps.

SET A PURPOSE **Think about** the title and genre of this text. What do you know about exploration of Earth's oceans and atmosphere? What do you want to learn? Write your ideas below.

CRITICAL VOCABULARY

- vast
- mariners
- cosmic
- ascend
- principle
- forged

Meet the Author and Illustrator: Stewart Ross and Stephen Biesty

INTO THE UNKNOWN: ABOVE AND BELOW

BY STEWART ROSS • ILLUSTRATED BY STEPHEN BIESTY

THE LAYERS OF EARTH'S ATMOSPHERE

Outer space

THERMOSPHERE
Scorchingly hot: 12 times boiling point, 32 times human body temperature

Around 50 miles up

MESOPAUSE
Temperatures here can fall to –150°F

MESOSPHERE
Temperatures as low as the lowest ever recorded on Earth

Around 30 miles up

STRATOPAUSE
Temperatures can rise to 32°F

STRATOSPHERE
Not enough air for breathing and temperatures as cold as at the poles

Around 10 miles up

TROPOPAUSE
Completely dry

TROPOSPHERE
Wet and oxygen-rich

The earth's surface

1 By the early 1930s, explorers had traveled to every corner of the earth and mapped nearly all its land surface. Some said there was nowhere new to go. However, many remote places remained that had not yet been visited. Who knew, for example, what lay in the stratosphere, that vast blue canopy above the clouds? Or what lurked in the depths of the deepest, darkest oceans? Were there monsters there?

2 Manned balloon flights had already risen to the lower reaches of the stratosphere, and recently invented submarines had dived 900 feet or more below the surface of the sea. But such journeys were extremely dangerous. The air is so thin in the stratosphere that there is not enough oxygen for breathing, and human bodies collapse. Equally terrible, in deep seas, water may weigh a crushing 8 tons per square inch, enough to squash an ordinary submarine like an empty soda can.

3 One family faced these dangers—and triumphed. Auguste Piccard and his son, Jacques, were among the bravest explorers of all time. Unlike adventurers of the past, they were not steely soldiers or hardy mariners; rather, they were scientists.

vast Something vast is very large.

mariners Mariners are people who navigate ships, such as sailors.

Swiss-born Auguste Piccard (1884–1962) studied engineering in Zurich before becoming a professor of physics in Brussels, Belgium. There he grew interested in new theories about the cosmic rays that were believed to be active in the stratosphere. To learn more, he decided to go and observe them directly.

4 In those days, the stratosphere was beyond the reach of any airplane, so the only way to travel there was by balloon. In 1862, scientists James Glaisher and Henry Coxwell had risen more than six miles in a balloon. In 1912, Victor Hess, the scientist who discovered the existence of cosmic rays, had reached over three miles. But all three had nearly died in the process. So how could Piccard ascend to seven and a half miles, as he hoped, and still return safely to Earth?

5 Backed by Belgium's FNRS (National Fund for Scientific Research), Auguste constructed a remarkable balloon. Its enormous canopy was made from very light cotton, sealed with a thin coat of rubber. To make it rise, the canopy was inflated with lighter-than-air hydrogen. To descend, the crew pulled a cord to release hydrogen from the top of the canopy, making the whole balloon heavier.

cosmic Something that is cosmic is beyond Earth and its atmosphere.

ascend To ascend is to go up.

6 Below the canopy hung a lightweight aluminum sphere. This specially designed cabin, with eight tiny portholes and two hatches, was just large enough for a two-man crew and their instruments. Once the balloon had risen to 5,000 feet, the hatches were sealed and the cabin became airtight, so the pressure inside remained constant no matter how high the balloon went. (The same principle applies to the pressurized cabins that are standard on all modern high-flying passenger aircraft.) In order for Piccard and his assistant to breathe safely, the cabin was equipped with around ten hours' supply of pure oxygen and a system for recycling stale air.

7 On May 26, 1931, the *FNRS* (the balloon was named after its sponsor) lifted off from Augsburg, Germany. Up and up and up it went, climbing into the stratosphere. Amazingly, some seventeen hours later, it floated safely down again and landed in the Swiss Alps. On this first flight, Piccard and his assistant, Paul Kipfer, had reached a world-record 51,775 feet. However, an air leak and the tangling of the hydrogen-release valve had made it too dangerous to gather any scientific data.

principle A scientific principle is a rule that explains how something in the natural world works.

INSIDE THE GONDOLA

Crossbar for sealing and unsealing hatch
Hatch, sealed shut at 5,000 feet
White-painted aluminum **gondola**
Auguste Piccard
Porthole
Altimeter: measures height above ground
Oxygen tanks
Food for flight
Lightweight wicker **seat**
Radio aerial lowered from hatch

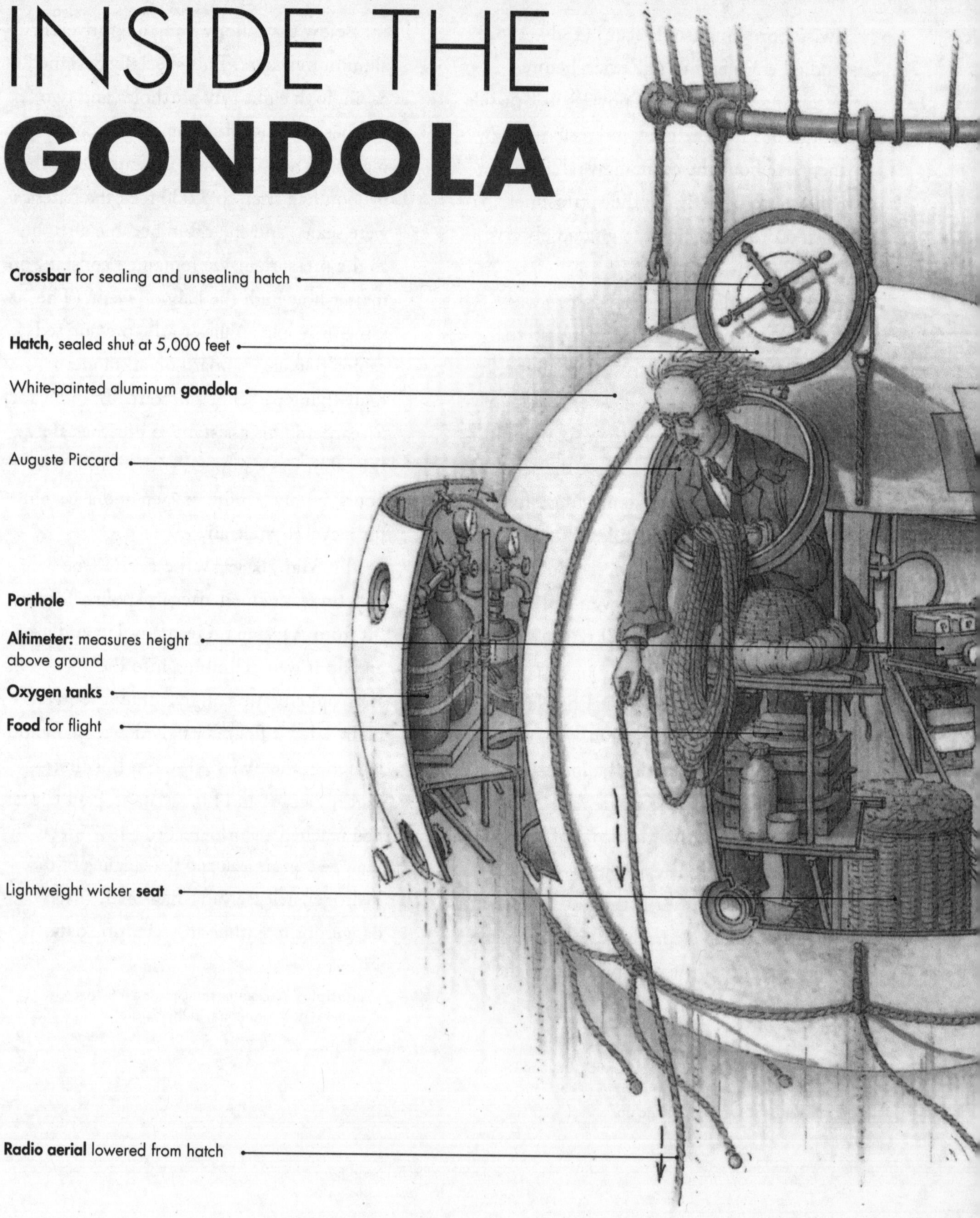

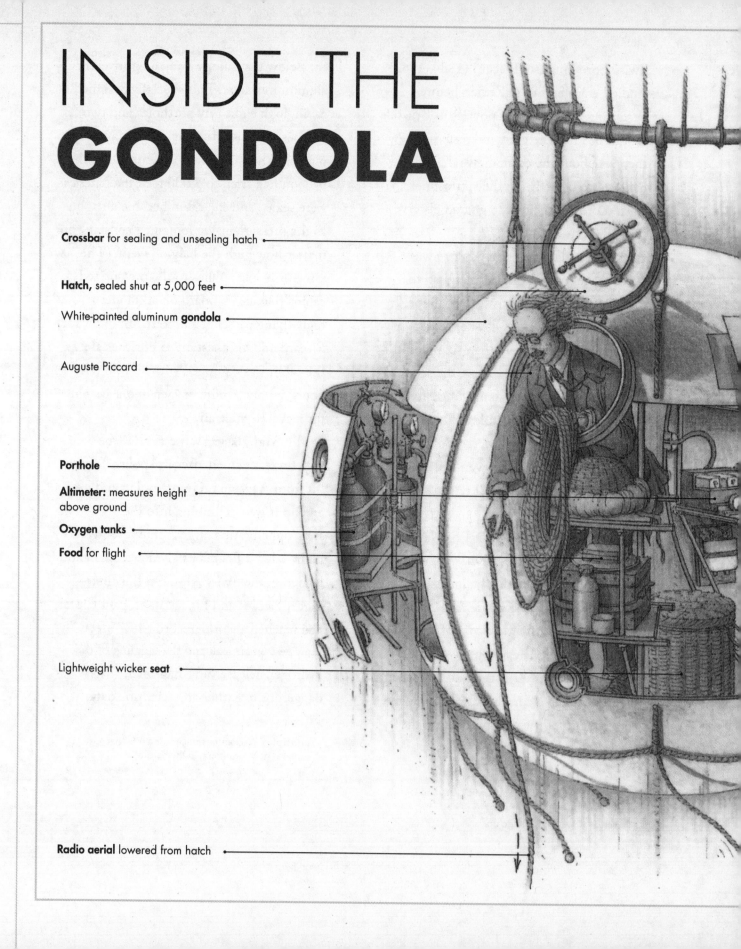

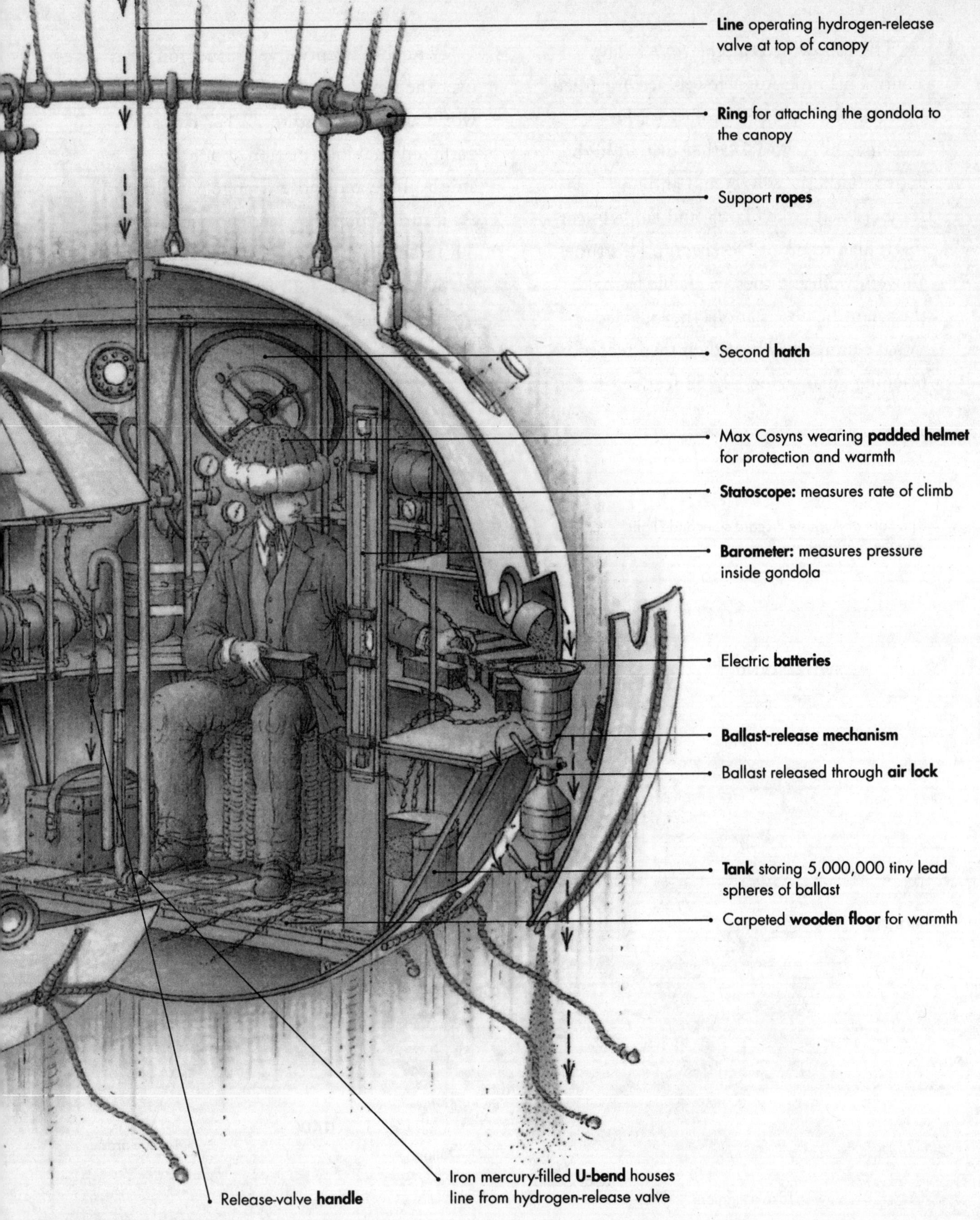
Line operating hydrogen-release valve at top of canopy
Ring for attaching the gondola to the canopy
Support ropes
Second hatch
Max Cosyns wearing padded helmet for protection and warmth
Statoscope: measures rate of climb
Barometer: measures pressure inside gondola
Electric batteries
Ballast-release mechanism
Ballast released through air lock
Tank storing 5,000,000 tiny lead spheres of ballast
Carpeted wooden floor for warmth
Iron mercury-filled U-bend houses line from hydrogen-release valve
Release-valve handle

myNotes

8 The following year, the *FNRS* flew again. This time Auguste was accompanied by a Belgian engineer, Professor Max Cosyns. On August 18, they drifted high above southern Switzerland and northern Italy, crossed Lake Garda, and landed near the Italian resort of Desenzano. This time all went well, and they were able to make the scientific observations they needed. What's more, they beat their own record, reaching an amazing 52,152 feet.

9 A further twenty-five ascents followed over the next few years. Piccard pushed the world altitude record to 72,177 feet and gathered vital information about the stratosphere and those strange cosmic rays. As it turned out, they were not rays at all, but minute space invaders: subatomic particles zooming into Earth's atmosphere from elsewhere in the universe.

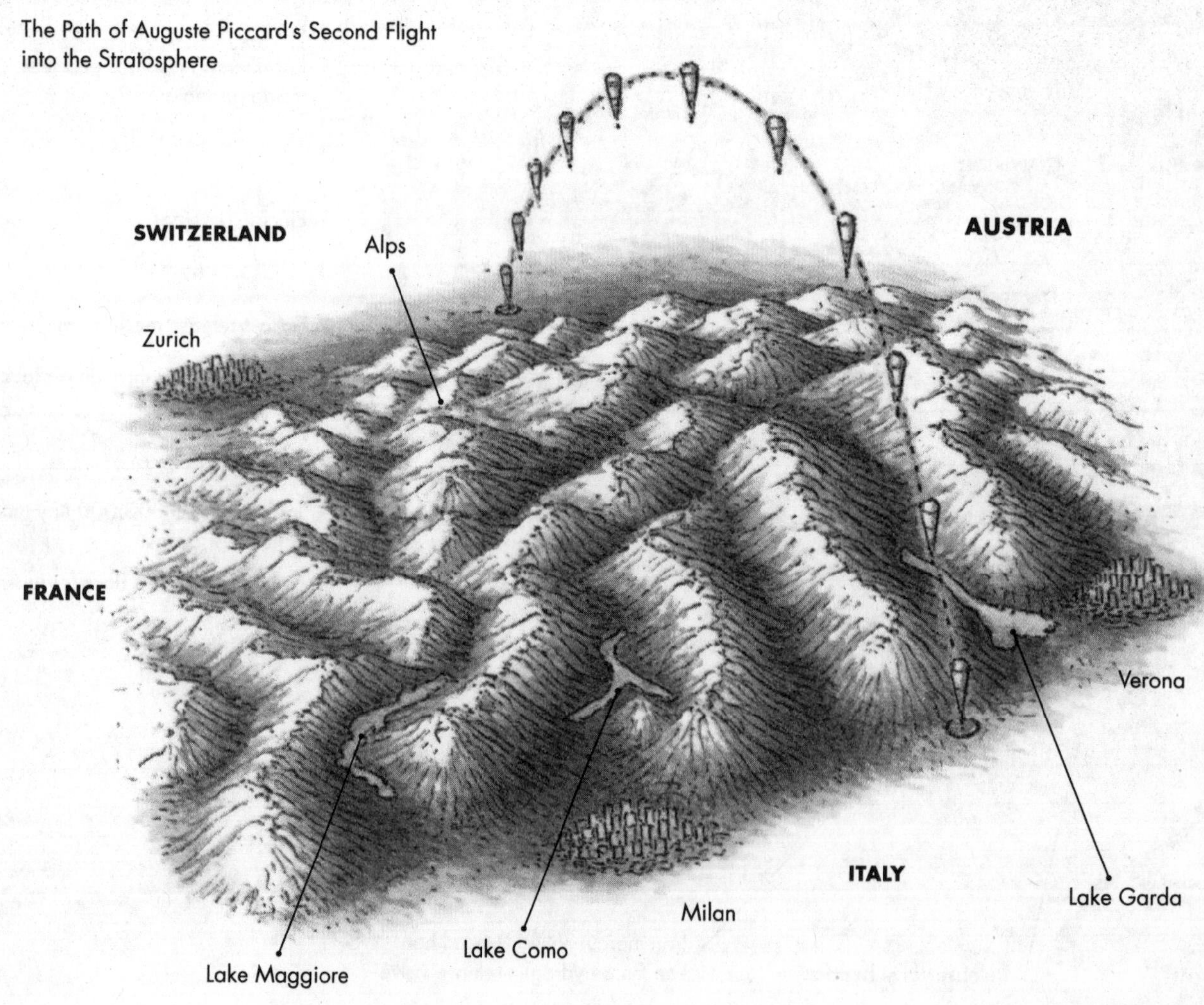

10 By the time of his last balloon adventure, Auguste Piccard knew that the principles of his pressurized cabin could also take him to the depths of the ocean. Working with his son, Jacques, he began to design an extraordinary deep-sea craft, or bathyscaphe. They named it the *Trieste.*

11 Instead of a balloon canopy, the *Trieste* had a long cylinder-shaped float. Inside the float were a large gas tank and two air tanks. Gasoline and air are lighter than water, so when all three tanks were full, the craft remained on the surface. To make it sink, the air tanks were flooded with seawater. The float also contained two hoppers filled with iron pellets to release when the bathyscaphe needed to rise again.

12 An airtight cabin was welded beneath the float. Like the cabin of the *FNRS*, it was a perfect sphere, but instead of aluminum, its walls were forged in steel 5 inches thick. It had two windows made of strong artificial glass called Lucite. And it had an air supply and purification system that allowed two crew members to breathe safely for up to twenty-four hours.

13 Built in Italy, the *Trieste* was bought by the U.S. Navy in 1958. The following year, the freighter *Santa Maria* transported it west from California to Guam. The USS *Wandank* then towed it to a site above the deepest part of all the world's seas: the mysterious Challenger Deep.

forged A metal object that was forged was heated in a special furnace and hammered into shape.

Piccard and Walsh recorded the depth of water under the *Trieste* with an electrical device called an echo sounder.

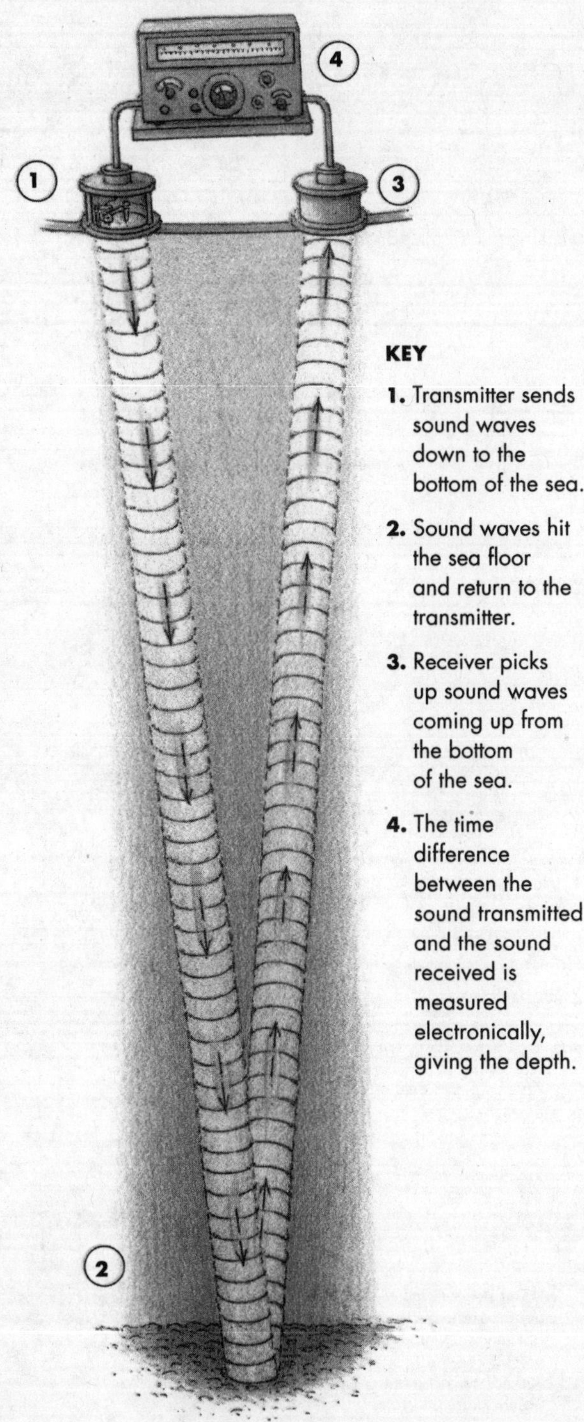

1
2
3
4
KEY
1. Transmitter sends sound waves down to the bottom of the sea.
2. Sound waves hit the sea floor and return to the transmitter.
3. Receiver picks up sound waves coming up from the bottom of the sea.
4. The time difference between the sound transmitted and the sound received is measured electronically, giving the depth.

myNotes

TO THE OCEAN FLOOR

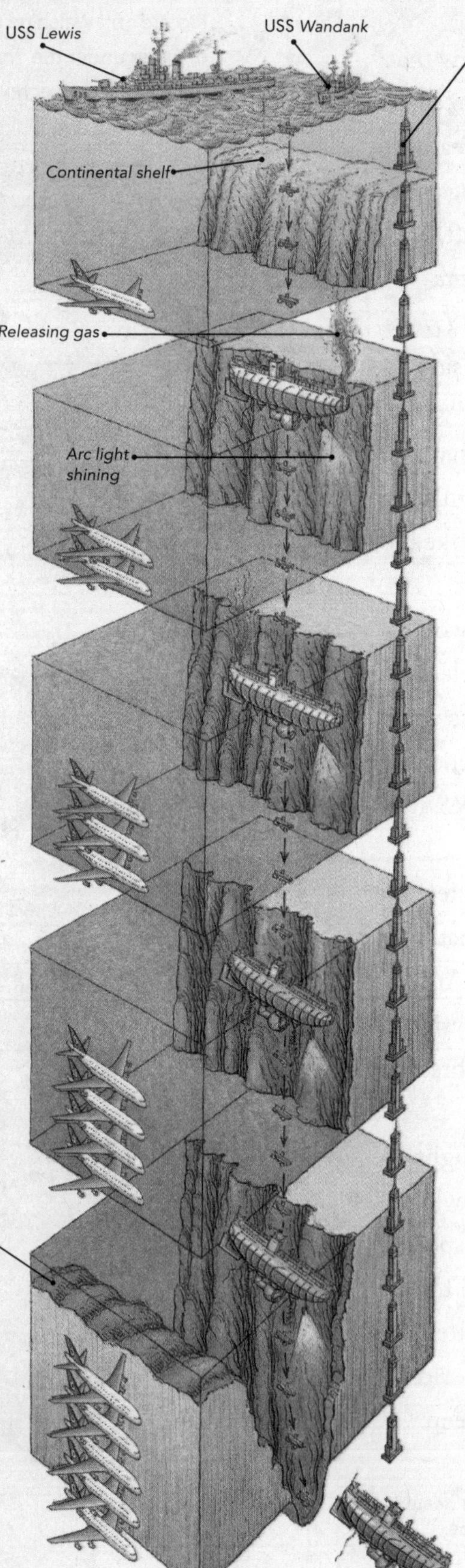
USS Lewis
USS Wandank
Depth measured in Empire State Buildings: 1,450 feet each
Continental shelf
Releasing gas
Arc light shining
Abyssal plain: level of the Pacific Ocean floor.
Water pressure increases with depth. At the bottom of the Challenger Deep, the total pressure on the Trieste was 220,500 tons (1.24 tons per square centimeter), equivalent to the weight of five A380 Airbuses.

At sea level
Trieste's air tanks are flooded with seawater, and she begins to sink.

325 feet below
Piccard releases gas to allow *Trieste* to desend through a cold layer.

985 feet
Arc lights are switched on.

1,970 feet
Speed of descent now increases from 4 inches per second to 36 inches per second.

2,400 feet
Total darkness from here on down.

18,000 feet
Cabin springs a leak but seals itself.

23,000 feet
Trieste sets a new record for the deepest-ever dive.

27,200 feet
Piccard dumps some ballast to slow the rate of descent.

30,000 feet
Alarm sounds as outer windowpane cracks.

31,000 feet
Piccard uses echo sounder to detect bottom of trench.

36,000 feet
Trieste comes to rest on the bottom of the Challenger Deep.

The great gash in the earth's surface, deeper than Mount Everest is high, lies in the Mariana Trench on the floor of the Pacific Ocean.

14 Here, in rough seas, Jacques Piccard and Lieutenant Don Walsh of the U.S. Navy undertook one of the most nerve-rattling journeys ever made. On the morning of January 23, 1960, the two men climbed through the hatch and sealed themselves into their steel bubble. At precisely 8:23 a.m., they let seawater into the air tanks above them and began a 288-minute descent down, down to the funeral-black floor of the ocean.

15 To Jacques's surprise and dismay, at about 340 feet below the surface, the *Trieste* came to a stop. It had met a dense layer of cold water (a thermocline), which blocked their descent. After a quick calculation, he made his craft less buoyant by releasing some of the gas from the tank above, and the *Trieste* continued dropping into the darkness.

16 At 1,000 feet, Jacques tested the *Trieste's* quartz arc lights, casting bright white beams into the surrounding sea. Plankton streamed past. By 2,400 feet, they had moved from the twilight zone to the abyssal zone, where not a trace of sunlight can reach. Staring out at the grim blackness, the men felt the cabin grow colder and colder.

17 Around 18,000 feet, the cabin sprang a small leak, which a little later mended itself. Now dropping at 200 feet a minute, the *Trieste* plummeted beyond 23,000 feet, reaching a new record depth for any dive. At 29,500 feet, Jacques could feel the steep walls of the Mariana Trench rising around them. The *Trieste* had not been tested to this depth, and he released some iron ballast to slow her speed. The ocean floor was still about a mile away.

18 Suddenly, the men were shaken by what sounded like a muffled explosion. The outer skin of one of the windows had cracked. For a second, they thought they were finished. Luckily the inner layer of Lucite held fast, and not long afterward the *Trieste* came to rest at the bottom of the Challenger Deep. Switching on their lights again, they stared out in wonder at the fish and slime around them. It was certainly eerie and strange—but at least there were no monsters.

19 As it would be dangerous to surface at night, the *Trieste* could not stay long. After just twenty minutes, Piccard lightened his craft by releasing 10 tons of iron pellets from the hoppers in the float. The *Trieste* immediately began to rise. Faster and faster she climbed, until she was moving upward at 5 feet per second. Just over three hours later, she broke the surface of the warm, bright Pacific. The sailors on the *Wandank* and the escorting destroyer *Lewis* hurried to winch her from the water and release her crew.

20 The amazing Piccards are still the only explorers to have traveled, literally, to both the heights and depths of our world.

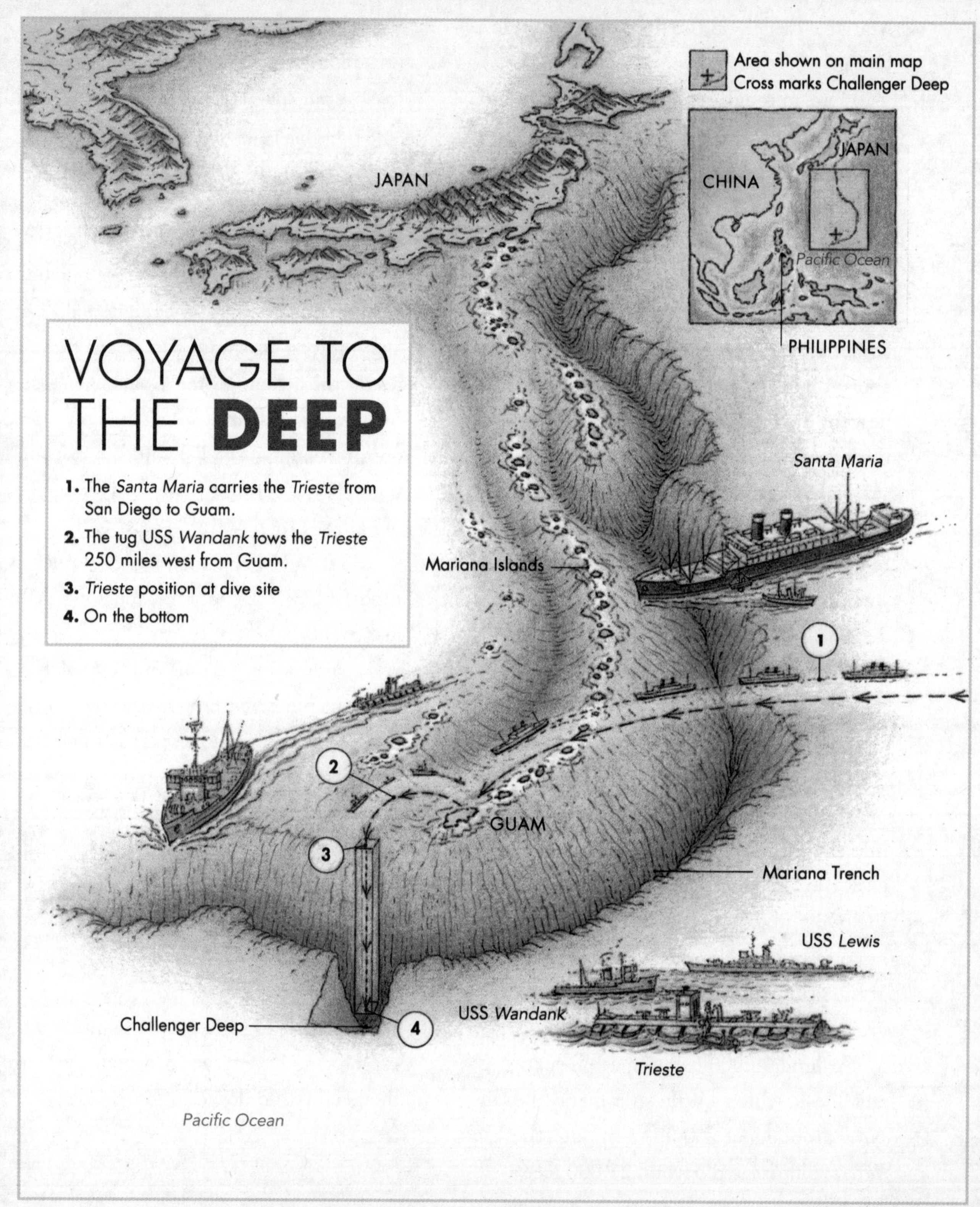

Area shown on main map
Cross marks Challenger Deep
JAPAN
CHINA
JAPAN
Pacific Ocean
PHILIPPINES
VOYAGE TO THE DEEP
1. The Santa Maria carries the Trieste from San Diego to Guam.
2. The tug USS Wandank tows the Trieste 250 miles west from Guam.
3. Trieste position at dive site
4. On the bottom
Santa Maria
Mariana Islands
1
2
GUAM
3
Mariana Trench
USS Lewis
USS Wandank
Challenger Deep
4
Trieste
Pacific Ocean

Respond to the Text

Collaborative Discussion

Look back at what you wrote on page 84. Tell a partner two things you learned from the text. Then work with a group to discuss the questions below. Use details from *Into the Unknown: Above and Below* to support your answers. Choose a group leader to guide your team's conversation.

1. Review pages 86–90. What do his efforts to explore the stratosphere tell you about Auguste Piccard?

2. Reread pages 91–93. What made the voyage of the *Trieste* "nerve-rattling"?

3. In what ways were Auguste Piccard's balloon and the *Trieste* alike? In what ways were they different?

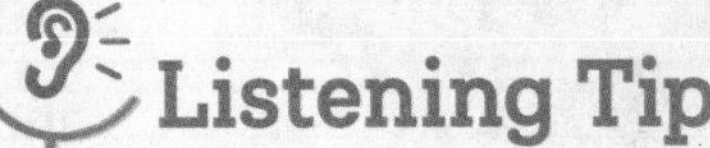

Listening Tip

Listen carefully as the group leader reads aloud the question your group will discuss next.

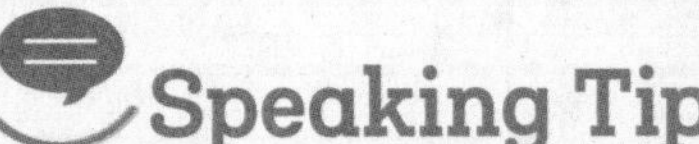

Speaking Tip

Take turns. Wait until you are called on by the leader before sharing your thoughts.

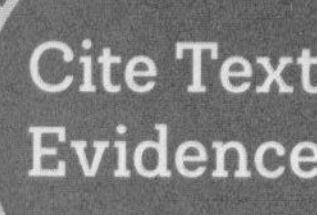

Write a News Script

PROMPT

Into the Unknown: Above and Below tells about Auguste and Jacques Piccard's fascinating explorations of the stratosphere above the earth as well as the ocean's depths.

Imagine that you are a news reporter assigned to report on one of the explorations. Choose an exploration as the focus of your report and write a script. Use evidence from the text to describe the exploration, its dangers, and the discoveries it uncovered. Include some scientific terms and explain what they mean. Include an introduction and a conclusion. Don't forget to use some of the Critical Vocabulary words in your writing.

PLAN

Make notes, using text evidence, about the important details of the exploration. Explain a few scientific terms in your own words.

WRITE

Now write your news script about one of the explorations.

Make sure your news script
☐ introduces the topic.
☐ includes facts and details from the text.
☐ uses and explains the meanings of scientific terms.
☐ contains a concluding statement.
☐ is easy for a non-scientific audience to understand.

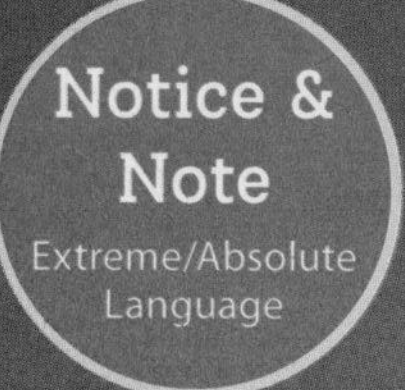

Prepare to Read

GENRE STUDY **Informational texts** give facts and examples about a topic.

- Informational texts may organize ideas using headings and subheadings. They may also have main ideas supported by key details, including facts and quotations.
- Social studies texts may include words that are specific to the topic.
- Informational texts include text features such as captions, which explain what readers see in photos and illustrations.

SET A PURPOSE **Think about** the title and genre of this text. What do you know about history's great discoveries? What do you want to learn? Write your ideas below.

CRITICAL VOCABULARY

- ransacked
- outskirts
- precious
- authorities
- ruthless

Meet the Author: Claire Llewellyn

Great DISCOVERIES and Amazing ADVENTURES

The Stories of Hidden Marvels and Lost Treasures

BY CLAIRE LLEWELLYN

myNotes

A Hidden City in the Andes

1 Between C.E. 1100 and 1500 the mighty Inca civilization flourished high up in the Andes mountains of Peru in South America. In 1532 Spanish adventurers known as *conquistadores* (conquerors) invaded the region and ransacked many Inca cities in search of gold. The Incas abandoned their other cities, which fell into ruin. One of these cities was Machu Picchu.

"I know of no place in the world [which] can compare with it."

—HIRAM BINGHAM, HISTORY PROFESSOR

The Professor

2 Hiram Bingham (1875–1956), a history professor at Yale University, studied South American history for many years. In 1911, during a visit to Lima, Peru, he came across an old book that told of the downfall of the Incas. He was inspired by the description of the Inca retreat and the ancient mountain cities that they had abandoned. Bingham decided to try to find the ancient Inca capital city.

Machu Picchu

Hiram Bingham's discovery of Machu Picchu brought him worldwide fame. He was the inspiration for the movie hero Indiana Jones. Possibly the greatest archaeological site in the Americas, Machu Picchu reveals fascinating facts about the Inca civilization and encourages many tourists to visit Peru.

ransacked If someone ransacked a place, he or she damaged it while looking for something.

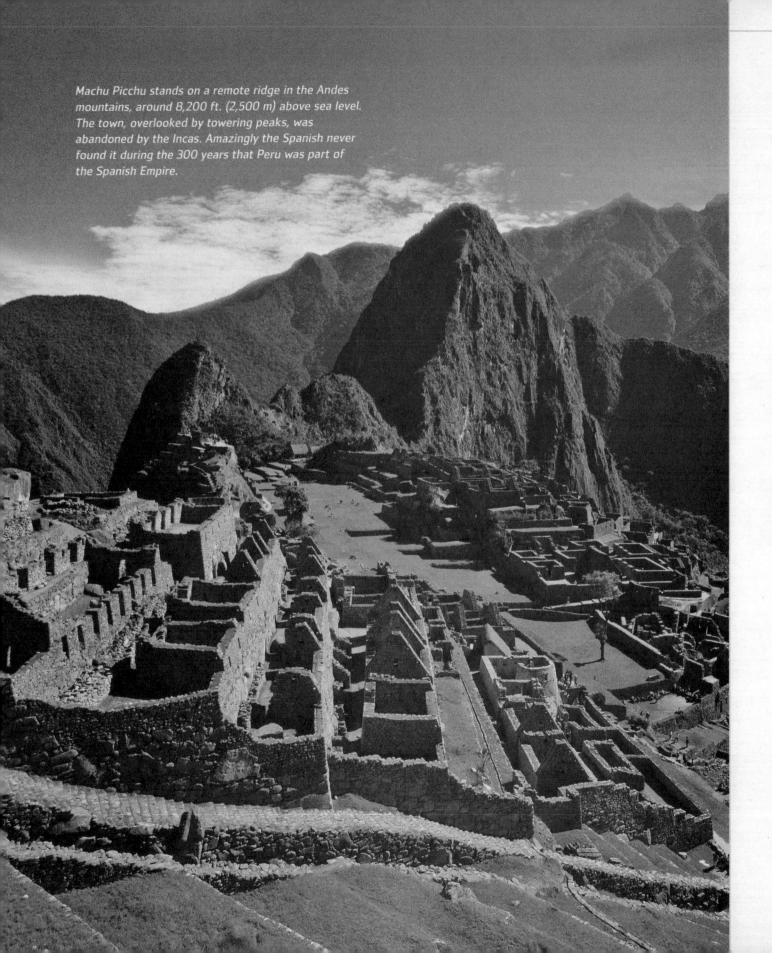

Machu Picchu stands on a remote ridge in the Andes mountains, around 8,200 ft. (2,500 m) above sea level. The town, overlooked by towering peaks, was abandoned by the Incas. Amazingly the Spanish never found it during the 300 years that Peru was part of the Spanish Empire.

myNotes

A Nerve-Racking Climb

3 Bingham led an expedition to Peru. He went with his party to Cuzco in the foothills of the Andes. From there they climbed into the Urubamba gorge. On July 23, 1911 the group camped on the land of a local farmer, who told Bingham about ruins on top of a ridge. Bingham paid the farmer to guide him there, and the two set out one cold, drizzly morning. It was a nerve-racking climb up steep, rocky slopes and along narrow mountain paths. At times the professor had to crawl on his hands and knees across narrow bridges stretching over terrifying gorges.

A Sensational Find

4 At the top of the ridge Bingham and the farmer rested in a hut, where locals told them about the nearby ruins. An 11-year-old boy escorted the professor past overgrown terraces to some white granite walls. Bingham saw palaces, temples, terraces, and towers. Astonishing! It was an ancient Inca city, known to locals as Machu Picchu. Bingham was overwhelmed. He led three additional expeditions to Machu Picchu over the next four years.

Building Machu Picchu

Built in 1450, Machu Picchu, or "old mountain," is a spectacular, highly ordered city covering a site of around 3 square miles (8 square km). Its houses, temples, workshops, and other buildings were built using a simple design. Large granite blocks were shaped and sanded by hand until they fit together perfectly without needing mortar. There were no rounded arches or decorative carvings. On the outskirts of the city the steep hillsides were terraced for farming, and fertile soil was brought up from the valley to grow sweet potatoes, sugarcane, yucca, and corn.

outskirts The outskirts of a city or town are its outer edges, farthest away from the center.

Ancient Pictures in a Hidden Cave

5 In September 1940 four boys were walking in the grounds of Lascaux (lah-SKOH), an old mansion in southwest France. When their dog fell through a crack in some rocks, the boys went to rescue it and found that the hole led to a cavern. It would prove to be one of the most exciting archaeological discoveries of the 1900s.

Finding the Cave

6 The four teenage boys who discovered the cavern were Marcel Ravidat, Jacques Marsal, Georges Agnel, and Simon Coencas. The next day they returned to explore. They brought ropes, ladders, and lights with them and lowered themselves down through the hole. Their eyes gradually adjusted to the darkness. They saw that the walls of the cavern were covered in pictures. They could see images of horses, deer, and other animals. The boys knew they had made an amazing discovery.

The insides of the Lascaux caves are covered with pictures—some are painted, and others are engraved or drawn. The pictures were made around 17,000 years ago during the early Stone Age, when people had not yet discovered metals and were using stone to make tools.

myNotes

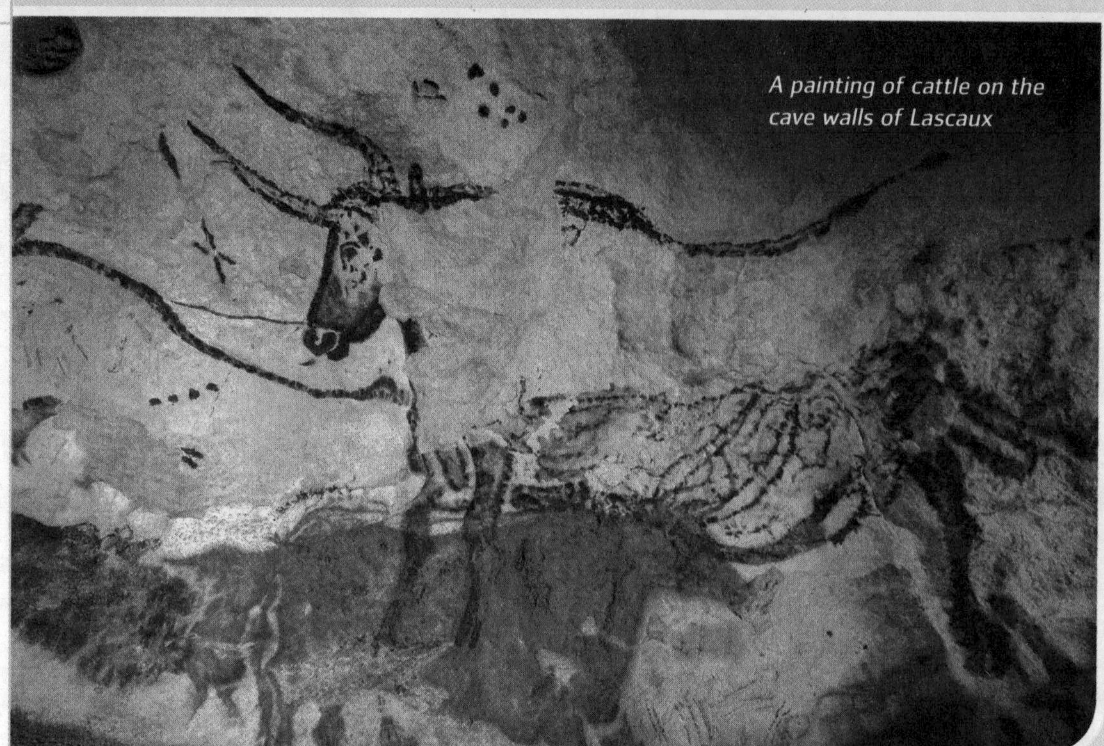

A painting of cattle on the cave walls of Lascaux

Cave Art

The artists who painted the pictures in Lascaux drew animals that were important to them. They might have thought that the paintings would help them while hunting. It must have been difficult to work in the dark, remote caves. The artists would have needed torches to see and ladders to reach the high ceilings. The paints they used were made from natural pigments, plant roots, charcoal, and sap and were dabbed on using their fingers or with sticks or pads of moss or fur.

The First Visitors

7 News of the discovery traveled fast. People were soon flocking to explore the caves. In all, they found seven underground chambers connected by narrow passageways, with paintings and engravings on the ceilings and walls. A team of top archaeologists soon arrived at the caves. They were amazed by the sensational find—the paintings dated from around 15000 B.C.E. and were perfectly preserved. Archaeologists were worried about what to do with the caves. Europe was involved in World War I, so there was no spare money to spend on developing and protecting the site. They decided to seal the caves until after the war.

Visits to the Cave

8 The caves were opened to the public in 1948, and thousands of people visited them. But it soon became clear that the visitors were having a harmful effect. The gases and water vapor in their breath dampened the cave walls and damaged the precious paintings. Attempts were made to protect them, but in 1963 it was decided to close the caves. Twenty years later a life-size replica of the biggest cave was opened nearby.

precious Something that is precious has value and should be treated with care.

A group of tourists visit the replica cave.

The Caves of Lascaux

The caves of Lascaux were one of the great archaeological discoveries of the 1900s. The paintings of prehistoric animals captured the world's imagination. They offer us a glimpse of the lives of our ancestors in the distant past.

myNotes

Silent Warriors Guard a Tomb

9 In 1974 a group of farmers were digging a well near the city of Xi'an (shee-ahn) in northern China when they stumbled across something surprising. Buried in the ground were several carved heads made out of pottery. The men took the statues home and informed the authorities. Soon an archaeologist arrived in Xi'an to study and learn more about the statues. He set up a tent in the middle of the field and began digging. It was not long before he made a sensational discovery.

authorities Authorities are the people in charge, who have the power to make decisions or give orders.

A terra-cotta warrior silently stands guard by the emperor's tomb. In the early civilizations servants were often sentenced to death to serve their ruler in the afterlife. Rather than sacrifice an entire army, Emperor Qin was buried with a symbolic army of life-size, terra-cotta soldiers.

The Imperial Burial Site

10 When archaeologist Yuan Zhongyi (yoo-ahn jong-ee) was sent to a field in northern China to investigate some buried figurines, he thought he would be there for around one week. But after digging in the ground for a few days his team uncovered something. Extraordinary! It was a gigantic pit covering almost 3.5 acres (14,300 square meters). It had a wooden roof made out of pine logs and a floor paved with brick, and it contained row upon row of life-size statues. They were an army of warriors beautifully crafted out of baked clay known as terra-cotta. Yuan Zhongyi soon realized that this must be part of the burial site of Emperor Qin Shi Huangdi (chin shir hwong-dee) (259–210 B.C.E.). He was the first emperor of China and was buried in a tomb in the area.

The Emperor

11 Emperor Qin Shi Huangdi was a major figure in Chinese history—a leader, conqueror, and ruthless tyrant. He successfully united six warring states into the land of modern-day China. As soon as he became emperor, Qin ordered 700,000 slave laborers to begin working on the tomb in which he would one day be buried, and he commanded craftsmen to make a terra-cotta army to protect him in the afterlife.

Qin Shi Huangdi, first emperor of China and founder of the Qin Dynasty

The Excavation

12 Archaeologists continued digging at the site. In 1976 they found a second pit and then two more pits. One of the pits was empty, but the others contained almost 8,000 statues. The archaeologists faced a huge task, and in order to protect the fragile figurines, they temporarily refilled the new pits. Since then two of the pits have been excavated. The figurines have been displayed in Qin Shi Huangdi's museum, which was built near the site. It is now one of the greatest tourist attractions in the world.

ruthless Someone who is ruthless shows no concern for other people and is very cruel.

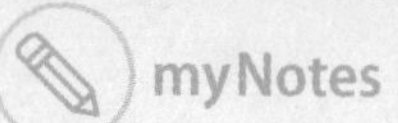

Making the Warriors

Each warrior in the Terra-Cotta Army is a unique individual and can be distinguished from all of the others. Their heads were made from one of around 12 different molds, and the eyes and noses were sculpted by hand. Beards, mustaches, hairstyles, and headgear helped create an individual appearance, while arms, legs, and armor added additional variety. After being fired the figurines were painted and given bronze swords and wooden scabbards (cases), crossbows, and spears.

Originally painted in bright colors, this terra-cotta archer has faded and lost his wooden crossbow. Other members of the army include officers, cavalrymen, and charioteers with chariots and mighty horses. Tall, well proportioned, and physically alert, the warriors look like they are ready for battle. Their faces are intelligent, resourceful, and sincere. This is an emperor's ideal army—one that would defend him to the death!

Part of the Terra-Cotta Army

Terra-Cotta Army

The discovery of the terra-cotta warriors has brought a unique work of art to the world's attention. The intricate detail of the figurines provides historians with a rich source of information about the early years of the Chinese Empire, and the discovery of his army has provided Emperor Qin Shi Huangdi with the glory and immortality he desired.

Respond to the Text

Collaborative Discussion

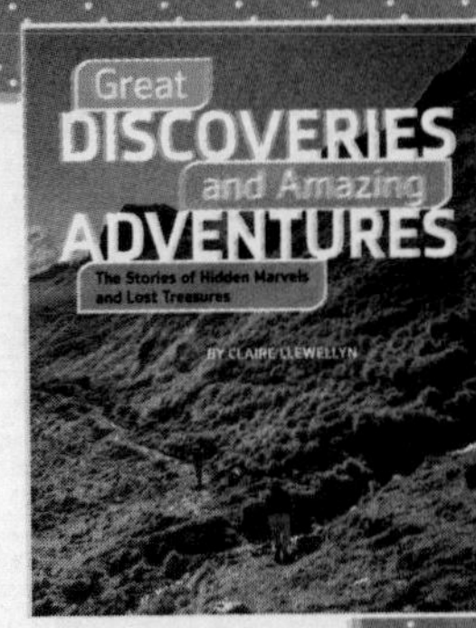

Look back at what you wrote on page 98. Tell a partner two things you learned from the text. Then work with a group to discuss the questions below. Look for details and examples in *Great Discoveries* to support your ideas. Ask and answer questions to help make the discussion worthwhile for everyone.

1. Review pages 100–102. Why is Machu Picchu described as a hidden city?

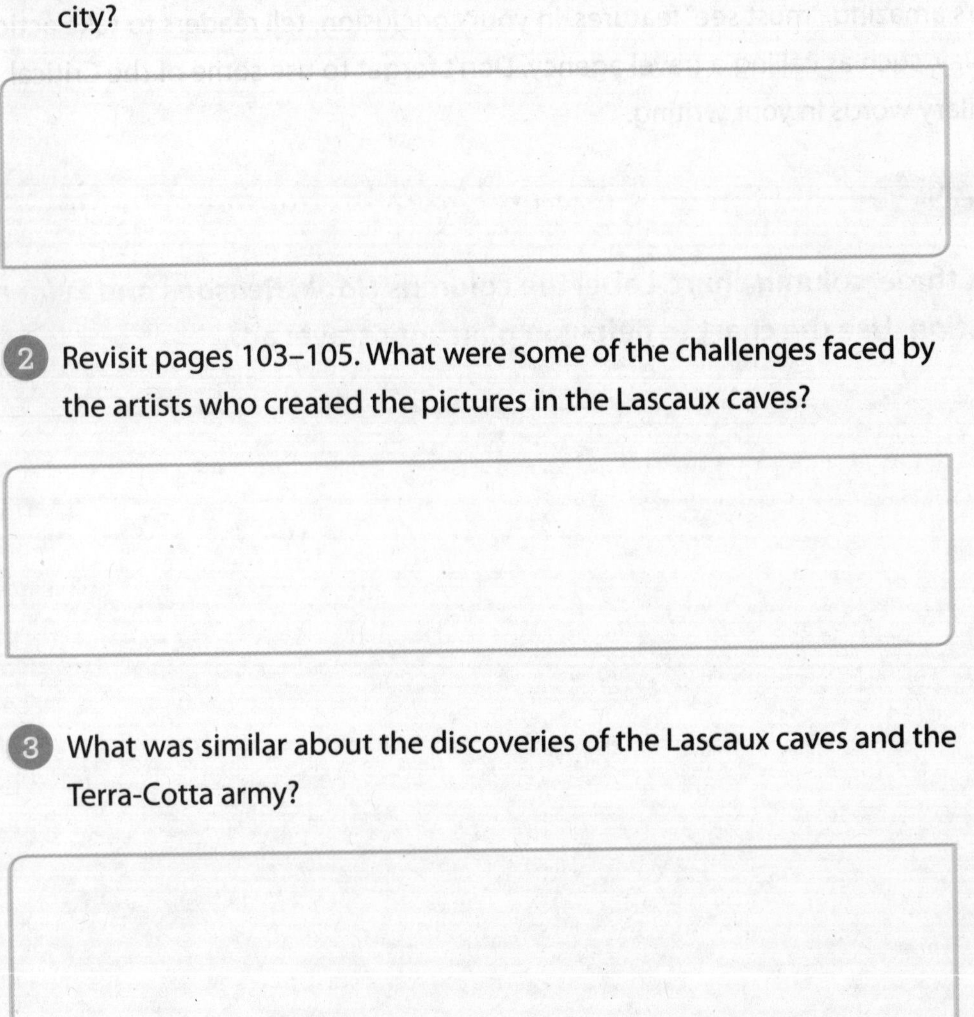

2. Revisit pages 103–105. What were some of the challenges faced by the artists who created the pictures in the Lascaux caves?

3. What was similar about the discoveries of the Lascaux caves and the Terra-Cotta army?

Listening Tip

Did someone make a comment that wasn't quite clear? Think of a question that will get you the information you need to better understand.

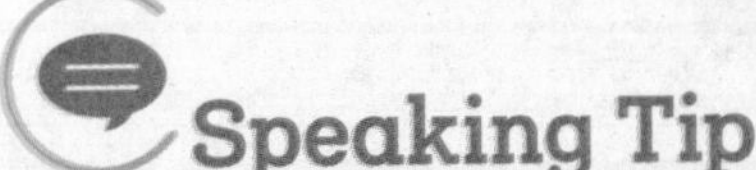

Speaking Tip

Once you've finished speaking, ask if anyone has a question about the information that you shared.

Cite Text Evidence

Write a Travel Advertisement

PROMPT

Great Discoveries and Amazing Adventures describes three amazing sites that have existed since ancient times. These wondrous places are popular with tourists who are interested in ancient history.

Imagine that your job is to write travel advertisements. Choose one of the three sites and write an ad that persuades tourists to visit that site. Introduce your destination with a "hook" that grabs the audience's attention. Use details from the text to highlight the site's amazing, "must see" features. In your conclusion, tell readers to take action in some way, such as calling a travel agency. Don't forget to use some of the Critical Vocabulary words in your writing.

PLAN

Draw a three-column chart. Label the columns *Hook, Reasons and Evidence,* and *Action*. Use the chart to help you plan your travel ad.

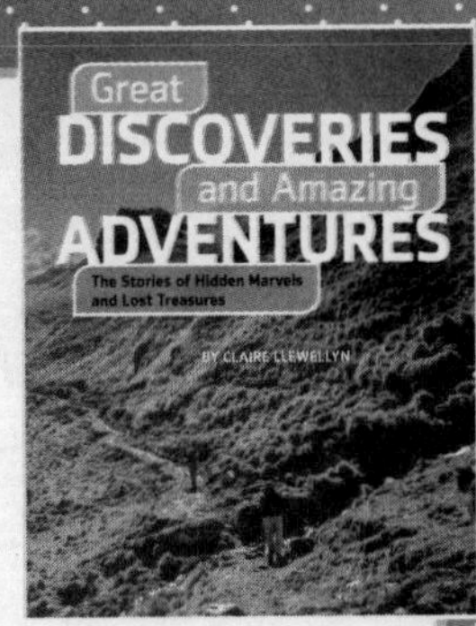

WRITE

Now write your travel ad persuading tourists to visit your chosen destination.

Make sure your travel ad

- ☐ begins with a strong hook that grabs the audience's attention.
- ☐ supports the hook using persuasive reasons.
- ☐ includes evidence from the text.
- ☐ concludes by telling the reader what to do next.

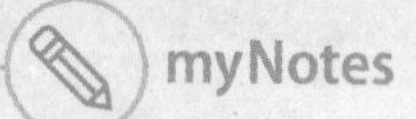

Notice & Note
Extreme/Absolute Language

Prepare to Read

GENRE STUDY An **autobiography** is the story of a real person's life written by that person.

- Autobiographies present events in sequential, or chronological, order to help readers understand what happened in the person's life and when.
- Autobiographies sometimes include literary devices, such as descriptive language and sensory words.
- Autobiographies include first-person pronouns such as *I, me, my, mine,* and *we.*

SET A PURPOSE **Think about** the title and genre of this text. What do you know about space travel? What do you want to learn? Write your ideas below.

CRITICAL VOCABULARY

- ignited
- hybrid
- synthetic
- exhaust
- physics
- institution

Build Background: Getting to Outer Space

SpaceShipOne

by Matthew Stinemetze
as told to Naomi Wallace

SpaceShipOne
A Paul G. Allen Project
N328KF

1 **"Holy cow, that was close!"** *SpaceShipOne's* engine ignited right by the mother ship, *White Knight*, which had just carried it on her underbelly to an altitude around 50,000 feet. My job was to ride in *White Knight* and pull the lever to release the spaceship. The sound of the rocket engine filled the cockpit. Through my small porthole window I could see the tiny spacecraft as it shot vertically into space. By the voices in my headphones, I could tell it was going to be an award-winning flight.

2 As a kid, I had always dreamed of going to space. I spent hours building different types of model aircraft, sometimes modifying the design. My brother and I even accidentally set a field on fire while shooting off our model rockets. Luckily, the firefighters got there quickly and put the fire out!

SpaceShipOne was part of a two-plane system. It attached to the belly of a mother ship, the *White Knight*. The *White Knight* carried *SpaceShipOne* to an altitude of 50,000 feet. When they reached the right altitude, *White Knight* crew member Matthew Stinemetze pulled a lever that released *SpaceShipOne*. Was he ever nervous when it was time to pull the lever? "Not nervous for me," he says, "nervous for the pilot that's about to get launched on an adventurous flight."

Once released from the mother ship, the pilot of *SpaceShipOne* was in control. He ignited his rocket engine and shot almost straight up into outer space. The rocket on the spaceship was a Lefler 2004, a hybrid rocket fueled by a mixture of two substances—in this case, laughing gas and synthetic rubber.

ignited Something that ignited caught fire or exploded.

hybrid Something can be described as hybrid if it is made up of two or more different things.

synthetic A synthetic item is artificial rather than natural.

3 My love for flight and aircraft design intensified as I grew older. I earned my bachelor's degree in Aeronautical Engineering in 1998, and a few months later I was hired on at Scaled Composites in Mojave, California. Through a little bit of luck and being in the right place at the right time, I was made project engineer for *SpaceShipOne*. Our one-of-a-kind spacecraft was being built for the Ansari X Prize competition, which was created to help develop the private spaceflight industry.

4 I spent the next couple of years working many long hours making dreams a reality. One of the toughest parts of my job was not being able to tell my family about it. My dad and my brother share my love for aircraft. They would love to have known all the details of what we were doing. But the project was top-secret, and I couldn't say a word. The one consolation was that my wife, Kit, also worked at Scaled. We had private discussions sharing our excitement during those top-secret years.

***White Knight* and *SpaceShipOne* take off together from the Mojave Airport runway.**

myNotes

5 The public was shown the finished project in April of 2003. My dad came out all the way from Kansas just to see it. I was so glad to have him there so I could show off what I had done. But there was still a lot of work to do. The spacecraft was made, but we had yet to run test flights. I felt honored to be a part of the test flight crew.

6 After many flights of varying difficulty, we were ready to make the first spaceflight. The date was June 21, 2004, and it would prove to be a historic day.

7 The sky was still black as we rolled the joined aircraft out of the hangar. I had hardly slept the night before. Every nerve in my body was filled with anticipation. This day would either prove that we had succeeded in making a spacecraft, or it would show that we still had a long way to go. I could feel the tension in the air. Everyone was aware of the dangers of this flight. Until now, no one but trained government astronauts had been to space. And even some of the government missions had ended in disaster. The possibility that someone could die was very real, but no one dared talk about it.

8 Even with all the danger, I was confident we would succeed. Burt Rutan, the president of Scaled Composites, had designed the aircraft and knew what he was doing. Every member of the team who helped build the planes and design the technology was exceptionally intelligent. We all knew what was at stake and had left nothing to chance.

At a news conference, aviation designer Burt Rutan describes how *SpaceShipOne* performed during its test flights.

SpaceShipOne **pilot Mike Melvill waves from the cockpit.**

9 I was in my flight suit by 4:00 a.m. The flight was scheduled to take off in a couple of hours. I tried to calm my nerves as I strapped on my parachute. Looking at the joined aircraft, my nervousness was replaced with excitement. I had looked forward to this day for months now. If all worked out as I expected, this would be our moment of glory.

10 As *White Knight* taxied onto the runway carrying *SpaceShipOne* under her, I looked out my small cockpit window at the crowd gathered to watch the flight. It was overwhelming! The fact that thousands of people came to watch a test flight proved that we weren't just a bunch of airplane geeks trying to build a spaceship. It showed that everyday citizens want to see space travel made a reality.

11 The flight to 48,000 feet took almost an hour. There is barely enough room to sit three people in the cockpits of *White Knight* and *SpaceShipOne*. Even though *White Knight's* cockpit is comfy, the parachutes and the flight-test gear made the space even more cramped, and it was difficult for me to move my arms and legs. After an hour I was getting sore, but it was worth it to make history. I anticipated the countdown for the release of *SpaceShipOne*. When the time came, I quickly pulled the small lever at my right side and heard "Clean release" from the chase aircraft, our extra eyes in the sky. Shortly after the spaceship was clear, the pilot, Mike Melvill, ignited the rocket engine and began his solo climb to space.

12 *White Knight* continued to circle in the sky as we waited to escort *SpaceShipOne* back to Earth. I studied the curvature of the earth and the darkness of space overhead as I listened intently to Mike's radio transmissions. Mission control called, "328,000 feet," and I cheered with joy. We later found out that Mike's actual altitude was 328,491 feet, a mere 408 feet past the boundary of space! We had done it! We'd sent a man into space in a spaceship we built with our own hands.

13 Although it took almost an hour for *White Knight* to carry *SpaceShipOne* to 50,000 feet, it took less than twenty minutes for the spaceship to come back to Earth. That's because it traveled back at over 100,000 feet per minute. That's about Mach 3, three times the speed of sound!

14 As *SpaceShipOne* landed, I could see the crowd on their feet cheering. Mike was led to a podium, and immediately flashbulbs started going off. News channels all over the world carried the story that the first civilian spaceship had made it safely to space and back again.

One of the cool things about *SpaceShipOne* was that it could take off from almost any airport in the world. The spaceships built by NASA have to take off from special launch pads several hundred yards from spectators. The large rocket boosters used to get them off the ground create a lot of heat and **exhaust**.

How hard is it to be part of a cool project like this? Sometimes, it's simply being in the right place at the right time. When Matthew Stinemetze was offered the position of project engineer, he had just finished working on another project and was able to jump right in. But it takes more than luck and timing. It takes a lot of hard work, too. Matt says the subjects that helped him land his job were math, **physics**, science, and art.

One of the biggest thrills he got from this project was just being a part of the team that changed history. "We are at the beginning of something huge," Matt says. "I can feel the wave forming. The support is huge, and this time the space race is here to stay."

exhaust Exhaust is the gas that comes out of an engine as a waste product.
physics Physics is the scientific study of matter and energy.

15 Three months later our team made the two flights that were required for the X Prize competition. The first flight, piloted by Mike Melvill, was on September 29, followed by the second flight on October 4, piloted by Brian Binnie. It was during the second flight that *SpaceShipOne's* engine ignited right outside my window. During this flight a new world record was set for the highest altitude reached by a single-wing craft. The previous record had been set in 1963 by the X-15, a military aircraft, with an altitude of 354,200 feet. *SpaceShipOne* beat that record with an altitude of 377,591 feet. Best of all, our team won the $10 million Ansari X Prize.

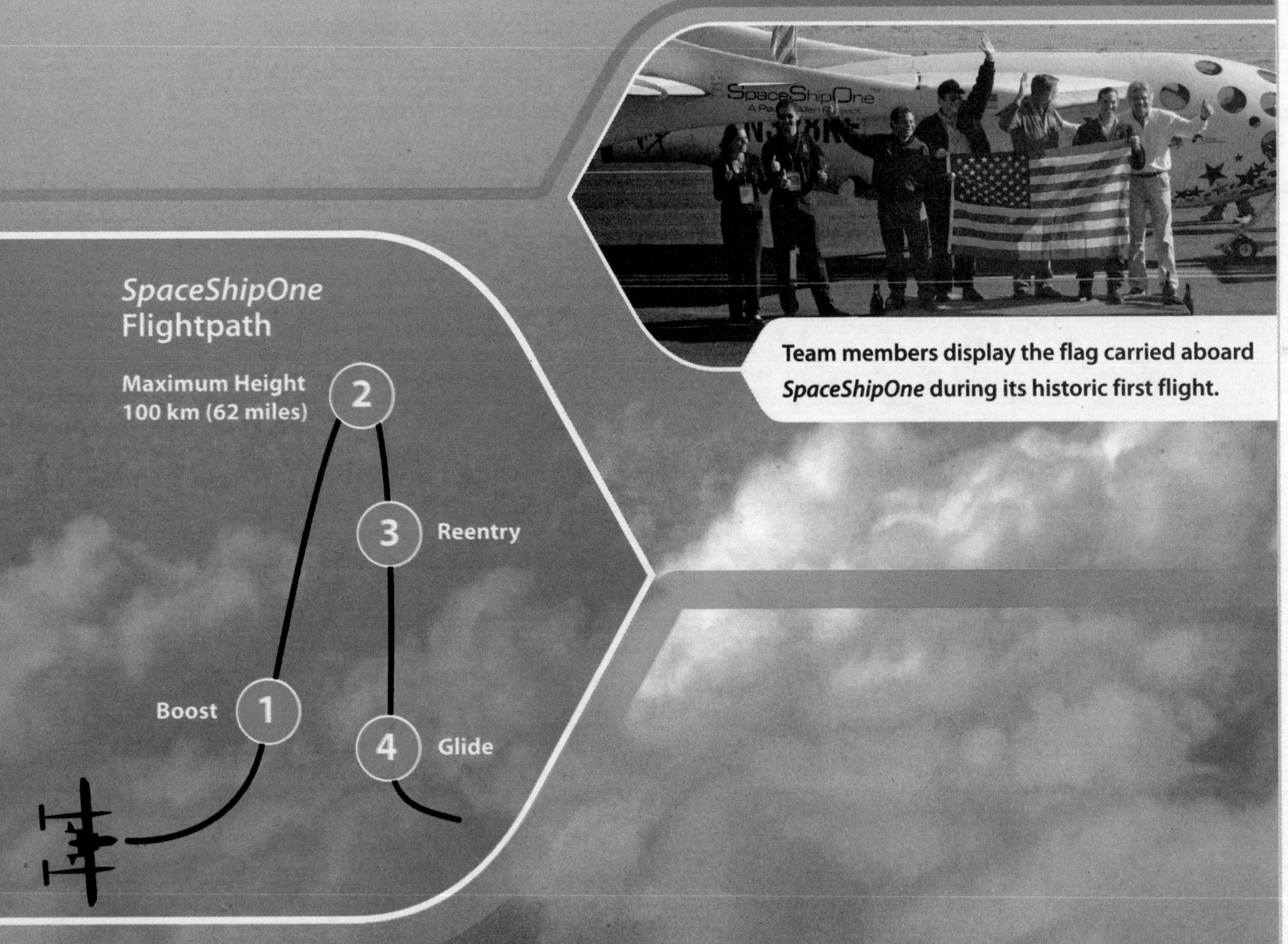

Team members display the flag carried aboard *SpaceShipOne* during its historic first flight.

myNotes

16 Although all the spaceflights were complete, life did not slow down for a long time. Burt Rutan and the pilots of *SpaceShipOne* made several appearances on talk shows, including *The Tonight Show with Jay Leno*. I was also asked to speak for several functions in my home state of Kansas, which included a trip to my mom's fifth-grade classroom and to my high school in McPherson. Anytime I gave a presentation, I tried to drive home the point that I'm just an ordinary guy who followed my dream. I was part of an amazing team of people that made this project a reality. No one person could have made this happen. It took a lot of teamwork and dedication from everyone.

17 This has been the coolest, most tiring experience of my life. But it will be worth it if by the time you are my age, space travel is as common as flying an airplane is today. As a kid, I'd look up at the stars and dream of going to space. Now, almost on a daily basis, I spend time 50,000 feet closer to my dream. And it's awesome!

18 With the records set and the goals achieved, *SpaceShipOne* has been retired to the halls of history. On October 5, 2005, *SpaceShipOne* was unveiled in its new home at the Smithsonian Institution in Washington, D.C. It was kind of sad to see the plane go as I had grown accustomed to seeing it around the shop. But I'm glad that it now hangs in its rightful place between Charles Lindbergh's

institution An institution is an organization that has a particular focus or goal.

SpaceShipOne now hangs in the Smithsonian Institution.

Respond to the Text

Collaborative Discussion

Look back at what you wrote on page 112. Tell a partner two things you learned from the text. Then work with a group to discuss the questions below. Include details from *SpaceShipOne* to support your answers. Be sure to follow your class's rules for an orderly discussion.

1 Revisit pages 114–115 of the selection. What events in Matthew's life led him to work on the *SpaceShipOne* project?

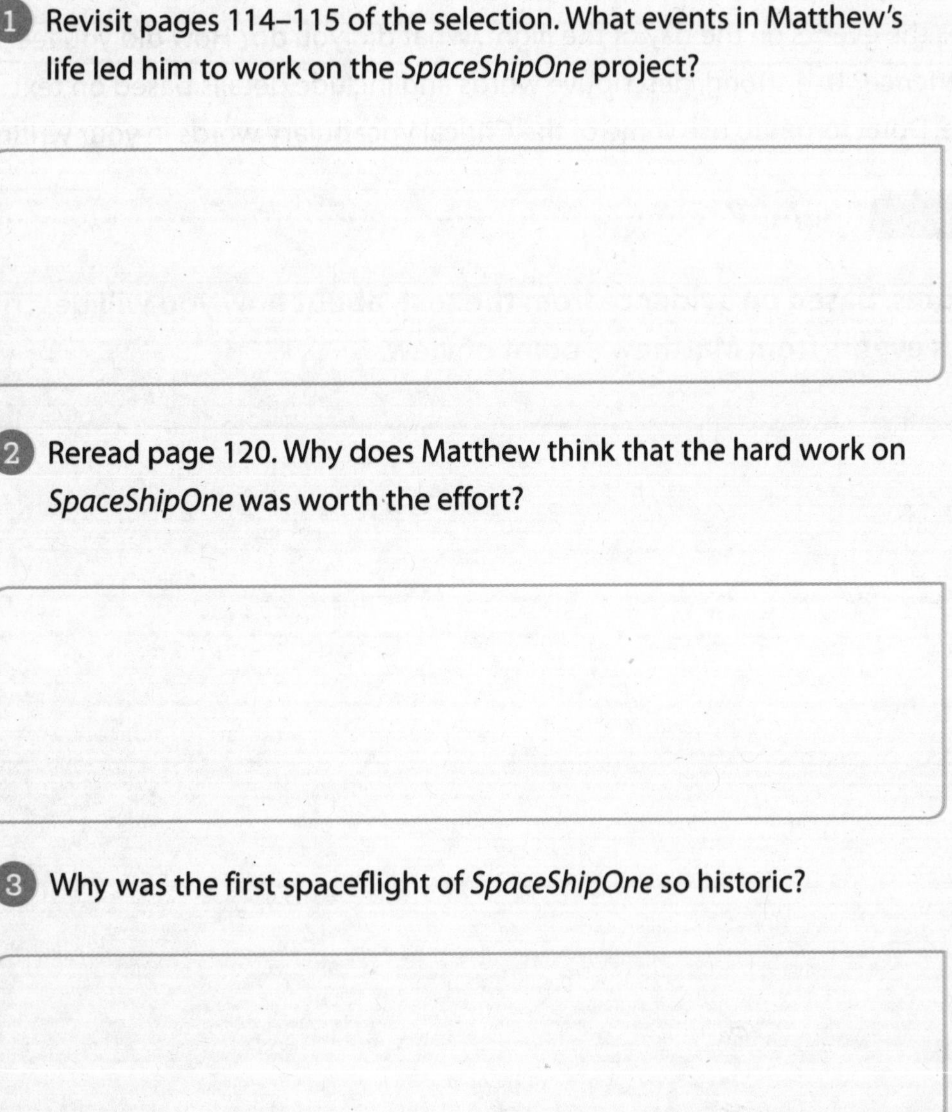

2 Reread page 120. Why does Matthew think that the hard work on *SpaceShipOne* was worth the effort?

3 Why was the first spaceflight of *SpaceShipOne* so historic?

Listening Tip

Listen politely to ideas that speakers share. If you are the recorder for your group, jot down key points.

Speaking Tip

Let your group's leader know when you want to speak, and then share your answer with a clear voice that others can hear.

Cite Text Evidence

Write a Journal Entry

PROMPT

In *SpaceShipOne,* you read about the experiences of engineer Matthew Stinemetze. In the text, Matthew recalls his experiences working on the historic flight of the first privately owned spacecraft to travel safely to space and back.

Imagine that you are Matthew. Write a journal entry from Matthew's point of view that describes the events on the day of the flight. What did you do? How did you feel about the experience? Use strong, descriptive words and include details based on text evidence. Don't forget to use some of the Critical Vocabulary words in your writing.

PLAN

Make notes, based on evidence from the text, about how you will describe the day's events from Matthew's point of view.

WRITE

Now write the journal entry describing Matthew's experience on the day of the historic flight.

Make sure your journal entry

- ☐ uses first-person pronouns such as *I*, *me*, *my*, and *our*.
- ☐ includes details about the events and Matthew's feelings that are based on text evidence.
- ☐ retells events from the text in sequence.

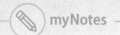

Notice & Note
Aha Moment

Prepare to Read

GENRE STUDY **Narrative nonfiction** gives factual information in a way that reads like a story.

- Narrative nonfiction presents events in sequential order.
- Texts about events that happened in the past feature real people and may include how they felt about events.
- Science-related texts may include words that are specific to the topic.
- Narrative nonfiction often includes visuals, such as photos and illustrations.

SET A PURPOSE **Think about** the title and genre of this text. What do you know about the planet Mars? What do you want to learn? Write your ideas below.

CRITICAL VOCABULARY

- deploy
- transition
- expanse
- resembled
- terrain
- international
- transmitted
- ailing

Build Background: The Red Planet

THE MIGHTY MARS ROVERS

THE INCREDIBLE ADVENTURES OF SPIRIT AND OPPORTUNITY

by Elizabeth Rusch

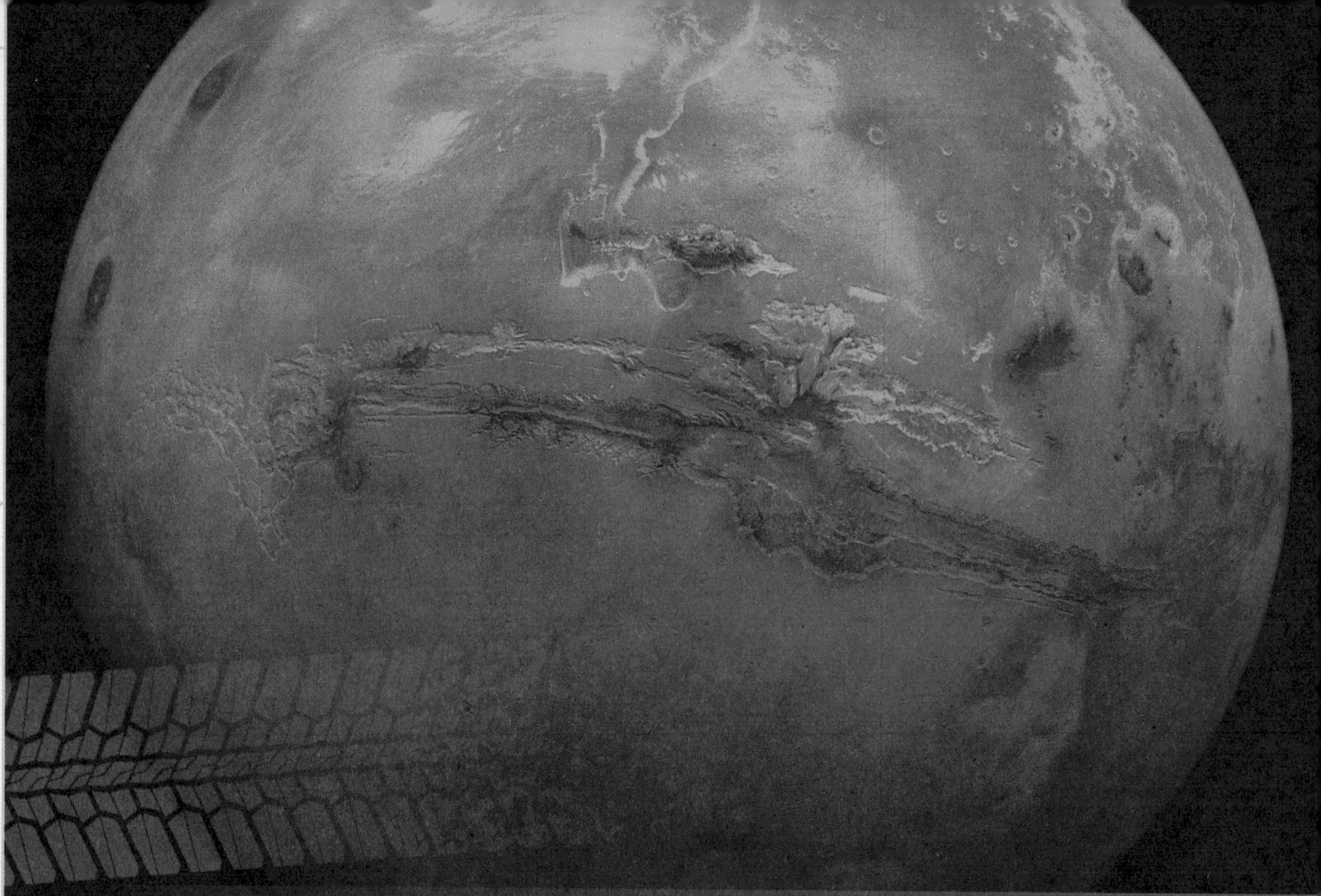

1 *For many years, astronomy professor Steve Squyres envisioned a robotic geologist that could explore Mars and collect data to send back to Earth. He and his team repeatedly proposed such a rover to the National Aeronautics and Space Administration (NASA). NASA repeatedly said "no." But Steve never gave up, and finally, NASA said "yes." Steve and a huge team of scientists and engineers worked feverishly to design and build two MERs (Mars Exploration Rovers) in time for a 2003 launch, at a time when Mars would be closer to Earth than usual. Despite many challenges and not enough time, the team made the deadline.*

2 *NASA launched the rovers, named Spirit and Opportunity, into space in the summer of 2003. In January 2004, Spirit was the first to arrive. Steve and the NASA team anxiously waited while Spirit made her historic descent toward Mars. (Note: In this selection, the author refers to Spirit as "she" and Opportunity as "he.")*

myNotes 

3 **As expected, Spirit approached the Martian atmosphere first.** She had made it this far, but landing on Mars would be tricky, requiring split-second timing. Many things could go wrong, fatally wrong. If the lander didn't pass through the atmosphere just right, it would burn up from friction. A parachute and retrorockets were supposed to slow the rover's screaming descent, but if they didn't deploy, the spacecraft would be smashed to a million pieces. The final stage of landing would be free fall, from 30 feet (9 m) in the air, protected only by a cushion of airbags that encircled the robot. Even if all went well, Spirit would bounce like a superball—as much as six stories high—time and time again. Finally she would roll to a stop, but no one knew where or in what condition.

4 Steve Squyres and his team knew that the landing would take about six minutes. They also knew that radio signals from Mars take ten minutes to reach Earth. This meant that for ten minutes of terror, scientists couldn't correct anything that went wrong. "We would be helpless," Steve said. "Watching . . . waiting . . ."

deploy If you deploy something, you move it into position so it can be used.

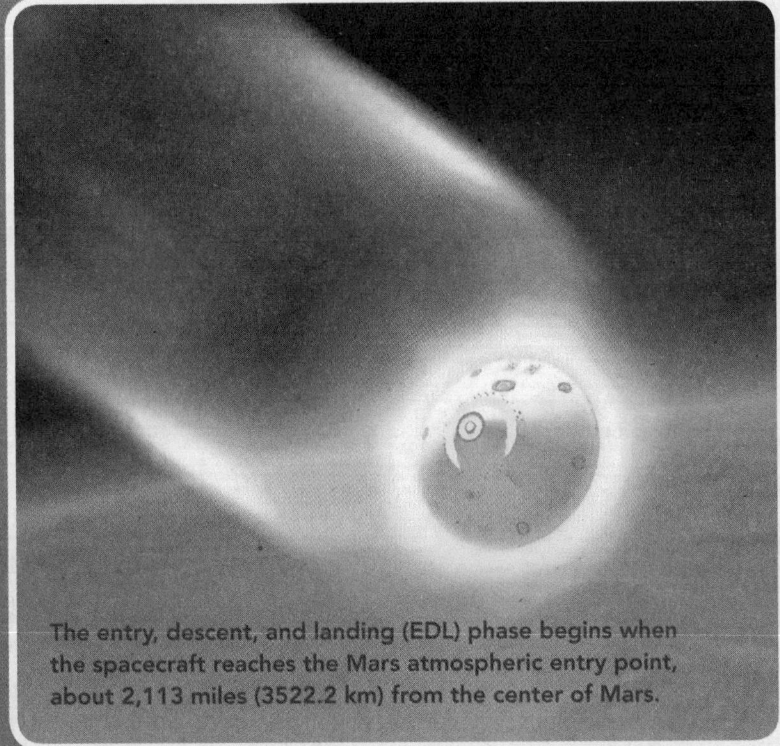

The entry, descent, and landing (EDL) phase begins when the spacecraft reaches the Mars atmospheric entry point, about 2,113 miles (3522.2 km) from the center of Mars.

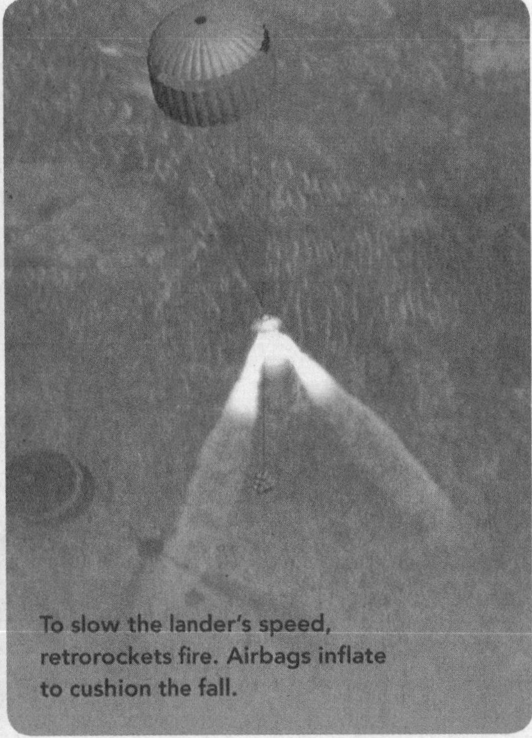

To slow the lander's speed, retrorockets fire. Airbags inflate to cushion the fall.

myNotes

5 In the large room at the Jet Propulsion Laboratory that served as Mission Control for the landing, rows of computers made a semicircle around wide screens and people packed in where they could find room. For good luck, all the scientists and engineers at Mission Control munched peanuts, because once when someone had brought peanuts to share during a landing, all had gone well. "I tore mine open and began to munch immediately, the one and only thing I could do to improve our chances of a safe landing," said Steve.

6 The six-minute landing began. Scientists hoped that Spirit would separate from her rocket properly. They worried about her burning through the Martian sky at twenty-five times the speed of sound. They prayed that the parachute and retrorockets would do their jobs as Spirit plummeted toward the ground. And they hoped that the precious little rover, wrapped in its cocoon of airbags, would survive all the bouncing.

7 The first announcement came over a loudspeaker from the landing manager, who handled the transition from flight operations to surface operations.

8 The room became hushed.

9 "We have a signal indicating bouncing on the surface."

10 Mission Control exploded with hugs, cheers, and tears. Steve pounded his fists on the tabletop, eyes pressed tightly closed. *Are we really on Mars?*

11 Then everything stopped.

12 The signal was lost.

13 The room went silent again.

14 A long minute.

15 The flight team reestablished contact. "We see it! We see it! We see it!"

transition In a transition, one thing changes to something else.

16 Then the words Steve had been waiting for from the flight team: "Surface, Flight. Spirit is yours."

17 Spirit shook off her airbags and stretched her solar wings to charge her batteries. The scientists couldn't wait for her to start snapping pictures. From Mars orbiter photos, Gusev Crater, her landing spot, appeared to be a ninety-five-mile-wide lakebed with a river channel feeding into it. Scientists thought Gusev was their best shot at finding signs of water.

18 And there on the screen was the first image from Mars.

19 Steve gasped. The colors were so perfect, and the details so sharp, it was like being there. "It works, man . . . It works," he muttered.

20 The red, rocky expanse resembled the Mojave Desert, with windblown dust and small, dark rocks casting shadows in the afternoon sun. The area was flat, with no big boulders or hills.

21 Could this be what a Martian lakebed looked like up close?

22 Scientists wouldn't learn more until Spirit, the mobile geologist, started driving, digging, poking, and analyzing the dust and rocks. It took days to maneuver Spirit off her landing pad. Then the rover drivers directed Spirit toward a small pyramid-shaped rock, which the scientists called Adirondack, about 10 feet (3 m) straight ahead.

expanse An expanse is a very large area of land, sea, or sky.
resembled If two things or people resembled each other, they looked like each other.

Steve Squyres, center, reacts as NASA administrator Sean O'Keefe, left, looks on as they get a signal from the Mars rover Spirit after she landed.

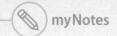

23 This is more complicated than it sounds. Signals from the rover, such as a photo of a dangerous ditch in her path, took ten minutes to reach Earth. Commands back to the rover, like "STOP!," took another ten minutes. Driving a rover is not like playing a video game—you can't just move your joystick and watch the rover obey. Instead, rover drivers carefully study the terrain ahead of time so they can safely map out the rover's moves. Roughly once a day, the team gets photos of the rover's surroundings, and about once a day, they send commands that tell the rover what to do.

24 Spirit crept along, with her drivers correcting her direction daily. It took three days, but finally she pointed her tools directly at the rock.

25 Would she find signs of water?

26 "We haven't heard anything from the spacecraft all day," Jennifer Trosper, the mission manager, told Steve the day they were set to use the RAT (rock abrasion tool) on the rock. They kept trying.

27 "Earth to Spirit."

28 Silence.

29 "Earth to Spirit. Come in Spirit!"

30 Lead engineer Pete Theisinger called all the mission managers and flight directors on the team into the conference room. Ideas flew. Maybe Spirit had shut herself down to cool off. Maybe her batteries were too low. Maybe the software had failed. Steve held on to one hope: maybe Spirit would phone home the next day as if nothing had gone wrong.

terrain The terrain of an area is what the surface of the land looks like.

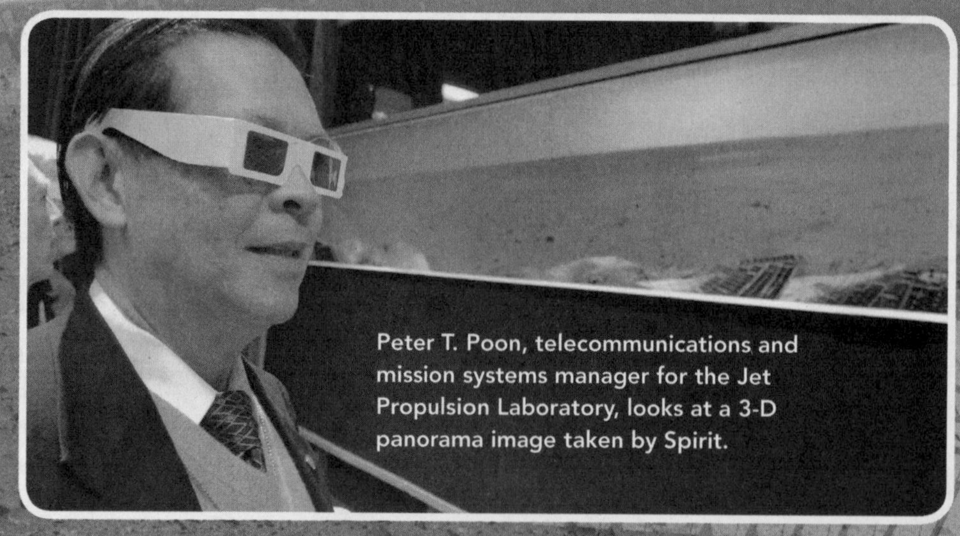

Peter T. Poon, telecommunications and mission systems manager for the Jet Propulsion Laboratory, looks at a 3-D panorama image taken by Spirit.

Naming Names

When Steve and his team talked about what the rovers saw around them on Mars, they couldn't just say "that crater" or "this rock" or "those hills." It would be too confusing. The International Astronomical Union (IAU) is responsible for naming land features on planets other than Earth. But the team had to discuss what the rovers should do daily, so they couldn't wait. Jim Rice, a geologist at Arizona State University and a rover science-team member, suggested that features studied on the mission be temporarily named according to themes. "OK," Steve said. "You're in charge."

The team decided to name craters near Spirit's landing site after lakes on Earth (Bonneville, for instance). Craters near Opportunity's landing site would be named after famous ships of exploration, hence Eagle (the *Apollo 11* lunar lander) and Endurance (after Ernest Shackleton's Antarctic expedition). The Columbia Hills were named after the space shuttle *Columbia*, and each of the seven peaks were named after the lost *Columbia* astronauts.

But there were so many features to name that soon the rules fell apart. Basically whoever started studying a rock or hill or crater got to name it. So there are place names (Adirondack and Stone Mountain), people names (Burns Cliff and Larry's Leap), and even foods (Mudpie, Chocolate Chip, and Cookies and Cream). "Whenever explorers go somewhere, we always want to name things," says Jim Rice. "It's just something we humans like to do."

international Something that is international is shared or worked on by multiple countries.

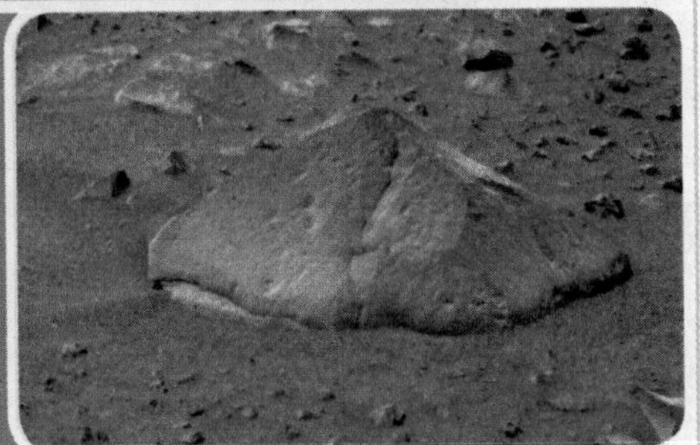

Adirondack, Spirit's first target rock, selected because its dust-free, flat surface was perfect for grinding. Spirit traversed the sandy Martian terrain at Gusev Crater to arrive in front of the football-size rock just three days after the rover successfully rolled off the lander. Scientists named the angular rock after the Adirondack mountain range in New York.

How to Drive a Rover

Rover driver Scott Maxwell sat down at his computer and called up an image of Mars. But the image didn't look like a photo. It had the sharp angles and flat, bold colors of a video game. Using his mouse, Scott started to move the scene around. The sky was a dusty butterscotch color—as it is on Mars. The beige areas were parts of the scene the rover couldn't see because its body got in the way. "We can spin it around," Scott said—the photo whirls—"zoom in on things that are interesting"—a rock grows large on the screen—"even mark off areas that we think are dangerous"—Scott drew red circles around two large rocks and a small crater. He clicked a rover into the middle of the scene and moved it around. "Now we can sketch out a path that we want the rover to drive along," he added.

It looks fun—and easy—but it's not so simple. The rover drivers test the maneuvers many times before sending drive commands to the rovers. "Part of the game is figuring out what things could possibly go wrong," said Scott. "If something goes wrong and you break the rovers, there is no way to fix them."

Rover driver Scott Maxwell on his first rover drive: "That night, I lay in bed looking up at the ceiling and thinking that right at that moment there was a robot on another planet doing what I told it to do. That was an incredible thrill. That feeling has never left me, when I'm about to make something happen on my computer. I'm going to reach my hand across a hundred million miles of empty space and move something on the surface of another world. I have the coolest job."

The control room for the rovers at NASA's Jet Propulsion Laboratory ▼

Another tense moment at Mission Control.

31 The whole team was there the next day when Spirit was scheduled to send a signal. "We've got data!"

32 Steve phoned his wife. "We got it," he said, his voice cracking.

33 But too soon the cheering died down and the smiles faded. Spirit transmitted gibberish for two minutes and then shut off.

34 "It hit me then," Steve said. "The whole mission could be over before it ever really began."

35 While Spirit's engineers struggled to fix the ailing rover, another team of engineers was guiding her twin, Opportunity, toward his fiery landing on the red planet. They all knew that if Spirit couldn't communicate and Opportunity crashed, all would be lost.

36 The mission would be a complete failure.

37 Opportunity neared the red planet. *Crack!* Off came his rocket. Opportunity burned through the Martian sky. *Whoosh!* His parachute ballooned. *Roar!* His retrorockets thrust against gravity. Airbags deployed! Free fall! BOUNCE . . . way up high . . . BOUNCE . . . high to the sky again . . . BOUNCE . . . plummeting down and rebounding up again . . . BOUNCE . . . and again . . . BOUNCE . . . and again! Opportunity bounced about twenty-six times before rolling to a halt.

38 "BEEP!" Opportunity signaled that he had landed.

transmitted When an electronic message is transmitted, it is sent from one place to another.

ailing Something that is ailing is not doing well or is getting weak.

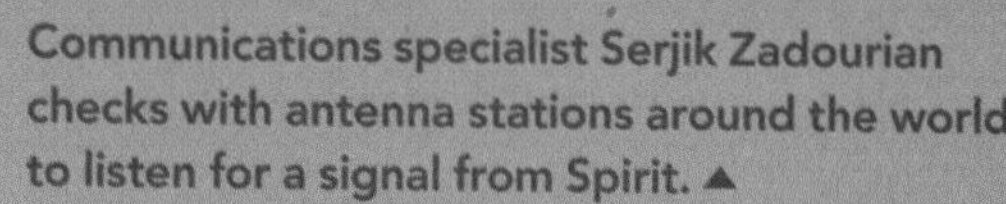

Communications specialist Serjik Zadourian checks with antenna stations around the world to listen for a signal from Spirit. ▲

Dawn shot of an antenna at the Goldstone Deep Space Communications Complex, located in the Mojave Desert in California, one of three complexes in NASA's Deep Space Network (DSN). The DSN provides radio communications for all of NASA's interplanetary spacecraft, including the rovers. ◀

Chatting with the Rovers

In this story, the scientists and rovers seem to speak to each other using words. But scientists can't really "talk" to the rovers. To communicate, scientists type codes and commands that they beam to one of the three huge satellite dishes in Earth's Deep Space Network (DSN). The dish passes the commands to a spacecraft that is orbiting Mars, usually the *Mars Odyssey*, which beams them to the rovers at an appointed time.

"You get a beep from the rover that means 'Thank you, I got my commands.' Then you don't hear from it for the rest of the day," said Matt Golombek, who manages rover planning. "You can't watch the rover; you can't listen to it. You really have no idea what is happening."

The team hopes the rovers follow the commands, driving, taking photos, and testing and measuring rocks. At a scheduled time, the rovers radiate the information they have gathered to *Odyssey* via their low-gain UHF antennas. *Odyssey*, directed to listen at that time, collects the signals. Sometime later, it downlinks the data to the Jet Propulsion Laboratory through Deep Space Network.

The rovers can phone home directly to Earth using their high-gain antennas, but they don't have to "yell" as loudly or use as much energy if they send messages through the orbiter. And they can send bigger messages, faster. That pleases the scientists who are eager for their rovers to phone home.

39 Mission Control erupted into cheers.

40 The team was thrilled. But they expected to find less at Opportunity's landing site than they had found at Spirit's. Scientists had chosen Meridiani Planum because it was the safest area to land, flat and featureless. Opportunity would probably have to drive around for a while over the fine red soil, they thought, to even find a rock worth studying.

41 Opportunity shook off his airbags, unfolded his instruments, and beamed his first photos to Mission Control.

42 "Holy smokes!" Steve Squyres exclaimed. "I'm sorry. I'm just—I'm blown away by this."

43 Just 10 yards away, large, layered slabs of rock jutted out in front of the rover. Opportunity had landed smack in a shallow crater, about 30 yards wide and a couple of yards deep. It was like scoring a great big interplanetary hole in one!

44 More pictures flashed on the screen. Opportunity's photos showed exposed rock layers that scientists had never seen before on Mars.

45 Steve's eyes widened. "That outcrop in the distance is just out of this world. I can't wait to get there. I've got nothing else to say. I just want to look."

46 Somebody called out, "Did we hit the sweet spot?"

47 "This is the sweetest spot I've ever seen!" is all Steve could manage in reply.

Steve Squyres celebrates with others in Mission Control at the successful landing of the second rover, Opportunity.

myNotes

48 Why was Steve so thrilled to see rock layers? On Earth and on Mars, rock layers tell us about the geologic, weather, and climate conditions that prevailed during the years and decades each layer was formed. It's like rings inside a tree stump: some rings are thick and others are thin, reflecting the weather conditions that accompanied the tree's growth. Steve and the other scientists looked at rock layers the rover photographed and wondered whether they were brought about by volcanic eruptions, blowing dust, flowing water, or all three.

49 Over the coming days and weeks, Steve and his team studied the images that filled their screens, and debated what they meant. Many of Opportunity's photos featured blueberry-shaped pebbles strewn across the soil, like beads spilled from a broken necklace. "They were the strangest-looking things I'd ever seen on Mars," Steve said.

50 Some team members thought the pebbles looked like volcanic hailstones. Others thought they might be droplets of lava that had cooled quickly.

51 Like detectives intent on understanding a clue, the team considered other possibilities. Maybe the rocks had rolled around in *water*, which smoothed them. Maybe material dissolved in *water* had dried out and solidified layer by layer to make the round forms. Was what they were seeing evidence that water had once existed on Mars?

52 To find out, Opportunity took close-up photos, tried RATing a blueberry, and took measurements. He discovered some salts!

This magnified photo of Eagle Crater, taken by the Microscopic Imager on Opportunity's arm, shows coarse grains that scientists nicknamed blueberries. The examined patch of soil is 1.2 inches (3 cm) across, and the largest blueberry shown is about the size of a sunflower seed. ▸

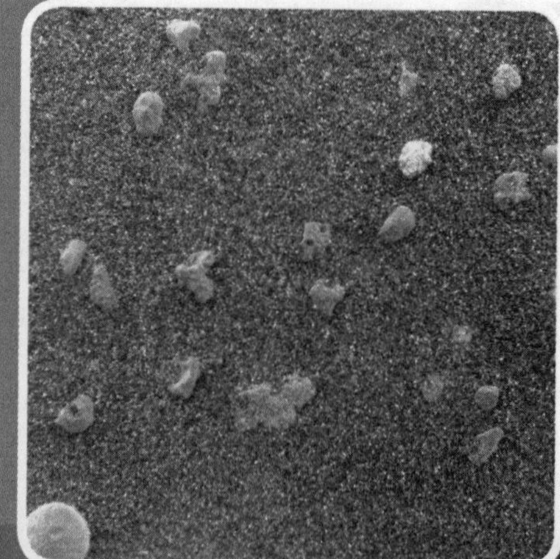

This high-resolution image captured by Opportunity's panoramic camera shows the rock outcrop on the rim of Eagle Crater, where the rover landed. These layered rocks measure only 4 inches (10 cm) high. Data from the panoramic camera's near-infrared blue and green filters were combined to create this approximate, true color image. ▾

53 Hmm, thought Steve and his colleagues. Salts are often left behind when water evaporates. But some team members needed more to convince them.

54 Opportunity kept exploring.

55 "We treated the rovers very carefully," said rover driver Scott Maxwell. "We didn't want to make them do things like drive over rocks, for fear of breaking them." Even so, discoveries poured in. Opportunity found jarosite—a kind of salt that on Earth forms in the presence of water, in acidic lakes or hot springs. Still, the scientists didn't want to jump to conclusions—maybe things are different on Mars?

56 The team pondered photos of ridges in the rocks. They looked just like ripples in the sand made by ocean waves on planet Earth.

57 As the clues poured in, Steve and the other scientists became convinced.

58 "Evidence pointed again and again to the existence at some time of a flowing, salty body of water on Mars," said Steve. "It was undeniable!"

59 Just weeks after landing, Opportunity had found evidence that water once pooled on the surface of this area of Mars. "We landed and *boom*, there it was, handed to us on a silver platter. We couldn't believe our luck," Steve said.

60 But important questions remained: Had the water been warm enough and deep enough, and had it been there long enough, for life to form?

(left) This view of Martian terrain includes Mount Sharp in the distance. ▶

(right) Opportunity took this self-portrait in March 2014. ▶

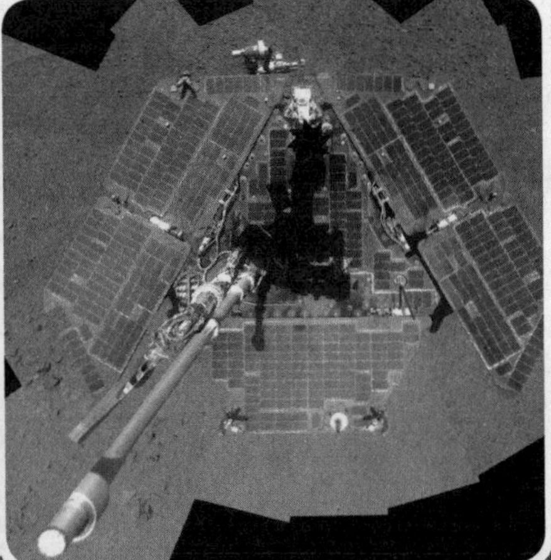

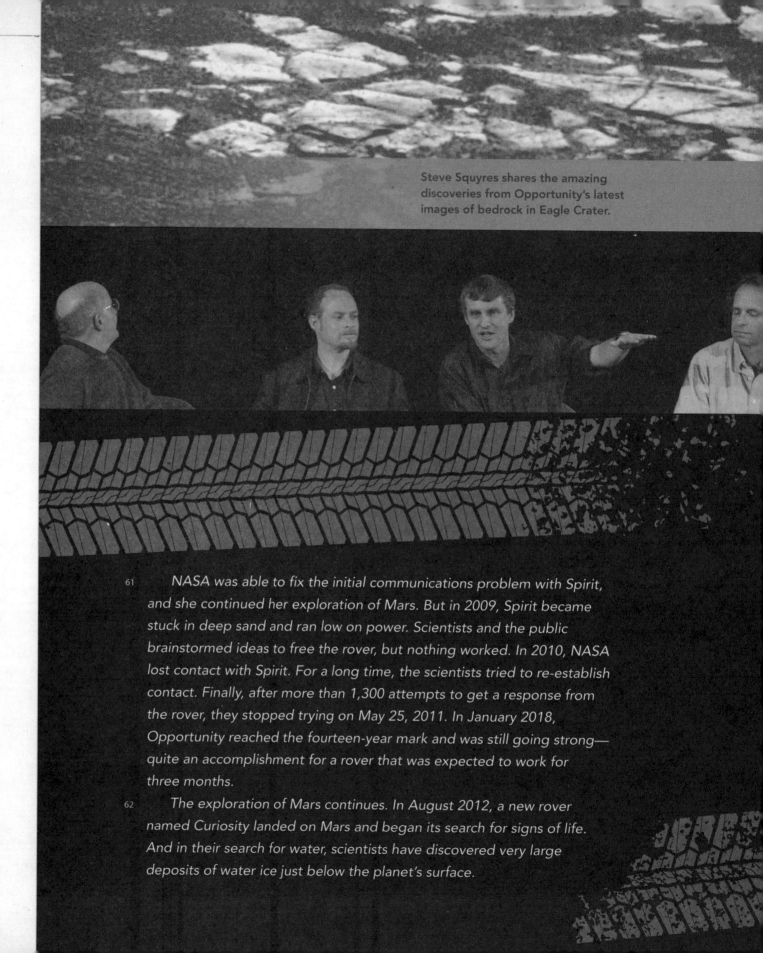

Steve Squyres shares the amazing discoveries from Opportunity's latest images of bedrock in Eagle Crater.

61 *NASA was able to fix the initial communications problem with Spirit, and she continued her exploration of Mars. But in 2009, Spirit became stuck in deep sand and ran low on power. Scientists and the public brainstormed ideas to free the rover, but nothing worked. In 2010, NASA lost contact with Spirit. For a long time, the scientists tried to re-establish contact. Finally, after more than 1,300 attempts to get a response from the rover, they stopped trying on May 25, 2011. In January 2018, Opportunity reached the fourteen-year mark and was still going strong—quite an accomplishment for a rover that was expected to work for three months.*

62 *The exploration of Mars continues. In August 2012, a new rover named Curiosity landed on Mars and began its search for signs of life. And in their search for water, scientists have discovered very large deposits of water ice just below the planet's surface.*

Respond to the Text

Collaborative Discussion

Look back at what you wrote on page 124 and talk with a partner about what you learned during reading. Then work with a group to discuss the questions below. Support your answers with information and details from *The Mighty Mars Rovers*. Work with your group to summarize key ideas from the text.

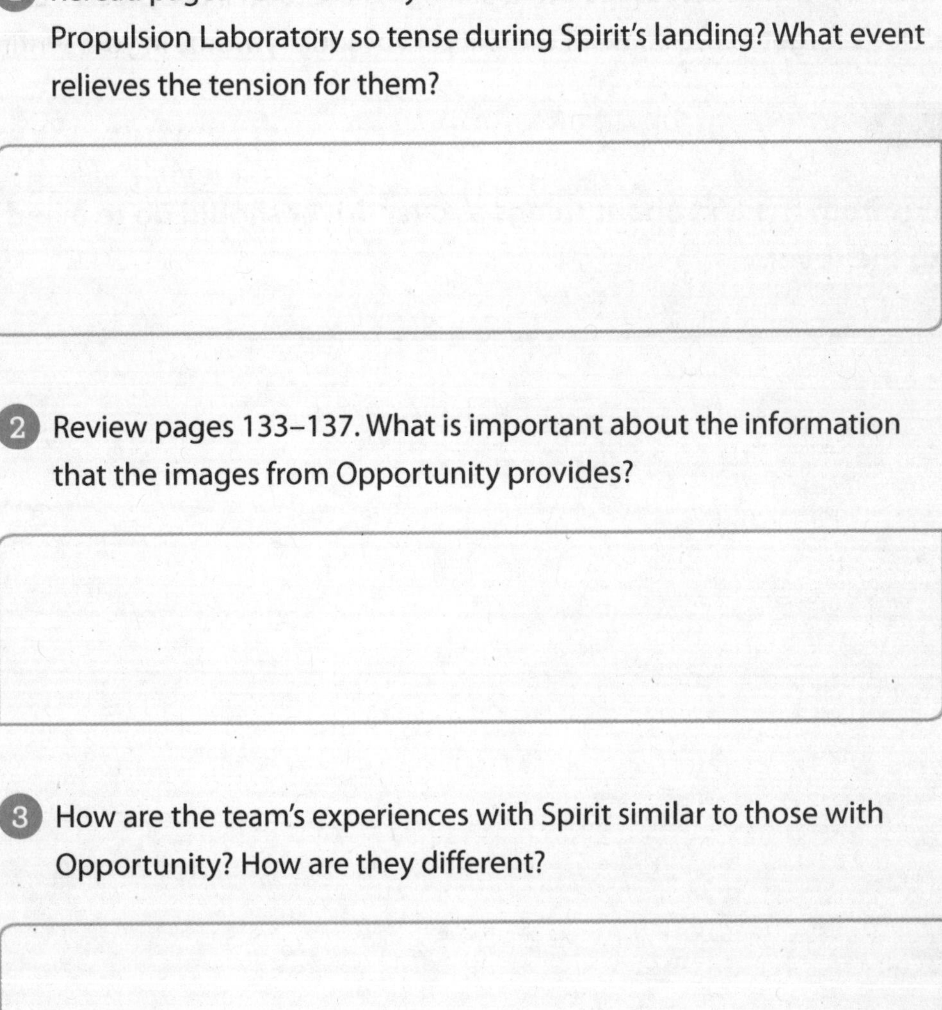

1. Reread pages 126–129. Why are the team members at the Jet Propulsion Laboratory so tense during Spirit's landing? What event relieves the tension for them?

2. Review pages 133–137. What is important about the information that the images from Opportunity provides?

3. How are the team's experiences with Spirit similar to those with Opportunity? How are they different?

Listening Tip

Listen for examples and details speakers share. What main idea do they tell about?

Speaking Tip

To help remember important points, take turns stating main ideas in your own words.

Cite Text Evidence

Write a Safety Checklist

PROMPT

The Mighty Mars Rovers describes what happened when the rover vehicles Spirit and Opportunity landed on and explored the surface of Mars.

Imagine that you train new rover drivers at NASA's Jet Propulsion Laboratory. You need to be sure the new drivers understand how to control the rovers and don't make mistakes that could cause damage. Use evidence from the text to prepare a safety checklist that new drivers can use to avoid damaging the rovers. Use precise, clear language. Don't forget to use some of the Critical Vocabulary words in your writing.

PLAN

Make notes from the text about things a rover driver should do to avoid damaging the rover.

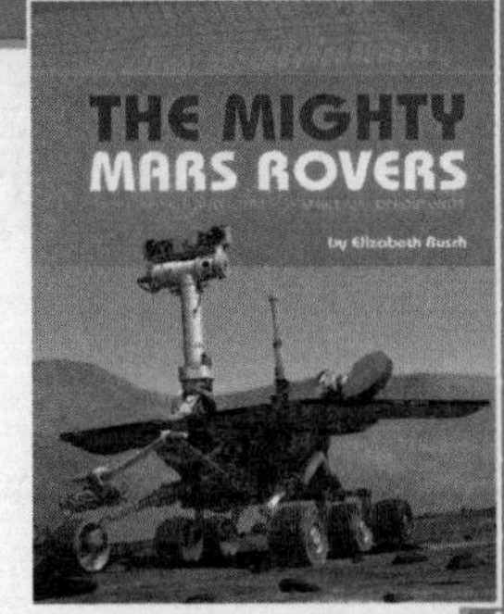

WRITE

Now write your safety checklist for a new rover driver.

Make sure your checklist

- ☐ states what the driver should do.
- ☐ uses evidence from the text.
- ☐ gives only one direction in each checklist item.
- ☐ uses precise words.

Performance Task

Essential Question

What role does curiosity play in exploration?

Write an Instructional Article

PROMPT Think about the scientific knowledge gained from the explorations in this module.

Imagine that your class is putting together a book on scientific discoveries. Each student will write an article to explain the science behind one of the discoveries in this module. Write an instructional article to contribute to the book. Use evidence from the text to support your ideas.

I will write about ____.

Make sure your instructional article

- ☐ has an introduction that clearly states the topic.
- ☐ supports central ideas with facts, examples, and definitions from the texts.
- ☐ uses text features such as headings to show key ideas.
- ☐ has a conclusion that sums up important points.

PLAN ·································· Gather information.

Which scientific concepts will you explain? How do they connect to one of the explorations you read about? Look back at your notes and revisit the texts for details.

Use the chart below to plan your article. Write your topic and overall central, or main, idea. Then use evidence from the texts to add supporting details for each important point.

My Topic: ______________________________

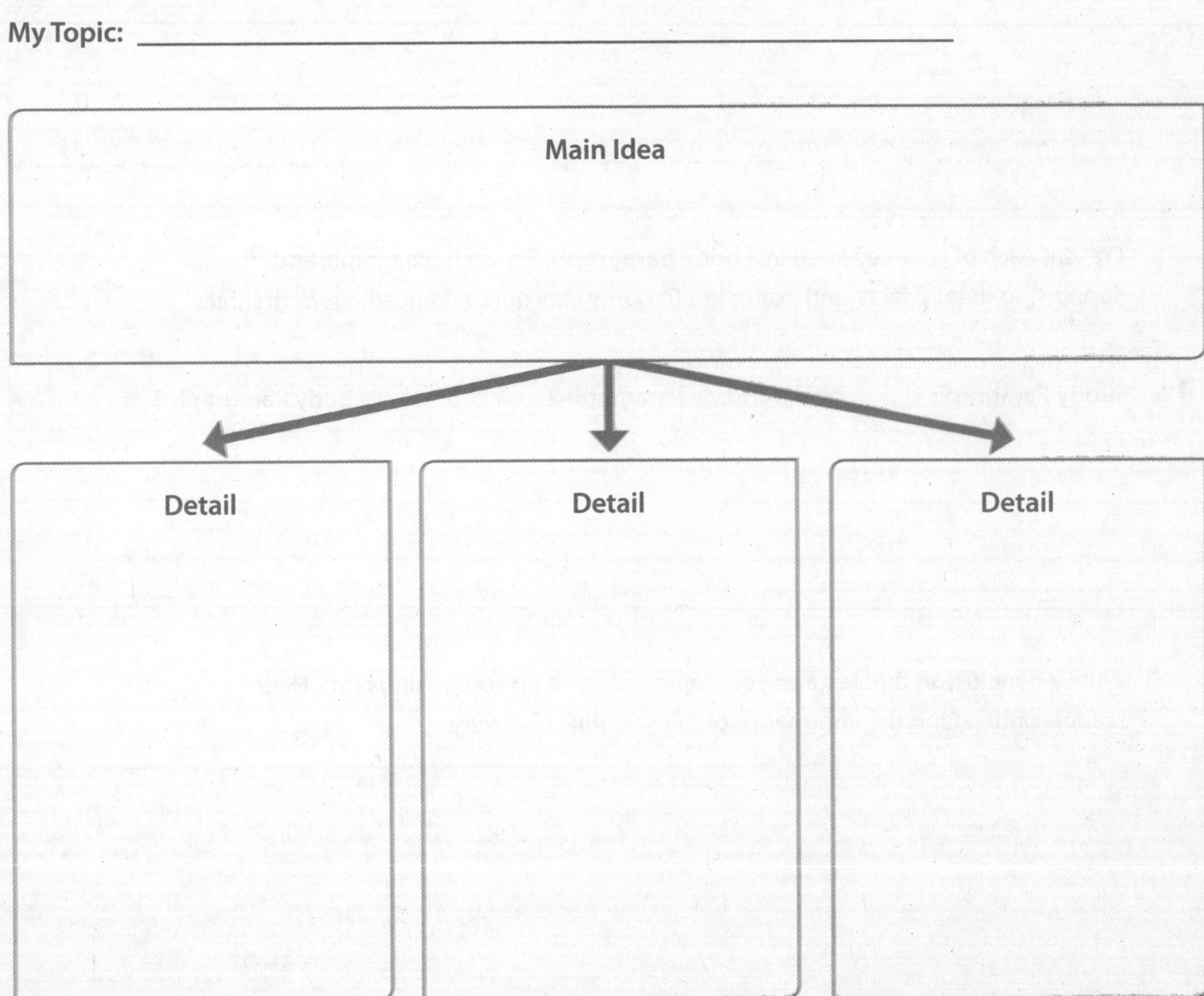

Performance Task

DRAFT .... **Write your article.**

Write an **introduction** that clearly states your topic and gives readers an idea of what they will be learning. Explain how a discovery led to this scientific knowledge.

Present each of your key ideas in a **body paragraph.** For each paragraph, add supporting details, facts, and examples. To clarify concepts, add headings or graphics.

Body Paragraph 1	Body Paragraph 2	Body Paragraph 3

Write a **conclusion** that restates your topic and sums up your main points. Help readers understand the importance of this scientific discovery.

REVISE AND EDIT ········ Review your draft.

Revise and edit your draft by carefully reviewing it and making changes to improve it. Work with a partner or small group. Read each other's articles and ask questions or offer feedback. Use these questions to help you focus on ways to improve your article.

PURPOSE/ FOCUS	ORGANIZATION	EVIDENCE	LANGUAGE/ VOCABULARY	CONVENTIONS
☐ Does my introduction state the topic and connect it to a scientific discovery? ☐ Does my conclusion show the importance of the discovery?	☐ Is the article organized into paragraphs that each focus on an important idea? ☐ Do headings show the focus of each paragraph?	☐ Have I included facts and examples from the text to support each main point? ☐ Do I need to add more evidence to strengthen my support?	☐ Did I use precise language and topic-specific vocabulary? ☐ Did I clearly define technical terms?	☐ Have I spelled all words correctly? ☐ Did I correctly use quotation marks, italics, and underlining?

PUBLISH ········ Share your work.

Create a Finished Copy. Make a final copy of your article. Include illustrations or graphic aids such as maps, charts, or diagrams. Consider these options for sharing your article:

1. Combine your article with those of your classmates to create a textbook on scientific discovery. Decide together on a title for the book.
2. Give an illustrated lecture to classmates or a science club. Read your article and display supporting visuals, such as diagrams and photographs. Invite the audience to comment and ask questions.
3. Post your article online to a school or science club website.

MODULE 8

A New Home

"There could be no place in the world to which he belonged so completely. That was why he'd always dreamed of leaving, and why he'd always been so afraid to go."

—Daniel Alarcón

Essential Question
How do people adapt to new experiences and make a new place home?
Get Curious
Video

Big Idea Words

Words About Moving to a New Home

The words in the chart will help you talk and write about the selections in this module. Which words about moving to a new home have you seen before? Which words are new to you?

Add to the Vocabulary Network on page 149 by writing synonyms, antonyms, and related words and phrases for each word about moving to a new home.

After you read each selection in this module, come back to the Vocabulary Network and keep building it. Add more boxes if you need to.

WORD	MEANING	CONTEXT SENTENCE
nomadic (adjective)	A nomadic person moves frequently and might not have a permanent home.	My aunt loves the nomadic life, so she moves to a new place every few months.
temporary (adjective)	Something temporary lasts for a limited time.	This tent is our temporary home while we are camping.
voice (noun)	An author's voice is that writer's style of expression.	This author writes about moving to a new country in a voice that is very humorous.
monologue (noun)	A monologue is a long, uninterrupted speech.	The audience cheered at the end of the speaker's monologue about immigration.

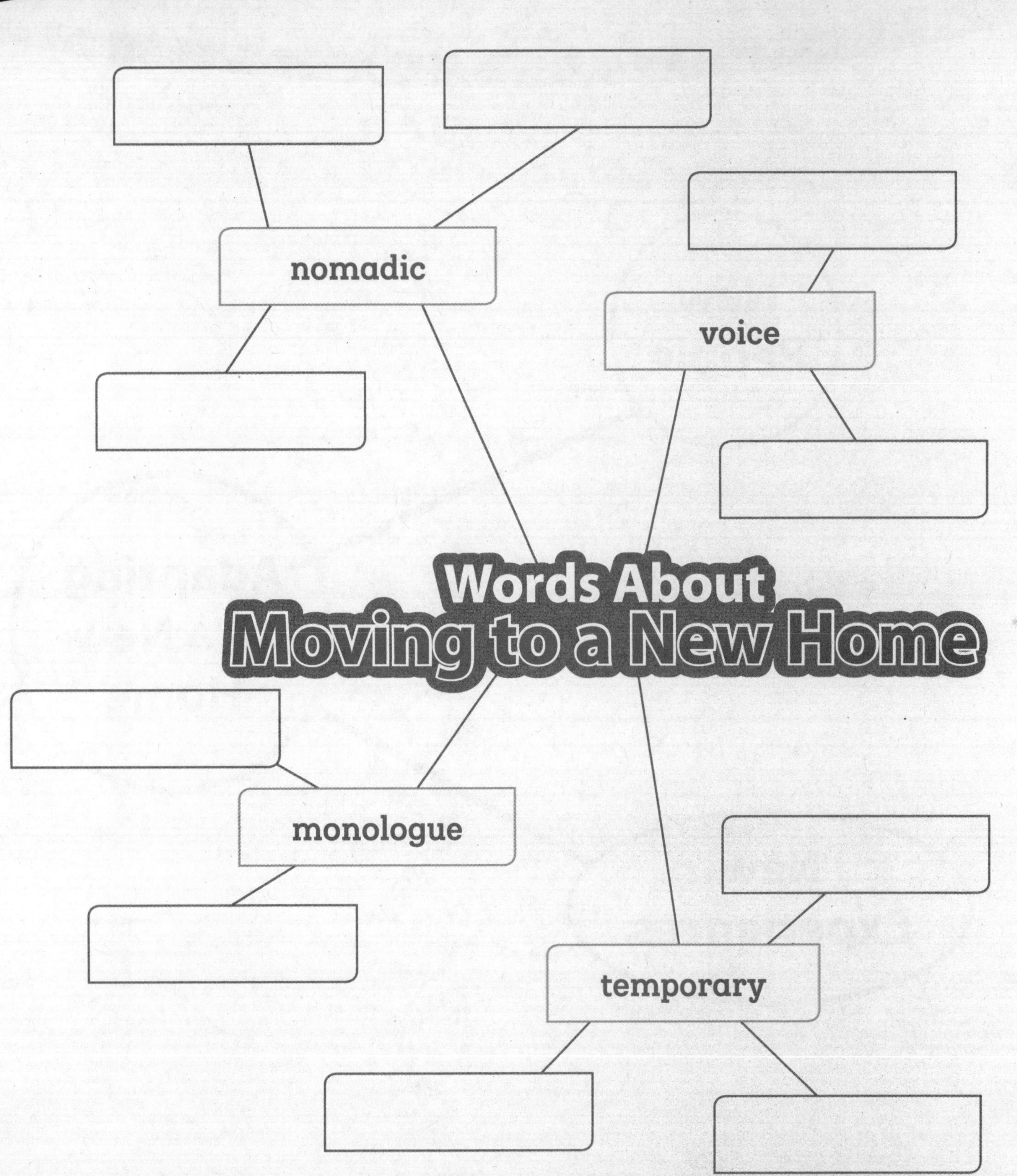
nomadic
voice
Words About
Moving to a New Home
monologue
temporary

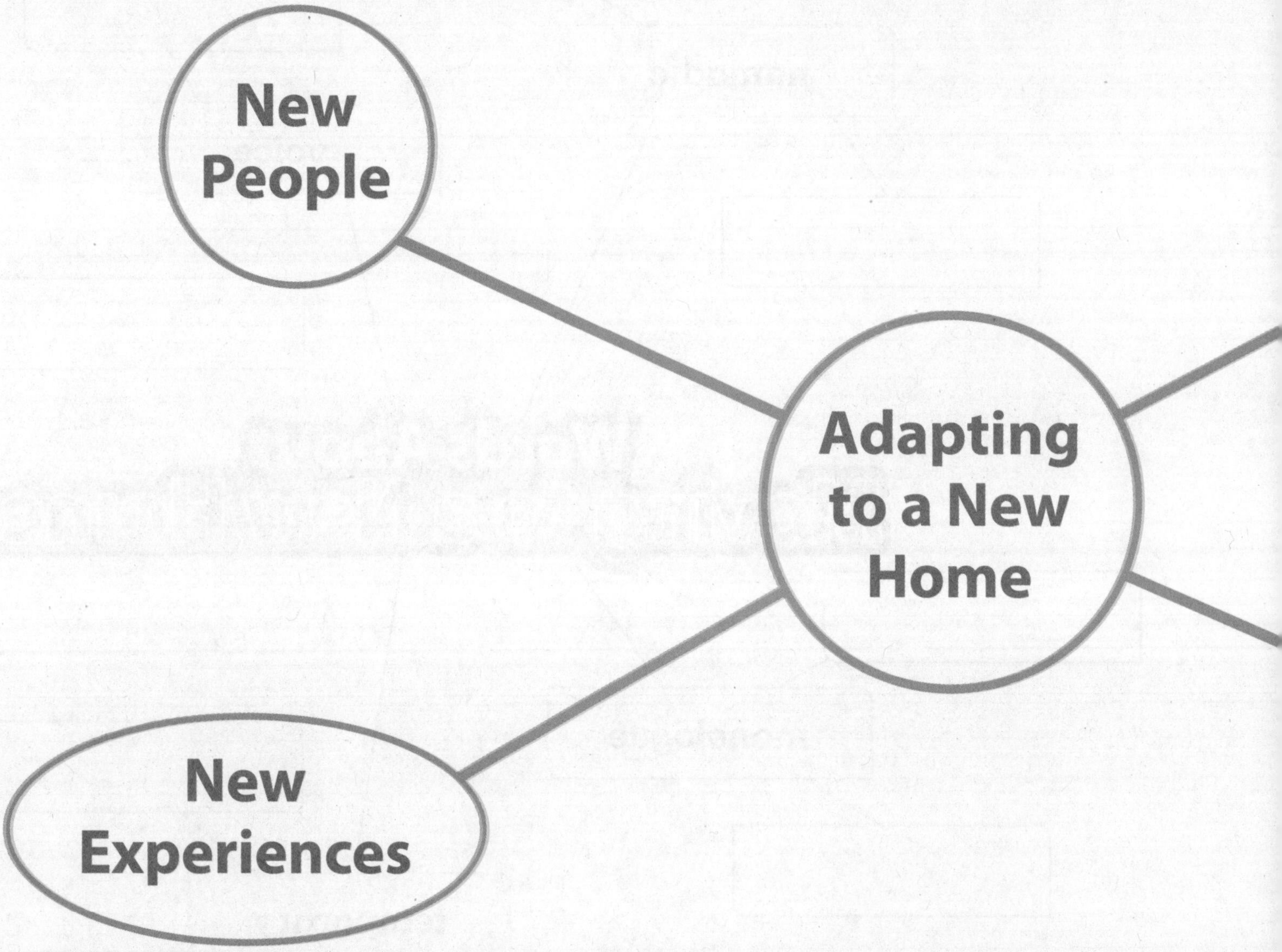

Knowledge Map

New People

Adapting to a New Home

New Experiences

Homesickness

New Places

myNotes

Short Read

Moving to a New Country: A Survival Guide

1 Long ago, many people were nomadic. They moved frequently to find food and other resources. Today, many people stay in the same area for long periods, maybe even for a lifetime. However, others make big moves—to a new country, maybe even a new continent.

2 Immigrating, or moving to a new country, can be a great adventure. There's no doubt about it, though: adjusting to a new country and culture is also a challenge, especially for kids. It's hard enough starting at a new school across town, let alone in a country that speaks an unfamiliar language! Fortunately, a few survival strategies can help make a big move a lot easier.

Curing Homesickness

3 For many people, one of the hardest parts of moving to a new country is leaving their old one behind. They miss their former homes, as well as their family and friends. They might miss their favorite sports teams, their favorite TV shows, and their favorite foods, too.

4 The good news is homesickness is usually temporary. One way to treat it is by staying in touch with people back home. Email, phone calls, and even letter writing make this easy. Chatting by live video is a lot like being in the same room, even when the chatters are thousands of miles apart.

Learning the New Language

5 Learning new languages is never easy, and it can be pretty frustrating when someone needs to know how to say, "Where is the bus stop?" right now, not four months from now. The good news for young people: scientists say it's easier for kids to pick up a new language. Also, living in a place where most people speak the same language speeds up learning. As they learn, new residents gain confidence and develop a voice to express their opinions, feelings, and sense of humor in their new language.

6 To get a head start, some people use language instruction books, classes, or computer-based programs. Good language instruction doesn't force learners to memorize long monologues or uncommon words. Instead, it teaches common, useful words and phrases that help newcomers meet new friends, find their way around, and keep themselves safe.

Celebrating Culture

7 When they move to a new country, many people worry they'll have to leave their culture behind. But as immigrants all over the world have discovered, people can carry parts of their culture wherever they go. They can continue to cook their favorite foods, sing their favorite songs, and celebrate their favorite holidays. They can share their culture with new friends, and those new friends will share their culture as well.

Finding New Friends at School

8 A new school in a new country might seem intimidating, and kids often worry they won't fit in. However, many schools are multicultural and include students from all over the world. That means teachers and students are used to welcoming people from other places.

9 School is obviously a great place to make new friends! It's a matter of finding a common interest, whether it's science, sports, or snapping photos. Being friendly works in pretty much any language, too.

myNotes

Notice & Note
Memory Moment

Prepare to Read

GENRE STUDY **Poetry** uses the sounds and rhythms of words to show images and express feelings.

- Poetry often includes figurative language, such as similes and metaphors, and sensory details.
- Poetry might be organized into stanzas, or a series of lines grouped together.
- Free verse poems do not rhyme or have a regular rhythm. In concrete—or shape—poems, the way the words appear helps to convey meaning.

SET A PURPOSE **Think about** the title and genre of this text. What do you know about poetry? What do you want to learn? Write your ideas below.

CRITICAL VOCABULARY

- yearning
- civil
- flourishing
- fortunate
- dedicate
- relatives
- discarded

Meet the Author and Illustrator:
Jorge Argueta and Elizabeth Gómez

A Movie in My Pillow

by Jorge Argueta

illustrations by Elizabeth Gómez

Introduction

1 I was born near San Salvador, the capital city of El Salvador. My house stood on the edge of the San Jacinto hill. It was a humble house with dirt floors, no running water, and no electricity. When it rained it was beautiful to hear the drops dancing on the tin roof. All around grew fruit trees. Parakeets and other multicolored birds arrived in the mornings to eat and sing.

2 Surrounded by all this beauty, I didn't realize how poor most of us were. We were yearning for change, but a few powerful people in our country didn't want change. The result was a bloody civil war. From 1980 to 1990, more than half a million of us fled to the United States. Today, there are flourishing Salvadoran communities in Los Angeles, San Francisco, Washington, D.C., and other cities.

3 These poems are based on my life when I first came to this country. How much I missed my homeland! How fortunate I was to be alive in San Francisco! These poems are my memories, my dreams—the movies in my pillow. I dedicate them to all the children from El Salvador—and to children everywhere—with the hope that we may all have a beautiful tomorrow.

—Jorge Argueta (HOR-hay ar-GEH-tuh)

yearning If you are yearning for something, you want it very much and feel sad not to have it.

civil A civil war is one that happens among groups of people living within a country.

flourishing If something is flourishing, it is growing and successful.

fortunate Someone who is fortunate is lucky.

dedicate Writers often dedicate their work to someone, usually in the first pages of the book, to show admiration or affection.

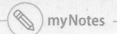

Wonders of the City

4 Here in the city there are
wonders everywhere

5 Here mangoes
come in cans

6 In El Salvador
they grew on trees

7 Here chickens come
in plastic bags

8 Over there
they slept beside me

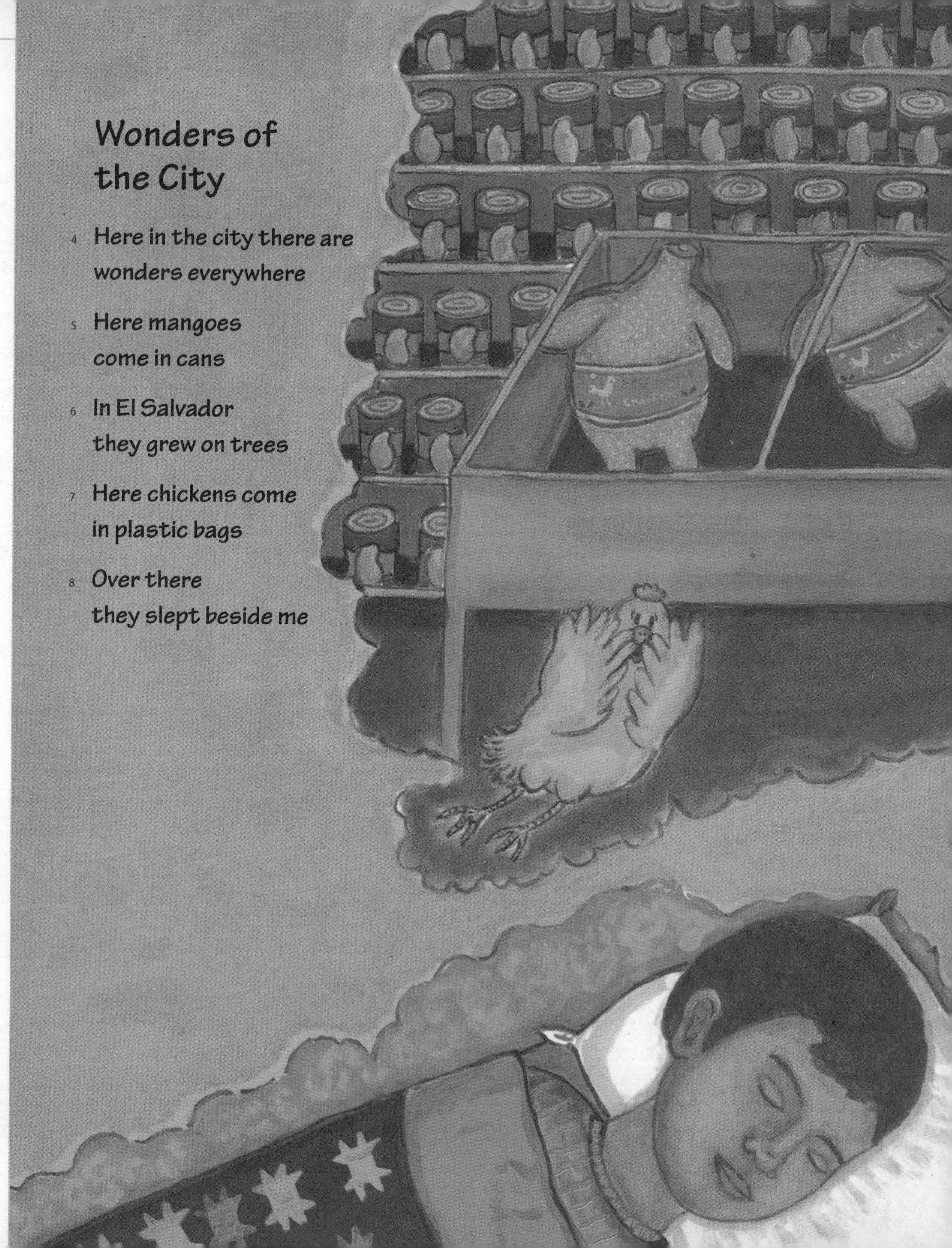

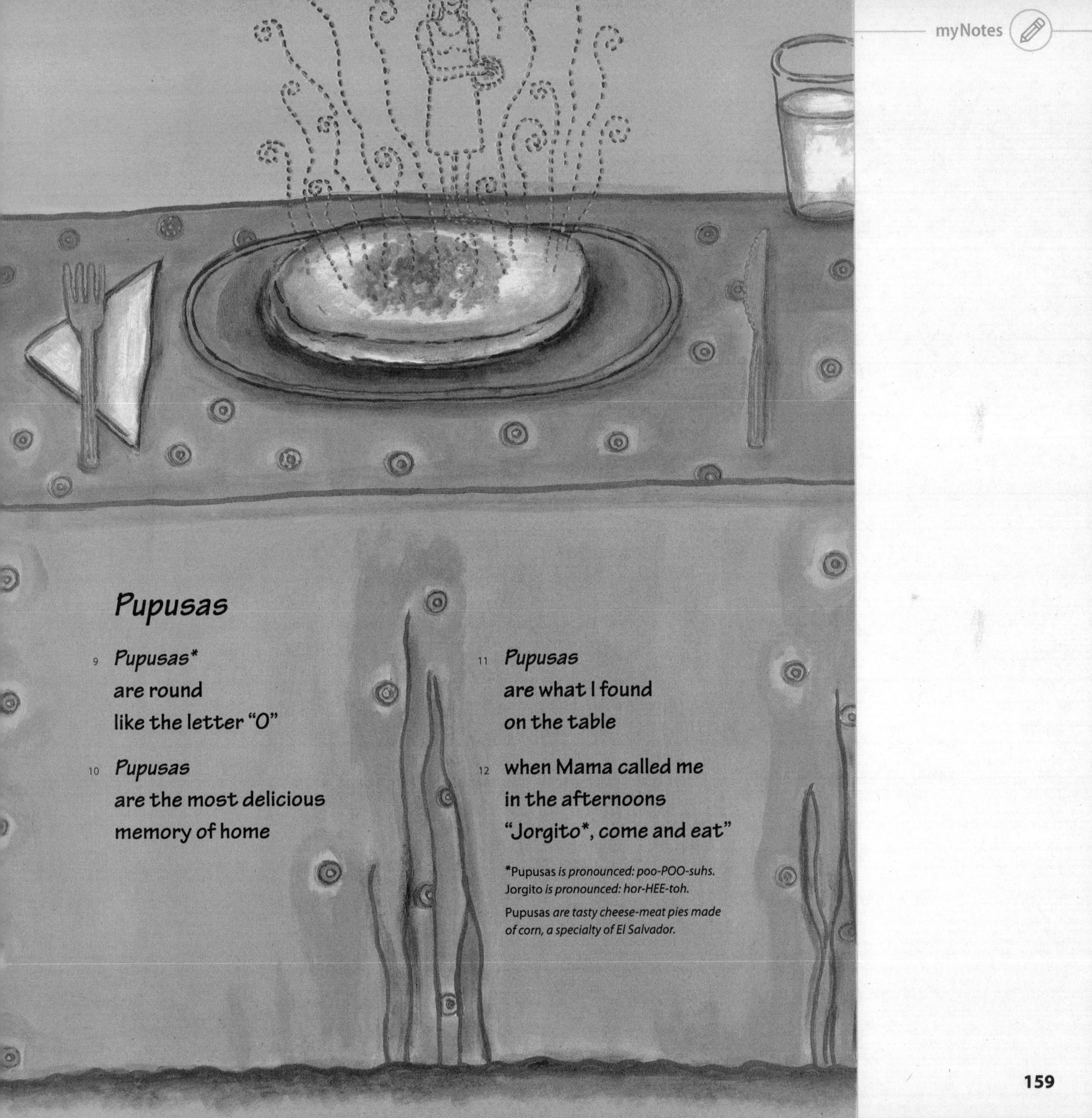

Pupusas

9 *Pupusas**
are round
like the letter "O"

10 *Pupusas*
are the most delicious
memory of home

11 *Pupusas*
are what I found
on the table

12 when Mama called me
in the afternoons
"Jorgito*, come and eat"

*Pupusas *is pronounced: poo-POO-suhs.*
Jorgito *is pronounced: hor-HEE-toh.*

Pupusas *are tasty cheese-meat pies made of corn, a specialty of El Salvador.*

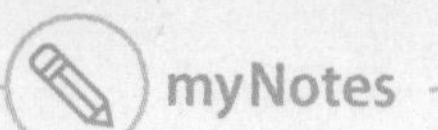
myNotes

When We Left El Salvador

13 When we left El Salvador
to come to the United States
Papa and I left in a hurry
one early morning in December

14 We left without saying goodbye
to relatives, friends, or neighbors
I didn't say goodbye to Neto
my best friend

15 I didn't say goodbye to Koki
my happy talking parakeet
I didn't say goodbye to
Miss Sha-Sha-She-Sha
my very dear doggie

16 When we left El Salvador
in a bus I couldn't stop crying
because I had left my mama
my little brothers
and my grandma behind

relatives Relatives are the people in your family.

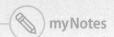

Soup of Stars

17 Many nights
we would go to bed
without eating

18 We would look up
at the stars—
the stars were our soup

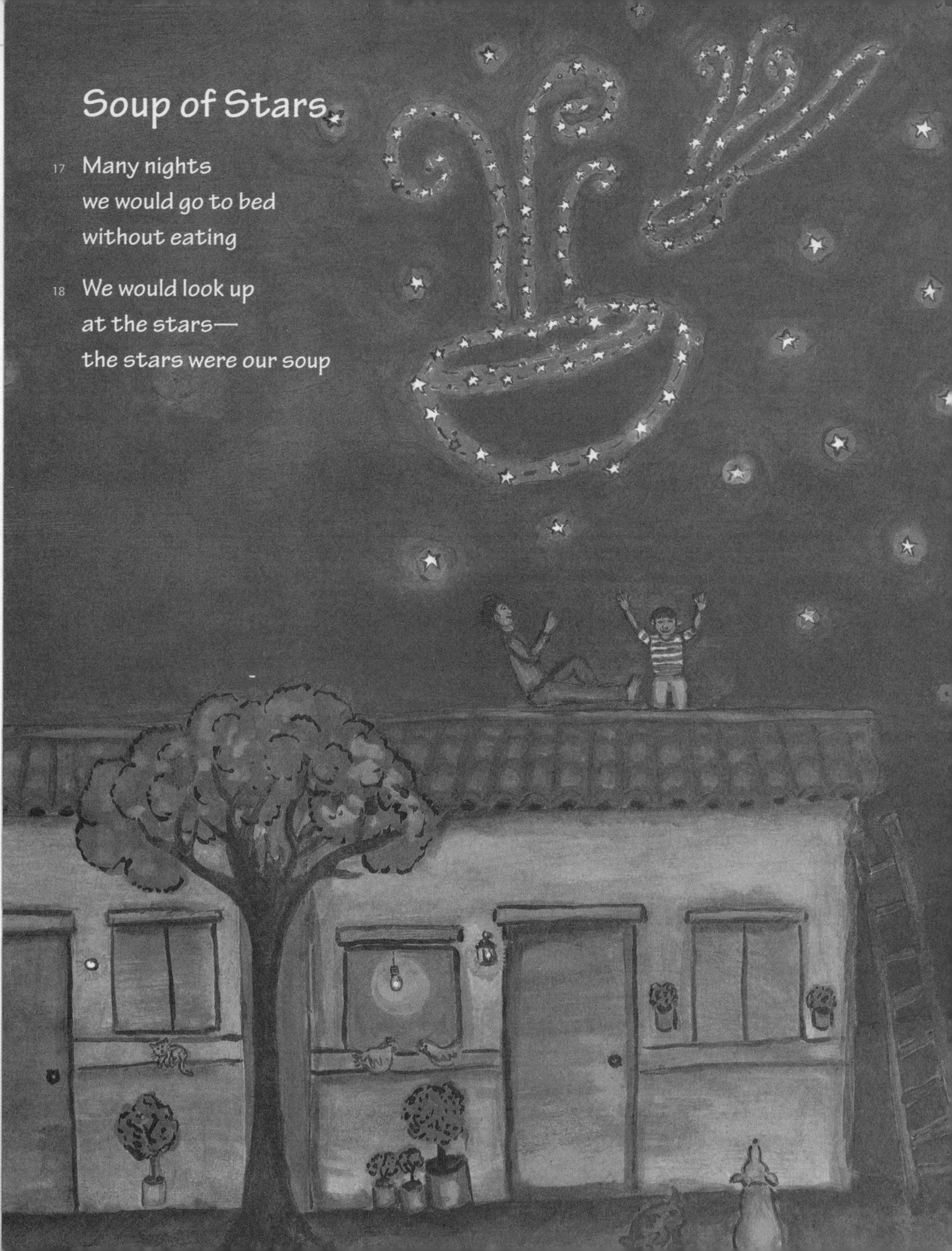

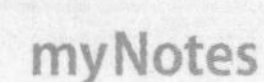

With the War

19 Streets
became so lonely

20 Doors
were made of metal

21 Wind
kept on howling

22 And we never
went out to play

My Bicycle

23 My bicycle
is purple
and taller than me

24 My bicycle
is a spotted horse
faster than the wind

25 My bicycle
is a dragon
dancing

26 *cumbias**
all the way
to El Salvador

*Cumbias *is pronounced: KOOM-bee-aws. The* cumbia *is a joyful tropical dance, very popular in Latin America.*

myNotes 

Shadow

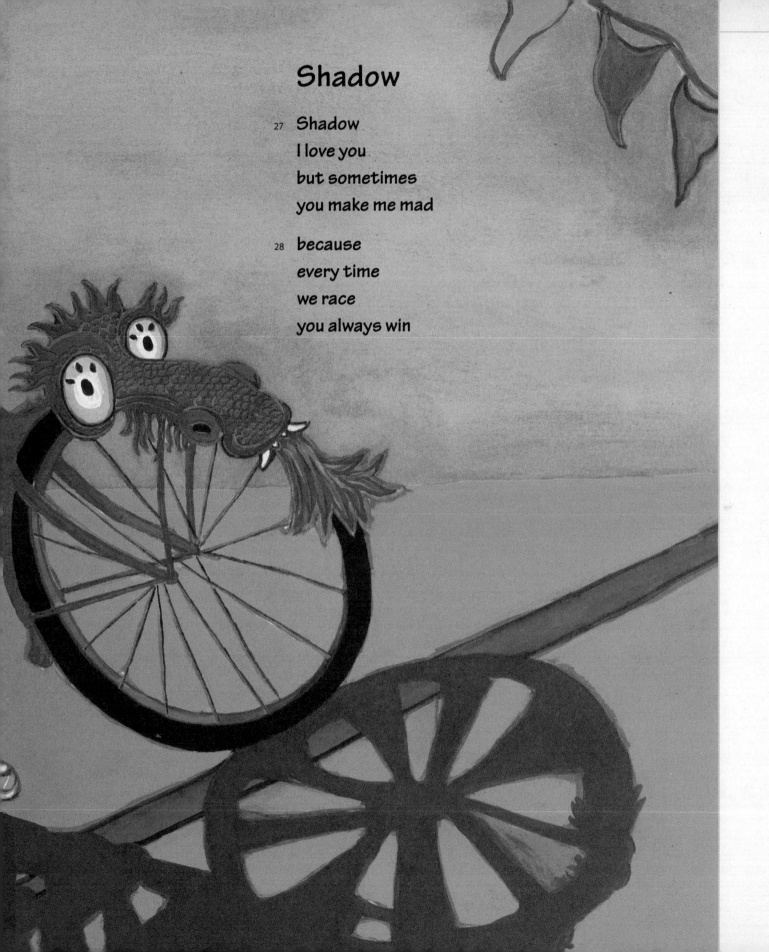

27 Shadow
I love you
but sometimes
you make me mad

28 because
every time
we race
you always win

My Papa's Orange Truck

29 *Vrrrooommm!*

30 My papa's orange truck
roars through the streets
every afternoon

31 When I see Papa
in his orange truck
in front of my school

32 I run and run
and take a big jump
to sit next to him

33 *Vrrrooommm!*

34 We go off laughing
looking for discarded
cardboard everywhere

35 I flatten the cardboard
boxes with my fists
pretending to be a boxer

36 Then I jump
on top of the boxes
like on a trampoline

37 Papa shakes my hand
and tells me: "*Gracias, mi' jo**"
(Thank you, my son)

38 *Vrrrooommm!*

39 Now my papa's orange truck
looks like
a pyramid on wheels

*Mi' jo *is pronounced: mee hoh*

discarded A discarded object is one that has been thrown away.

myNotes

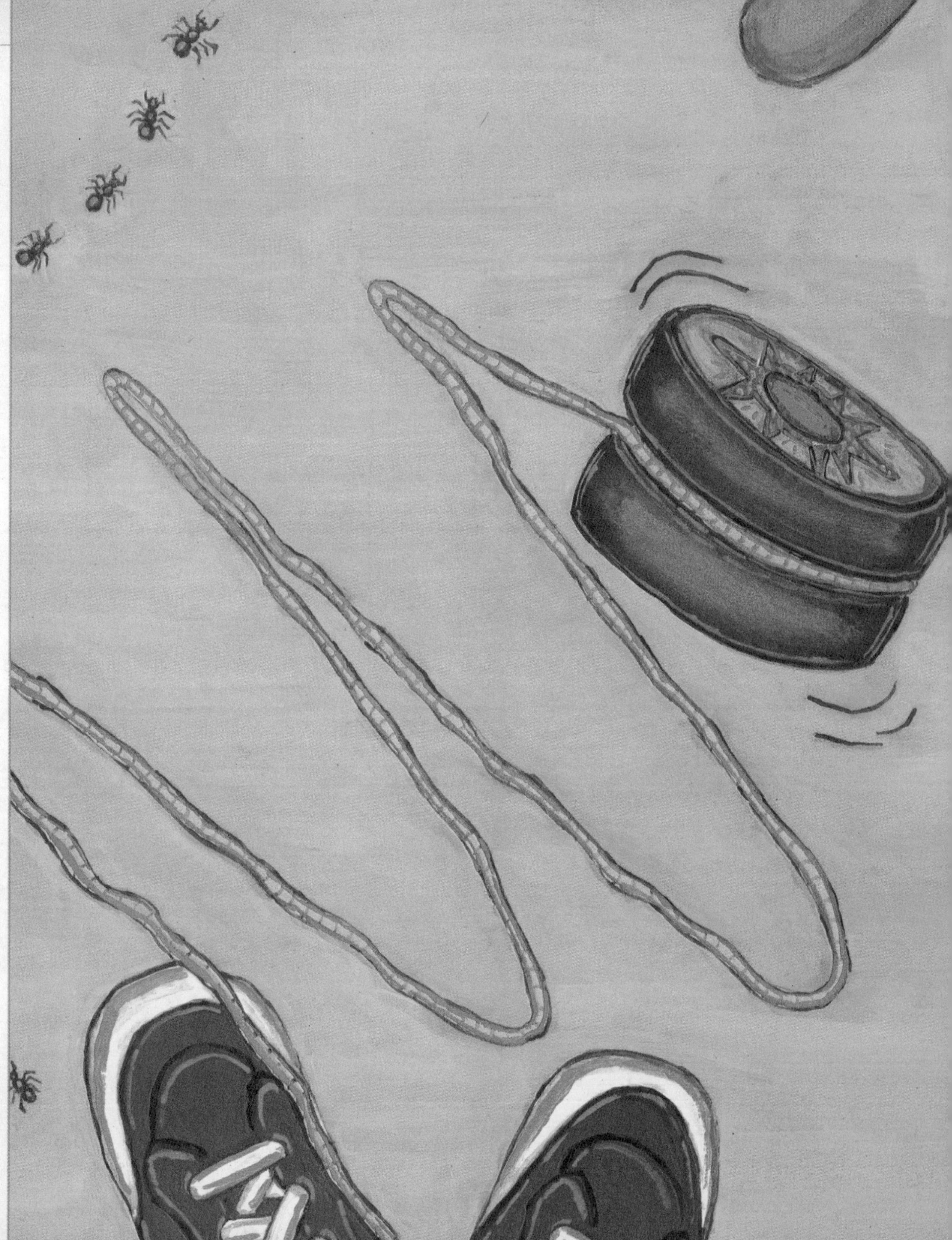

Yo-yo

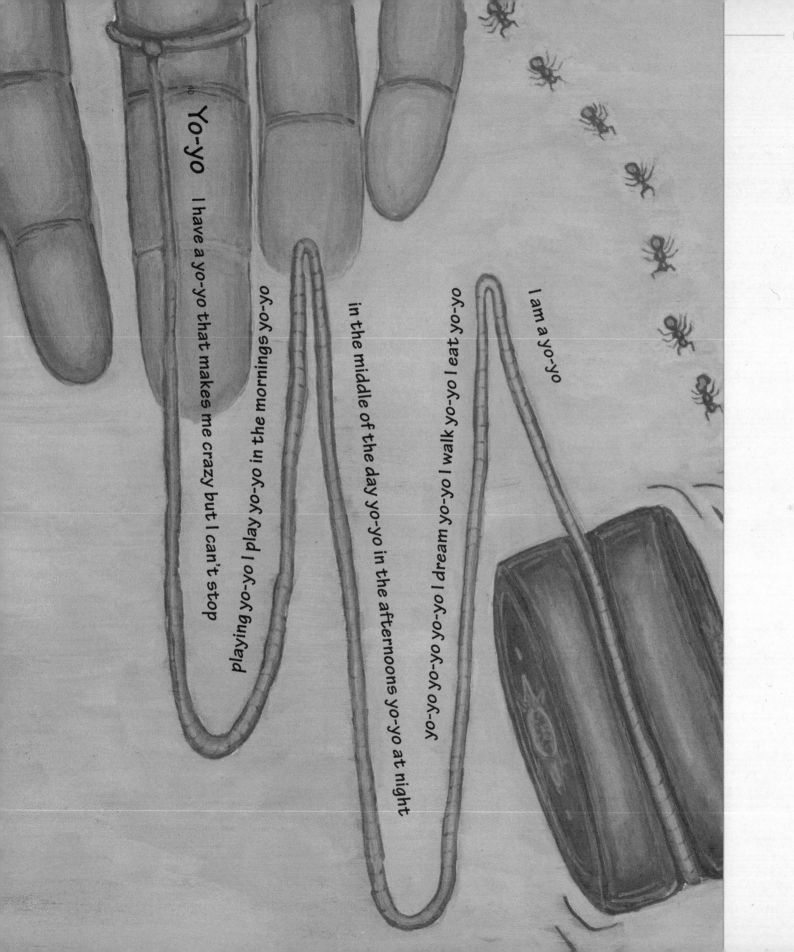

I have a yo-yo that makes me crazy but I can't stop
playing yo-yo I play yo-yo in the mornings yo-yo
in the middle of the day yo-yo in the afternoons yo-yo at night
yo-yo yo-yo yo-yo I dream yo-yo I walk yo-yo I eat yo-yo
I am a yo-yo

Voice from Home

41 From my uncle Alfredo
I received a great surprise—
a package in the mail
from El Salvador

42 Inside I found a tape
with my grandma's voice
talking and singing to me
in Nahuatl* and Spanish:

43 "Jorge, Jorge, maybe
you will never come back.
Remember when you sat
next to me on the river bank?"

44 "Jorge, Jorge, don't forget
that in Nahuatl 'tetl'
means 'stone' and 'niyollotl'
means 'my heart' "

*Nahuatl *is pronounced: NAH-wah-tuhl.*

Nahuatl *is an indigenous language spoken in parts of Mexico and El Salvador.*

Language of the Birds

45 I used to speak
only Spanish

46 Now I can speak
English too

47 And in my dreams
I speak in Nahuatl

48 the language
my grandma says

49 her people
—the Pipiles—

50 learned
from the birds

The Pipiles are an indigenous people of El Salvador who speak Nahuatl, the language of the Aztecs.

My Grandma's Stories

I call my grandma "Mita"—an affectionate term for "mi abuelita" ("my grandma").

51 Mita's stories
filled her shack
with stars

52 Mita's stories
put smiles
on our faces

53 Mita's stories
are old
like the mountains

54 Mita's stories
are like the songs
of the crickets

55 If I close my eyes
I hear them
in the wind

Family Nest

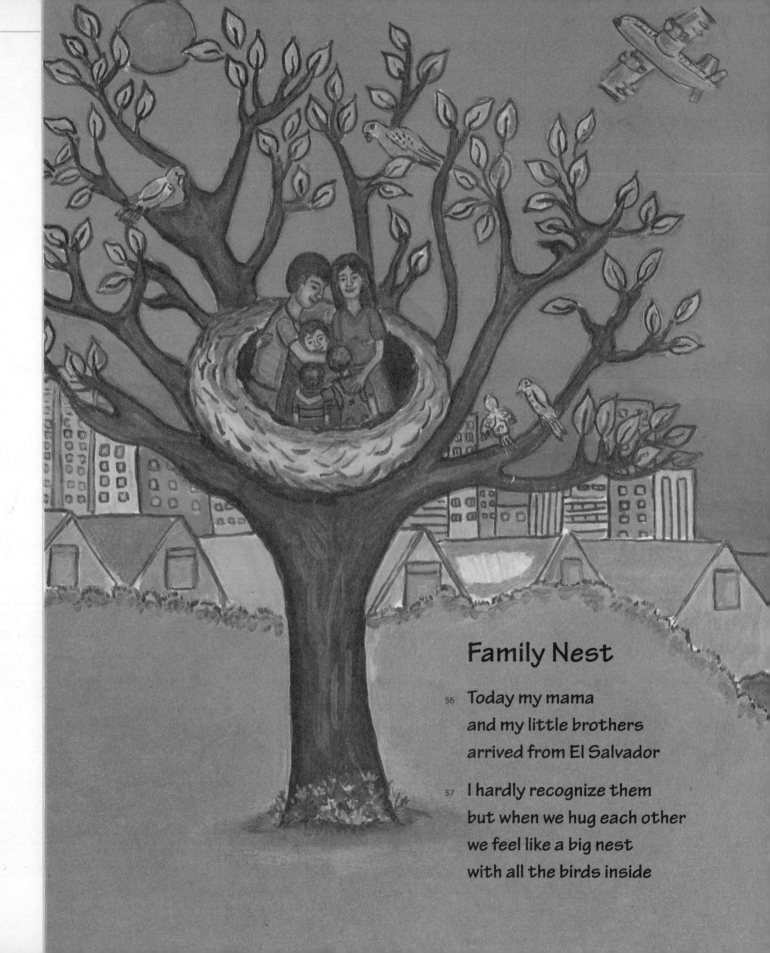

56 Today my mama
and my little brothers
arrived from El Salvador

57 I hardly recognize them
but when we hug each other
we feel like a big nest
with all the birds inside

The Best Guide in Town

58 "Let's go see the city
Today I'll be your guide"
I tell my mama
and my little brothers

59 There are so many things
I want to show you—
Gardens that walk by
on the hands of women

60 Little city trains
that go in and out
of the open mouths
of mountains

61 Giant buildings
that pick up stars
from the ground
and put them in the sky

A Band of Parakeets

62 Every Saturday morning
Mama and Papa
my little brothers
and I walk
on 24th Street

63 We are like a band
of parakeets flying
from San Francisco
to El Salvador
and back again

Respond to the Text

Collaborative Discussion

Revisit what you wrote on page 154 and tell a partner what you learned from the text. Then work with a group to discuss the questions below. Look for details in *A Movie in My Pillow* to support your ideas. Follow the class rules for good discussion.

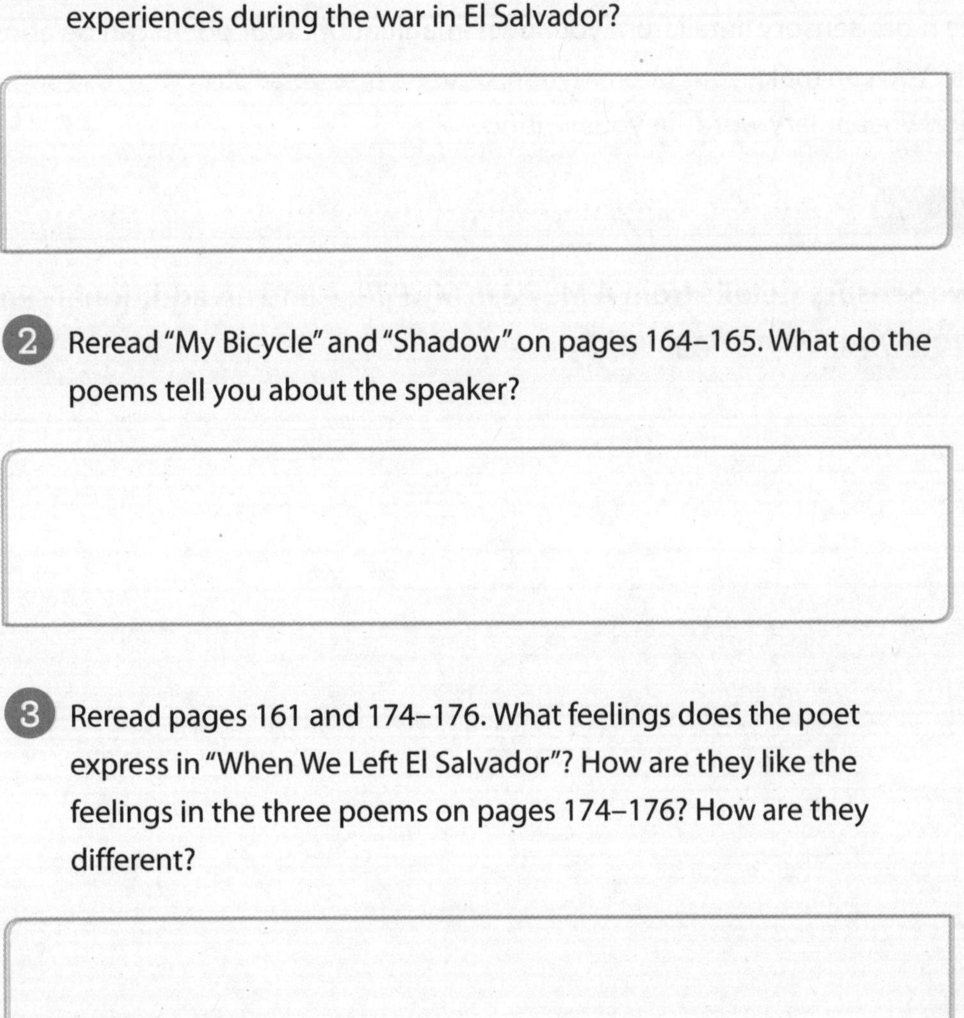

1. Reread pages 162–163. What do the poems suggest about people's experiences during the war in El Salvador?

2. Reread "My Bicycle" and "Shadow" on pages 164–165. What do the poems tell you about the speaker?

3. Reread pages 161 and 174–176. What feelings does the poet express in "When We Left El Salvador"? How are they like the feelings in the three poems on pages 174–176? How are they different?

Listening Tip

Listen politely and pay careful attention to each speaker's ideas.

Speaking Tip

Wait your turn to speak. If you disagree with someone, do so calmly and support your ideas with details from the poems.

Cite Text Evidence

Write a Poem

PROMPT

The poems in *A Movie in My Pillow* tell about important memories of the author's childhood. The reader experiences the sights, smells, and sounds the author remembers through the poems' sensory details.

Imagine you are writing a poem for your school's online poetry magazine. Choose two sensory details from *A Movie in My Pillow* and write a poem that includes them. Add at least one more sensory detail from your own imagination. Your poem can be about any topic. You can make your poem rhyme, or use a free-verse structure. Use some of the Critical Vocabulary words in your writing.

PLAN

Note two sensory details from *A Movie in My Pillow* and an additional sensory detail from your own imagination.

WRITE

Now write your poem.

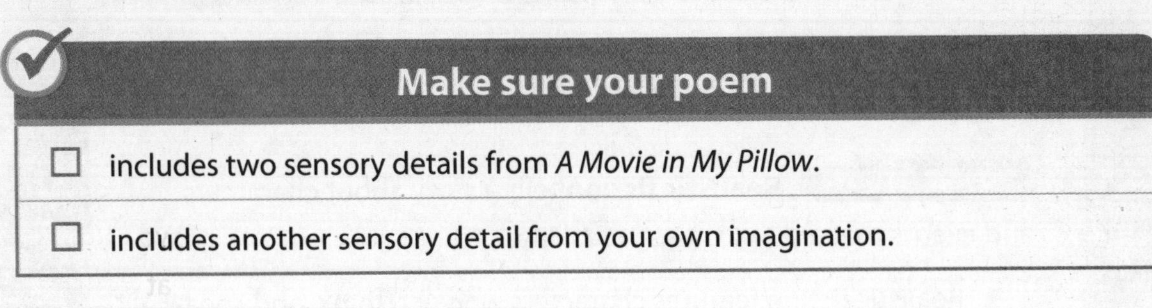

Make sure your poem

- ☐ includes two sensory details from *A Movie in My Pillow*.
- ☐ includes another sensory detail from your own imagination.

Notice & Note
Memory Moment

Prepare to Read

GENRE STUDY **Realistic fiction** tells a story about characters and events that are like those in real life.

- Realistic fiction features characters who act, think, and speak like real people would.
- Dialogue in realistic fiction is true to life and usually contains informal language.
- Most realistic fiction includes a theme or lesson learned by the main character.

SET A PURPOSE **Think about** the title and genre of this text. What do you know about Indian culture? What do you want to learn? Write your ideas below.

CRITICAL VOCABULARY

- reluctantly
- reserve
- casual
- nudged

Build Background: Diwali, Festival of Light

From Scratch

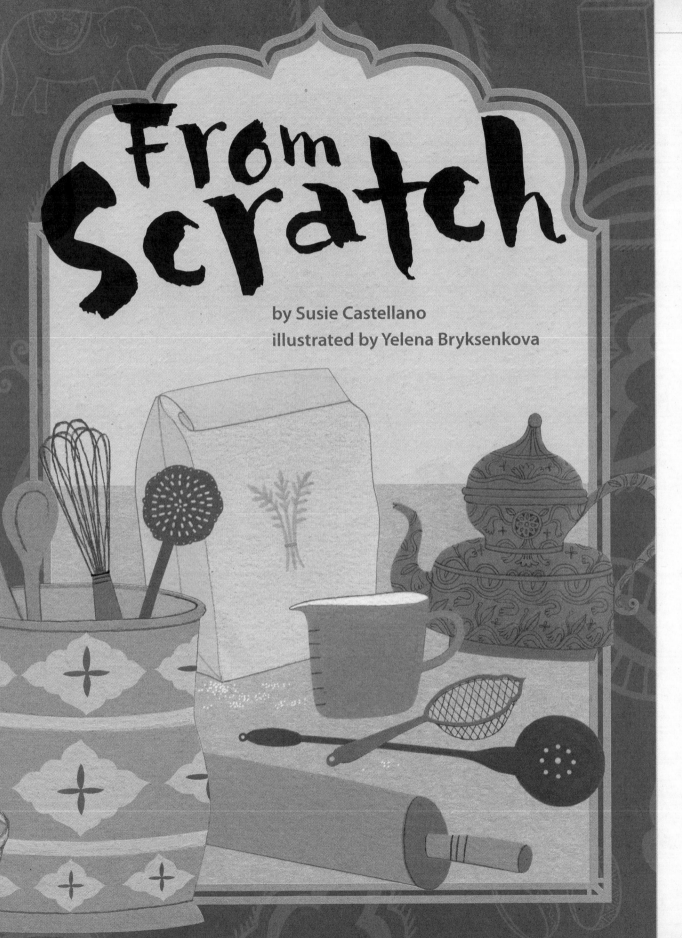

by Susie Castellano
illustrated by Yelena Bryksenkova

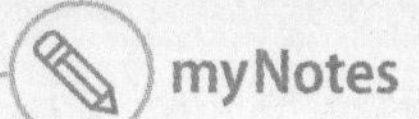

1 Priya's mother placed the pot of water on the stove, and Priya poured in the sugar. One, two, three, four cups of the sugary crystals glinted under the stove light. Priya peered into the pot as she stirred the sugar water. Soon it would be thick and syrupy.

2 "Mummy, what time is it back home . . ." Priya stopped and corrected herself. "I mean . . . in India?"

3 Her mother rattled around in the cabinet for another small pot. "Here it is seven at night, so in India it is six-thirty in the morning."

4 Time for *chai*, Priya thought. She pictured Ama squatting in their little kitchen, her orange-and-yellow sari draped around her shoulders and over her head in the traditional way. She'd sing a silly song in Hindi about the weather as she fixed the morning tea on the little electric stove: "*Dum dum diga diga, mosum biga biga . . .*" Priya felt a sharp pang in her chest as her grandmother's voice flooded her mind. She didn't want her mother to see her tears, so she stared into the pot, stirring absently.

5 Mummy placed a stick of butter in the second pot and adjusted the heat. Priya watched the waxy butter slowly turn to foamy liquid.

6 "Will you get out the dry milk and the baking mix?" her mother asked.

7 Priya opened the cupboard and stared at the prepackaged baking mix her mother had bought at the big indoor supermarket. Already her mother was adjusting to their new life, buying quick American ingredients to replace the traditional ones that were now hard to find. In India, everything was made from scratch. Reluctantly, Priya opened the baking mix and poured it into a bowl with the dry milk.

8 Priya hated the American supermarket. It felt cold and unfriendly, and the fluorescent ceiling lights hurt her eyes. Priya thought about the bazaar, the outdoor marketplace near Delhi. There were vegetable stands and crowds of chattering people, kiosks with colorful bindis, and the warm smell of spices from the dhaba. There were shops with rainbows of blankets, silver and gold jewelry glittering in the sun, and fabric shops where her mother bought material for her clothes. Best of all, there was the little bracelet stand, where shiny bangles painted the walls with splashes of red, purple, orange, and green. Every autumn, just before the Diwali holiday festival, her father would give her ten rupees to buy new bracelets. Priya hadn't worn her sparkling bangles since they'd stepped off the plane in Dallas, Texas, five weeks ago. They remained hidden in her drawer, in the little velvet pouch Ama had sewn for her.

reluctantly If you do something reluctantly, you do it without wanting to.

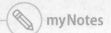

9 Priya thought about her mother browsing the long supermarket aisles with a clangy metal shopping cart, her dupatta swinging behind her in a wave of color. Suddenly her throat felt tight again. Mummy wanted so much for her to be happy here. “Do you want this for your lunch or this?” she would ask, offering Priya packaged snacks in colorful, cartoon boxes with big letters that shouted “New!” “Great Taste!” and “Quick and Easy!” In India, Priya might have traded all the bangles in the world for a box of the sweet, brightly colored treats. Now they just reminded her of the kids at school, the ones who stared as she unpacked channa dal and chapatis from her lunch bag in the cafeteria. For days she sat alone in the lunchroom, hiding her food behind her paper sack so no one would see that she didn’t have jelly and peanut butter or cartoon-shaped fruit snacks.

10 Finally she had selected a jar of peanut butter at the supermarket and described the sandwich for Mummy to make. It tasted sugary-sweet and made her mouth feel stuck shut. But she ate it anyway, grateful that at least no one stared or whispered.

11 Priya looked at her mother, who was busy grinding the beady black cardamom seeds to powder in a marble bowl. Her long, ebony hair was pulled into a braid, but as she worked at crushing the seeds, wisps of hair blew forward and back around her face, like a curtain near an open window. She was not like the other mothers, the American mothers with their short hair dyed and cut like movie stars and their wide, painted smiles. She loved her mother's soft, golden face and her thoughtful silence. She didn't want her mother to change; in fact, she much preferred Mummy's quiet reserve to the loud way some had of talking just to chase out the quiet. But Priya had seen how the other children stared at her mother when she came to school after the first day. Mummy had worn her beautiful green salwar kurta, more casual than a sari but still elegant and flowing. She had also worn a decorative bindi on her forehead, silver ankle bracelets that jingled when she walked, and matching toe rings. Everyone stared, and Priya's face grew hot. She felt embarrassed, and guilty for feeling embarrassed. She forced a smile and kissed her mother on the cheek, then choked back tears the whole way home.

reserve Reserve is a quiet, sometimes shy, way of behaving.
casual Casual clothing is not dressy and is meant for everyday use.

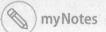

12 Priya's mother swept the cardamom powder into the baking mix, and Priya drizzled in the melted butter. As Priya stirred the mixture, her mother's eyes caught hers. They both smiled, and Mummy asked, "Did you make any new friends today?"

13 Priya stared into the bowl. "I met a girl from France," she said. Actually, the teacher had paired them together because they were the only ones left after everyone had chosen science partners.

14 "Ah," Mummy said, crumbling the dough with her fingers. "And what did you have for lunch?"

15 Priya thought about what to tell her mother. After the peanut butter sandwiches had grown tiresome, she had begun buying lunch at the cafeteria. But that, too, drew attention because she could only eat the vegetarian items, no meat or fish. Children watched as she passed over the hamburger patties and chicken nuggets, choosing only watery green beans and lumpy blobs of mashed potatoes. Lindsay, a blond girl in her class, had asked, "Why don't you eat meat?"

16 Priya had thought about telling her the story Ama had told a hundred times, about how the gods came to Earth in different forms, and how Brahma had once come to live amongst the people as a cow. Because of that, Hindus do not eat beef, fearing they might harm a god in disguise. She smiled as she remembered waiting in dusty traffic jams in Delhi, all because a cow had decided to nap in the road, and no one would disturb it.

17 But when Priya had looked at the girl's big, blue, wondering eyes in the cafeteria, she decided Lindsay wouldn't understand the story about Brahma and the cow. So she had mumbled an excuse and hurried away from the food line.

18 She couldn't be Indian anymore and she didn't know how to be American. She didn't fit anywhere.

19 "I had some green beans and salad," she said, looking down.

20 Her mother studied her closely, then glanced at the stove. "Time to test the syrup, chicaree."

21 Leaving the crumbly dough to her mother, Priya dribbled a tiny drop of syrup from the pot onto her finger, then pressed her finger and thumb together and slowly pulled them apart.

22 "It's ready, Mummy," she said, seeing the syrup form a threadlike string between her fingers.

23 Her mother nodded and was quiet.

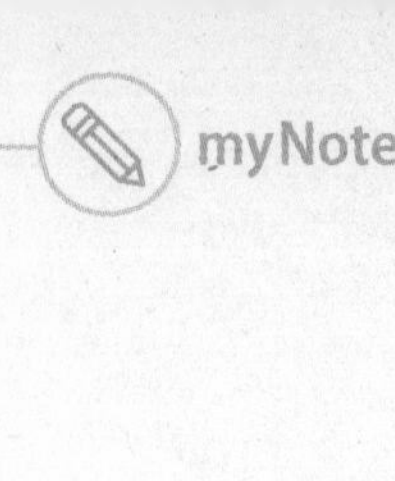

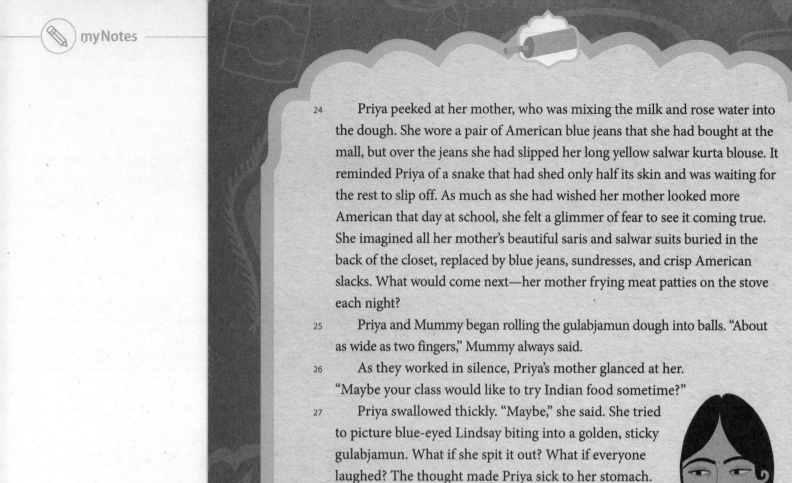

24 Priya peeked at her mother, who was mixing the milk and rose water into the dough. She wore a pair of American blue jeans that she had bought at the mall, but over the jeans she had slipped her long yellow salwar kurta blouse. It reminded Priya of a snake that had shed only half its skin and was waiting for the rest to slip off. As much as she had wished her mother looked more American that day at school, she felt a glimmer of fear to see it coming true. She imagined all her mother's beautiful saris and salwar suits buried in the back of the closet, replaced by blue jeans, sundresses, and crisp American slacks. What would come next—her mother frying meat patties on the stove each night?

25 Priya and Mummy began rolling the gulabjamun dough into balls. "About as wide as two fingers," Mummy always said.

26 As they worked in silence, Priya's mother glanced at her. "Maybe your class would like to try Indian food sometime?"

27 Priya swallowed thickly. "Maybe," she said. She tried to picture blue-eyed Lindsay biting into a golden, sticky gulabjamun. What if she spit it out? What if everyone laughed? The thought made Priya sick to her stomach.

28 Priya's mother melted shortening in a large frying pan, and one by one, Priya began dropping the little dough balls in.

29 "I spoke with your teacher today," Mummy said, wiping the counter with quick, practiced motions.

30 Priya silently nudged the little white balls with a spoon, turning them so they would brown evenly on all sides.

31 "She mentioned that there is a Muslim girl in your class . . . ?"

32 Priya flashed her mother a quick look. "Muslim?" The faces of the people at school flickered through her mind one by one. She didn't remember seeing any dark-haired Muslim girl.

33 Priya's mother began scooping the golden balls out of the oil. "Her name is Lindsay. Mrs. Swanson said she moved here from Iran last year. Apparently she had a hard time adjusting and has been very lonely."

34 Priya's head spun with confusion. Blond-haired, blue-eyed Lindsay? She seemed to fit in perfectly with the other kids. Priya shook her head. "The Lindsay in my class . . . is light skinned. She's American. She speaks English perfectly."

35 "Mrs. Swanson said her father is Iranian and her mother is American. They moved to Iran when she was very young, and she grew up there." Priya's mother eyed her pointedly. "She was raised bilingual, like you. She speaks Persian *and* English."

36 Priya thought back to the day in the cafeteria when Lindsay had asked why she didn't eat meat. She knew Muslims didn't eat pork, so could it be that Lindsay was trying to find something in common with someone? To connect with a culture that seemed similar to her own? Priya remembered how she had mumbled rudely and walked away. Suddenly, she felt ashamed. She had never given Lindsay a chance. Maybe Lindsay even thought *she* was unfriendly.

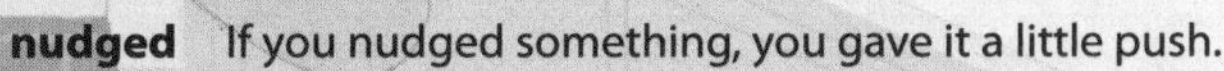

nudged If you nudged something, you gave it a little push.

37 Priya helped her mother scoop the rest of the gulabjamun out of the pan. They worked quietly and easily, dabbing the extra oil from the golden balls before dropping them gently into the syrup. When they were done, Priya admired the rich, glowing batch of sweets they had made. She thought how much Ama would have liked them. Then she took a deep breath.

38 "Maybe I could take these to school tomorrow, to share with my class," she said at last.

39 Priya's mother cocked her head lightly from side to side, the Indian way of saying O.K. It was a casual gesture, but Priya saw her mother smiling behind her dark curtain of hair. Their eyes met, and Priya smiled back. They never needed many words, Mummy and she.

40 As she stretched a thin sheet of plastic wrap over the bowl of gulabjamun, Priya wondered if Lindsay had beautiful things from her country hidden in a velvet pouch in her drawer. Maybe tomorrow she would ask.

Respond to the Text

Collaborative Discussion

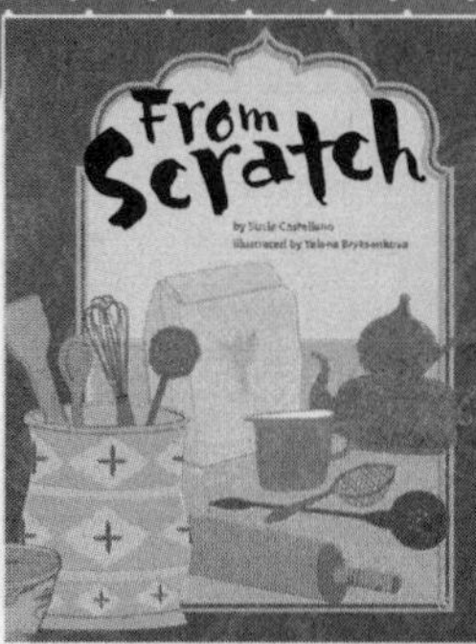

Look back at what you wrote on page 180. Tell a partner two things you learned during reading. Then work with a group to discuss the questions below. Look for details in *From Scratch* to strengthen your answers. Take an active role in your discussion and engage with other group members.

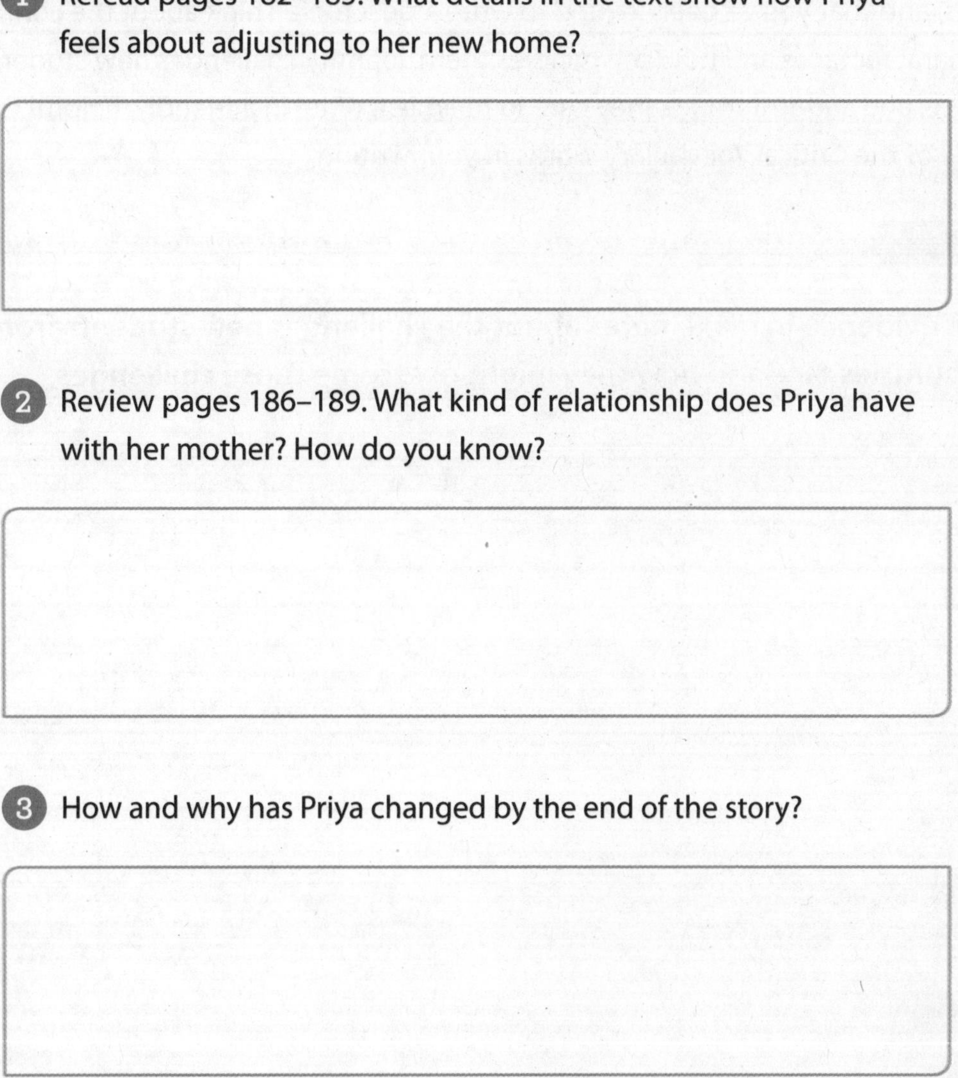

1. Reread pages 182–185. What details in the text show how Priya feels about adjusting to her new home?

2. Review pages 186–189. What kind of relationship does Priya have with her mother? How do you know?

3. How and why has Priya changed by the end of the story?

Listening Tip

Listen closely and look at the person who is speaking. Smile or nod to show that you agree with or understand the comments.

Speaking Tip

When you speak, make eye contact with other group members. Invite questions to keep the discussion moving.

Cite Text Evidence

Write a Blog Post

PROMPT

From Scratch tells the story of Priya, who has recently moved to the United States from India. She feels lonely and has trouble adjusting to her new life.

Imagine that your school's website includes a blog to welcome students from other countries, and that you've been invited to write a post for it. Think about the conflicts Priya's character faces and how she handles them. Identify challenges new students might face, and suggest things they can do to adjust. Write in a friendly, helpful tone. Use some of the Critical Vocabulary words in your writing.

PLAN

Use text evidence to make notes about the challenges new students from other countries face and how they might overcome those challenges.

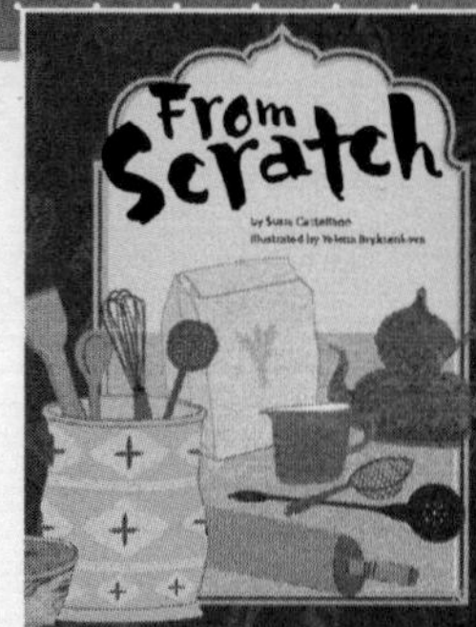

WRITE

Now write your blog post to welcome students from other countries.

Make sure your blog post
☐ is written for an audience of students who are new to America.
☐ uses a friendly, helpful tone.
☐ uses details from the text to point out challenges students might face and ideas for overcoming those challenges.

Notice & Note
Memory Moment

Prepare to Read

GENRE STUDY **Realistic fiction** tells a story about characters and events that are like those in real life.

- Realistic fiction tells the story through the plot, which includes a conflict and its resolution.
- Realistic fiction might include a flashback, which is an event that happened in the past.
- Realistic fiction includes natural-sounding dialogue that helps develop the characters.

SET A PURPOSE **Think about** the title and genre of this text. What do you know about moving to a new place? What do you want to learn? Write your ideas below.

CRITICAL VOCABULARY

- diary
- promptly
- semidarkness
- obvious
- comprehended
- officially
- preliminary

Meet the Author and Illustrator: Doris Luisa Oronoz and Byron Gin

Elisa's Diary

by Doris Luisa Oronoz
illustrated by Byron Gin

1 "Today is the saddest day of my life," Elisa wrote in her diary on March 25th. She was going to continue, but her father knocked on the door and said, "It's nine o'clock, dear. Turn off the lights and go to sleep." Elisa put her pen and notebook away in her backpack and promptly obeyed.

2 In the semidarkness she could just make out the objects in her new room. She had stayed in this room before, but it seemed to her as though it were the first time. The bright, vivid colors of her bedspread, which she liked so much before, now seemed cold and muted.

3 Elisa looked at the little porcelain squirrel and remembered the day it was given to her. It was the first time she had visited this country. She had come to spend some time with her grandmother, and one night she heard a sound like something scratching under the eave of the house. She became frightened, thinking that it might be mice, and she ran to ask her grandmother.

4 Grandma took her to the patio and motioned to her to be very quiet. When they reached the back, Elisa glanced up and saw two

diary A diary is a daily record of someone's experiences and feelings.
promptly When you do something promptly, you do it right away.
semidarkness A place that is in semidarkness is partially dark.

squirrels playing on the roof right above her room. They were sliding down a branch and leaping onto the roof tiles to gather acorns, then they would scurry back to the branch and repeat the process, over and over.

5 Since there were no squirrels in Elisa's country, this was a new experience for her. She enjoyed watching the squirrels so much that when her vacation was over, Grandma bought her a squirrel figurine and put it on her night table.

6 "It will be right here waiting for you when you come back to visit again."

7 "I'll be back soon, Grandma. I love this place. Maybe some day I'll come and live with you."

8 But that was then and this is now.

9 "Who needs squirrels?" she asked herself.

10 She closed her eyes and took a deep breath. She was exhausted; it had been a long day that for some reason had gone slowly. That morning she had been in Puerto Rico, and now she was in the United States of America—except that this time, supposedly, it was forever. A tear rolled down her cheek and landed on the pillow.

myNotes

11 Elisa was ten years old, and her brother Francisco was twelve. At least if they were going to go to the same school, she would have felt protected, but they weren't. And of course, boys at that age typically don't want anything to do with their little sisters anyway.

12 "He's unbearable," she thought aloud, just as her brother strolled into her room.

13 "Who's unbearable?" asked Francisco.

14 "You," answered Elisa, holding nothing back.

15 "Oh? And why am I so unbearable?" asked her brother, sounding a little surprised.

16 "Because you leave me alone all day while you're out running around, having fun."

17 "It's obvious that you're afraid to go out," answered her brother. "Look, I've met some neighbors, and they're nice."

18 "And in what language do you speak to them, huh?"

19 "Well, I speak to them in English," responded Francisco.

20 "I can imagine the crazy things you come up with."

obvious Something that is obvious is easy to see or understand.

21 "But at least I try," retorted her brother. "What you have to do is make an effort. If they don't understand me, I talk with my hands until something happens."

22 "I write well in English, and when I read, I understand a lot. But now, when they speak to me, I don't understand a word."

23 "Listen, the woman who lives in the house on the corner—"

24 "Which one?" interrupted Elisa.

25 "The one who gave me two dollars to take care of her cat."

26 "What about her?"

27 "She told me that she used to listen to the news on the radio and got used to hearing English that way. Then, little by little, she understood English better and better."

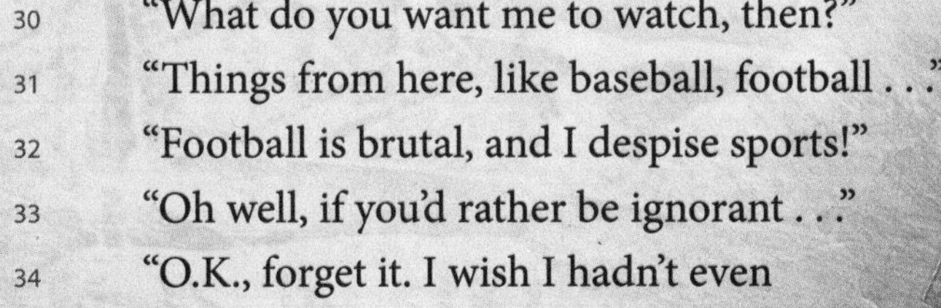

28 "I don't like the radio," declared Elisa.

29 "Turn on the TV, then, but not to those lovey-dovey soaps in Spanish and all that silly stuff you like."

30 "What do you want me to watch, then?"

31 "Things from here, like baseball, football . . ."

32 "Football is brutal, and I despise sports!"

33 "Oh well, if you'd rather be ignorant . . ."

34 "O.K., forget it. I wish I hadn't even mentioned it."

 myNotes

35 Elisa regretted ever having wanted to be in the same school as her know-it-all brother. She realized she'd have to solve her dilemma on her own, but she had no idea how.

36 The summer came to an end, and the school year commenced. That's when she met José. At the end of that day she wrote in her diary,

37 I met a student from Guatemala, named José. He's very quiet, and he spends all his time with his head down, drawing in a notebook. He has sad, dark eyes. I thought he was going to talk to me once, but he didn't. He just smiled and kept on drawing.

38 She read what she had written and added, "I think I'm going to like this school after all."

39 The fact is that she didn't like the school one bit. On the second day of classes, the English teacher called her name, pronouncing it more like "Alisha" than "Elisa." She arose from her desk expecting a disaster, and that's exactly what happened. She was asked a question that she didn't understand, and when it was repeated, she comprehended even less. She was so nervous that she could only stammer a few syllables "*eh, ah, ah, uh.*" She couldn't

comprehended If you comprehended something you understood it.

continue, and she collapsed in her seat in front of those forty faces—her opponents—some disbelieving, some mocking. Elisa had never felt so embarrassed in her whole life.

40 Around noon, when José's turn came, he stood up. He got up, and he spoke shyly of the customs and traditions of his country. He mentioned the quetzal—a bird with soft feathers, a green crest, and a red chest. He told how this gorgeous bird was the symbol of power for the Maya and that today it is officially the national bird of Guatemala. Finally, he showed them a color drawing and told them proudly that the quetzal on the Guatemalan flag was an emblem of national liberty.

41 The entire class applauded. José took his seat, and, as always, he put his head down and went back to drawing.

officially If something is done officially, it is approved by the government or someone in charge.

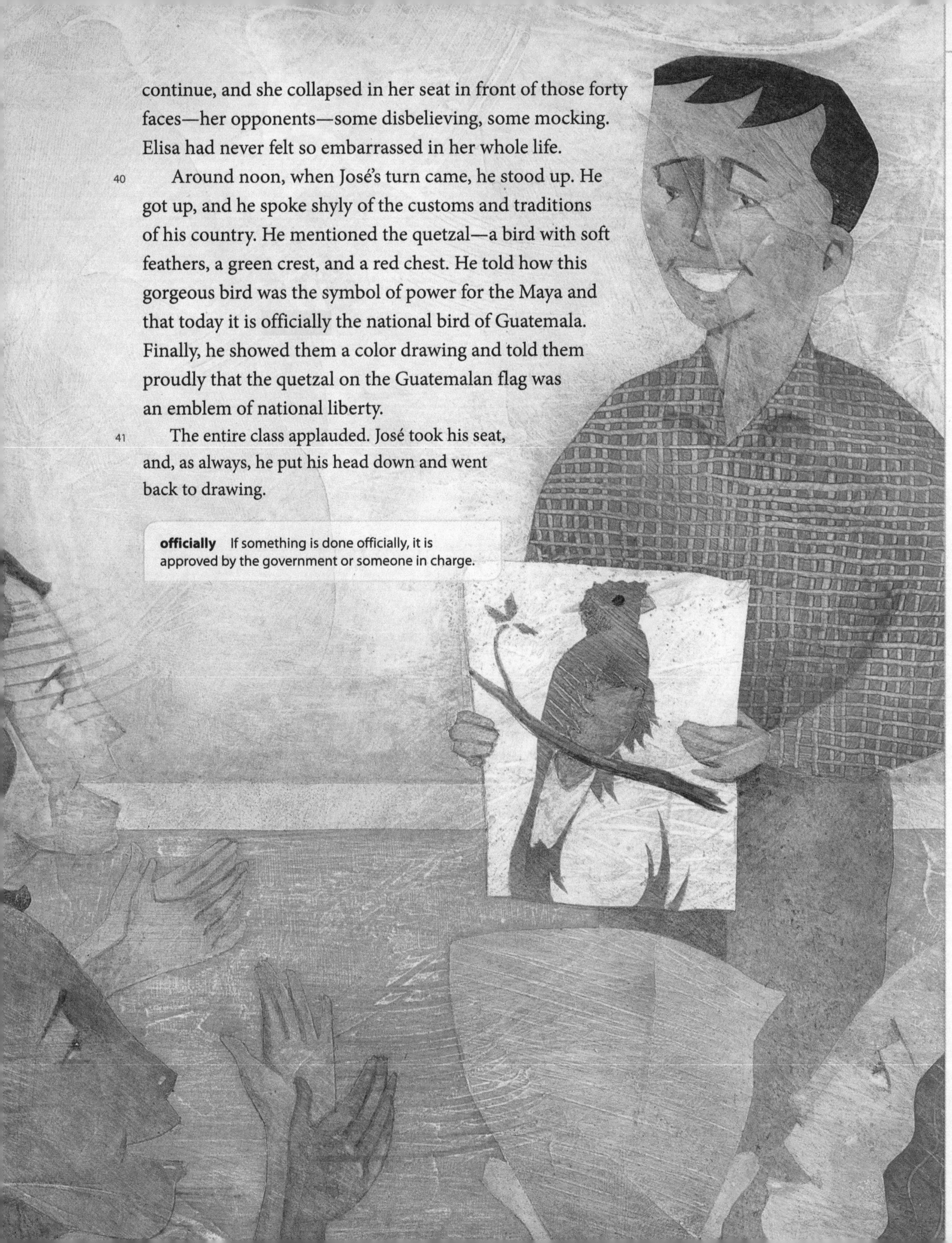

42 In the afternoon each student wrote a composition. Elisa wrote about her home, Puerto Rico. Like José, she described its customs and traditions and explained the symbolism of Puerto Rico's shield—a lamb, the emblem of peace and fraternity, appears in the green center. Above the lamb is a bundle of arrows, symbols of the creative force, and above the arrows is a yoke, which represents the joining of forces necessary to attain success. She thought it turned out pretty well, but writing was one thing and talking was another.

43 That night she didn't open her diary because she had grown weary of complaining, even if it was only to her diary.

44 The next morning Elisa smiled for the first time since classes had started. She received a good grade on her composition. She wanted to show it to everyone so that they'd see that she wasn't so dumb, but she refrained from doing that. She thought maybe she'd show it to José, though. Yes, she decided, she would show the composition to him. So during recess she called to him

and proudly showed him her paper. He looked at it and, lowering his eyes, he said with a fleeting smile, "Congratulations."

45 "Thanks." said Elisa. "And how did you do?"

46 "O.K."

47 "No doubt you got an A and you don't want me to be embarrassed."

48 "No, it's not that, Elisa. It's that . . . I picked up English by listening. You know, 'on the street.' I never took English in school. I write it like I hear it, and everything comes out wrong."

49 Elisa read the paper that he handed her, and in one sweeping glance, she saw what he meant. She didn't know what to say.

50 "But you speak English very well," Elisa tried to console him.

51 "Speaking is one thing and writing is another."

52 "And vice-versa," said Elisa.

53 "And the opposite."

54 "And the other way around."

55 They laughed so hard that the rest of the kids came over to see what was so humorous, but they didn't reveal their secret to anyone. That afternoon, they made a deal: she would assist him with writing, and he, in turn, would help her with pronunciation.

56 Twelve years later, Elisa was getting ready for work. She pulled down a box of shoes from the top shelf of her closet and in the rush, several things cascaded down on top of her. One of them was her old diary. It fell open to the last page, and Elisa picked it up and read.

57 Today I received my high school diploma. When I looked at myself in the mirror with my cap and gown and my gold honors tassels, I remembered the little girl who arrived here confused, scared, and sad. I'm happy now.

58 She put away the notebook, got dressed, and headed for work. When she entered the classroom, her students looked at her—some shy, some confused, some scared. She saw those sad, preliminary, first-day-of-school expressions that she knew so well.

59 She opened her lesson planner, considered it for a moment, and then shut it. She stood up and wrote on the board, "The joining of forces."

60 Then she said, "I'm going to tell you the story of a quetzal that came down to the plain with the gentleness of a lamb, and a lamb that soared to great heights on the wings of a quetzal."

preliminary Something that is preliminary happens at the very beginning of an event, or just before a main event.

Respond to the Text

Collaborative Discussion

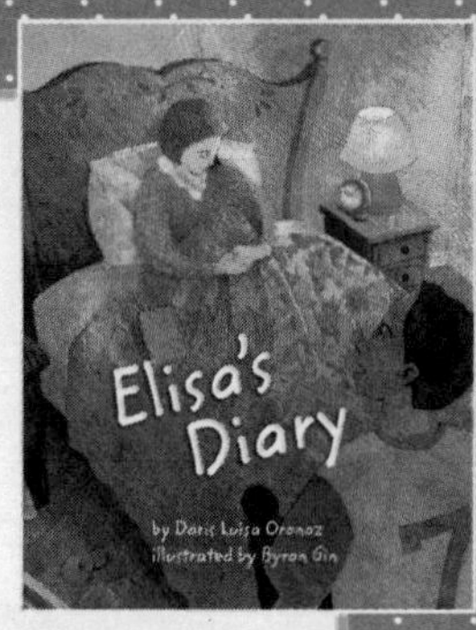

Look back at what you wrote on page 194. Tell a partner two things you learned from the text. Then work with a group to discuss the questions below. Look for details in *Elisa's Diary* to support your ideas. In your discussion, add ideas of your own that build on those of others in your group.

1. Revisit pages 196–197. What has caused Elisa's feelings about visiting her grandmother to change?

2. Review pages 200–203. Why is Elisa surprised by José's composition? What does she learn from him?

3. What experiences have shown Elisa that "the joining of forces" is important?

Listening Tip

Listen to each speaker's ideas. Think about how you can add to or build on what others have said.

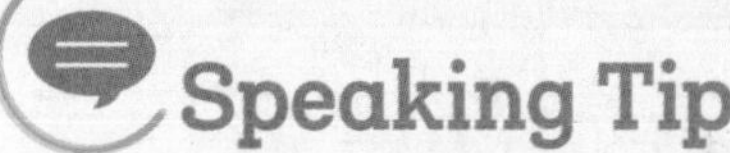

Speaking Tip

Point out how your ideas are connected to those of other speakers. If you do not agree with what someone else has said, be sure to explain why.

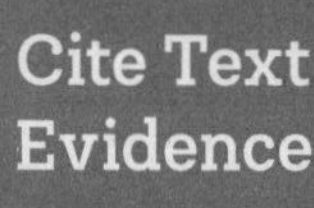
Cite Text Evidence

Write a Retelling

PROMPT

In *Elisa's Diary*, a girl writes about adjusting to a new home and a new language.

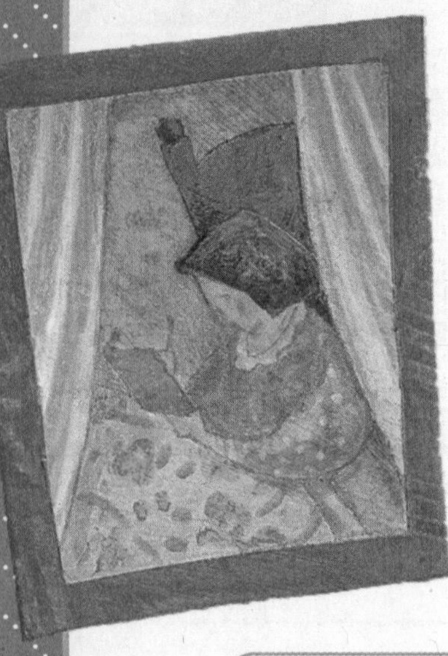

Imagine that you are one of the other characters in Elisa's story: a family member, a teacher, José, or another classmate. Retell an event from the story from that character's point of view. Use evidence from the text to retell what happens, in order. Describe things that Elisa says and does, but remember to tell it from your character's point of view. Use some of the Critical Vocabulary words in your writing.

PLAN

Makes notes about an event from the text and plan how your character will retell it.

WRITE

Now write your retelling of the text.

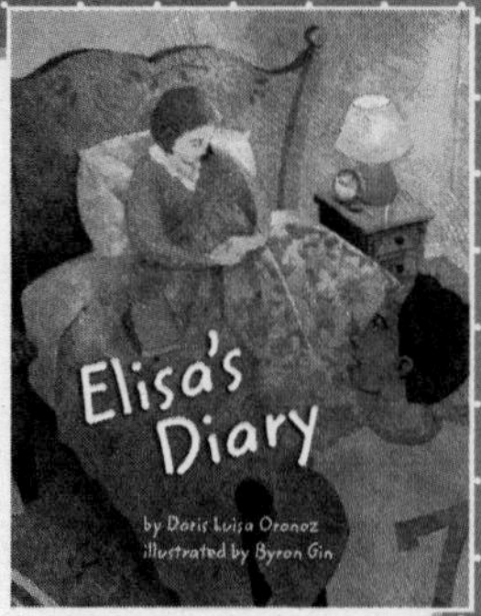

Make sure your retelling

- ☐ makes it clear which character you are.
- ☐ retells an event from the story from your character's point of view.
- ☐ uses evidence from the text.
- ☐ retells details in the correct order.

Elisa's Diary
by Doris Luisa Oronoz
illustrated by Byron Gin

myNotes

Notice & Note
Memory Moment

Prepare to Read

GENRE STUDY **Poetry** uses the sounds and rhythms of words to convey images and feelings.

- Poems include word sounds, such as onomatopoeia, to emphasize ideas. Onomatopoeia describes words that sound like what they mean, such as *hiss*.
- Poems may be organized into stanzas, or a series of lines grouped together.
- Free verse poems do not rhyme or have a regular rhythm. They sound more like natural speech.

SET A PURPOSE **Think about** the title and genre of this text. What do you know about feeling "inside out" in an unfamiliar place? Write your ideas below.

CRITICAL VOCABULARY

- sponsor
- generosity
- goodwill
- grateful
- exception
- sensible

Meet the Author: Thanhha Lai

Inside Out and Back Again

by Thanhha Lai

illustrated by Lisa Fields

1 *In 1975, ten-year-old Hà, her mother, and her older brothers fled from their home in Saigon, South Vietnam. Their country, along with the United States and other nations, had just lost a very long war with North Vietnam. As the American and other military allies of South Vietnam left the country, conditions became too dangerous for Hà and her family to stay. They left without Hà's father, who had been missing in the war for several years. The family first moved to the island of Guam, where they lived in a tent city with other refugees, then on to the United States. In Alabama, the immigrants moved in with their* ***sponsor****, Mr. Johnston. Hà thinks he's a cowboy. Next door to them lives Mrs. Washington, a kind, retired teacher who offers to teach the family to speak English.*

Our Cowboy

2 Our sponsor
looks just like
an American should.

3 Tall and pig-bellied,
black cowboy hat,
tan cowboy boots,
teeth shining,
red in face,
golden in hair.

4 I love him
immediately
and imagine him
to be good-hearted and loud
and the owner of a horse.

August 8

sponsor A sponsor helps an immigrant settle into his or her new country.

First Rule

5 Brother Quang says
add an *s* to nouns
to mean more than one
even if there's
already an *s*
sitting there.

6 *Glass*
Glass-es

7 All day
I practice
squeezing hisses
through my teeth.

8 Whoever invented
English
must have loved
snakes.

August 17

myNotes

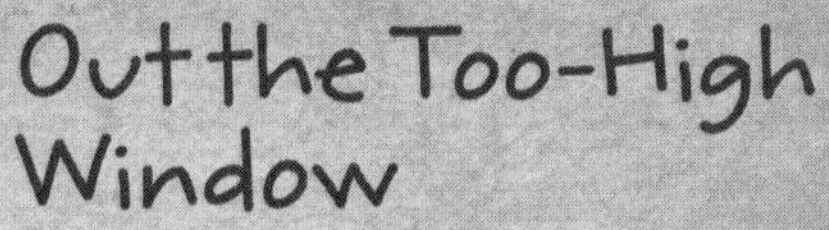

Out the Too-High Window

9 Green mats of grass
in front of every house.

10 Vast windows
in front of sealed curtains.

11 Cement lanes where
no one walks.

12 Big cars
pass not often.

13 Not a noise.

14 Clean, quiet
loneliness.

August 21

Second Rule

15 Add an *s* to verbs
acted by one person
in the present tense,
even if there's
already an *s* sound
nearby.

16 *She choose-s*
He refuse-s

17 I'm getting better
at hissing,
no longer spitting
on my forearms.

August 22

American Address

18 Our cowboy
in an even taller hat
finds us a house
on Princess Anne Road,
pays rent ahead
three months.

19 Mother could not believe
his generosity
until Brother Quang says
the American government
gives sponsors money.

20 Mother is even more amazed
by the generosity
of the American government
until Brother Quang says
it's to ease the guilt
of losing the war.

21 Mother's face crinkles
like paper on fire.
She tells Brother Quang
to clamp shut his mouth.

22 *People living on*
others' goodwill
cannot afford
political opinions.

23 I inspect our house.

generosity When people show generosity, they give something valuable or meaningful to someone.

goodwill When people show goodwill, they show kindness toward others and a willingness to help.

24 Two bedrooms,
one for my brothers,
one for Mother and me.

25 A washing machine,
because no one here
will scrub laundry
in exchange for
a bowl of rice.

26 The stove spews out
clean blue flames,
unlike the ashy coals
back home.

27 What I love best:
the lotus-pod shower,
where heavy drops
will massage my scalp
as if I were standing
in a monsoon.

28 What I don't love:
pink sofas, green chairs,
plastic cover on a table,
stained mattresses,
old clothes,
unmatched dishes.

29 All from friends
of our cowboy.

30 Even at our poorest
we always had
beautiful furniture
and matching dishes.

31 Mother says be grateful.

32 I'm trying.

August 24

grateful When people are grateful, they are happy and satisfied with what they have.

Third Rule

33 Always an exception.

34 Do *not* add an *s*
to certain nouns.

35 One deer,
two deer.

36 Why no *s* for two deer,
but an *s* for two monkeys?

37 Brother Quang says
no one knows.

38 So much for rules!

39 Whoever invented English
should be bitten
by a snake.

August 26

Fourth Rule

40 Some verbs
switch all over
just because.

41 *I am*
She is
They are
He was
They were

42 Would be simpler
if English
and life
were logical.

August 30

exception If something is an exception, it is left out of a group or list because it doesn't fit well.

The Outside

43 Starting tomorrow
everyone must
leave the house.

44 Mother starts sewing
at a factory;
Brother Quang begins
repairing cars.

45 The rest of us
must go to school,
repeating the last grade,
left unfinished.

46 Brother Vũ wants
to be a cook
or teach martial arts,
not waste a year
as the oldest senior.

47 Mother says
one word:
University.

48 Brother Khôi
gets an old bicycle to ride,
but Mother says
I'm too young for one
even though I'm
a ten-year-old
in the fourth grade,
when everyone else
is nine.

49 Mother says,
Worry instead
about getting sleep
because from now on
no more naps.
You will eat lunch
at school
with friends.

50 *What friends?*

51 *You'll make some.*

52 *What if I can't?*

53 *You will.*

54 *What will I eat?*

55 *What your friends eat.*

56 *But what will I eat?*

57 *Be surprised.*

58 *I hate surprises.*

59 *Be agreeable.*

60 *Not without knowing*
what I'm agreeing to.

61 Mother sighs,
walking away.

September 1

Sadder Laugh

62 School!

63 I wake up with
dragonflies
zipping through
my gut.

64 I eat nothing.

65 I take each step toward school evenly,
trying to hold my stomach
steady.

66 It helps that
the morning air glides cool
like a constant washcloth
against my face.

67 Deep breaths.

68 I'm the first student in class.

69 My new teacher has brown curls
looped tight to her scalp
like circles in a beehive.

70 She points to her chest:
MiSSS SScott,

71 saying it three times,
each louder
with ever more spit.

72 I repeat, *MiSSS SScott,*
careful to hiss every *s*.

73 She doesn't seem impressed.

74 I tap my own chest:
Hà.

75 She must have heard
ha,
as in funny *ha-ha-ha*.

76 She fakes a laugh.

77 I repeat, *Hà*,
and wish I knew
enough English
to tell her
to listen for
the diacritical mark,

78 this one directing
the tone
downward.

79 My new teacher tilts
her head back,
fakes
an even sadder laugh.

September 2
Morning

Rainbow

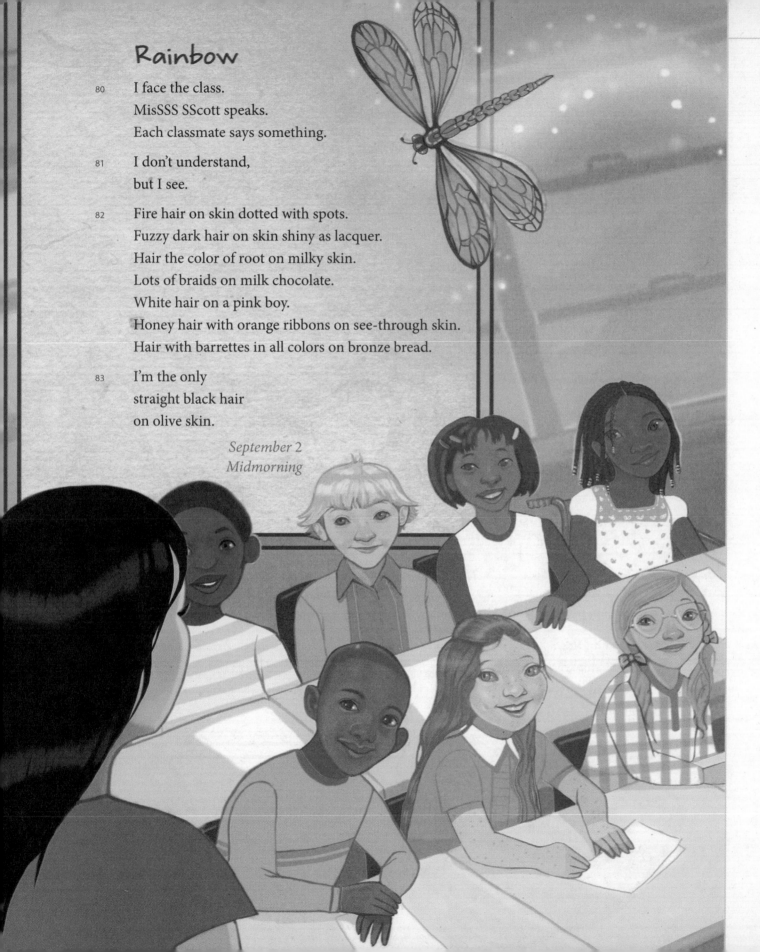

80 I face the class.
MisSSS SScott speaks.
Each classmate says something.

81 I don't understand,
but I see.

82 Fire hair on skin dotted with spots.
Fuzzy dark hair on skin shiny as lacquer.
Hair the color of root on milky skin.
Lots of braids on milk chocolate.
White hair on a pink boy.
Honey hair with orange ribbons on see-through skin.
Hair with barrettes in all colors on bronze bread.

83 I'm the only
straight black hair
on olive skin.

September 2
Midmorning

New Word a Day

84 MiSSSisss WaSShington
has her own rules.

85 She makes me memorize
one new word a day
and practice it
ten times in conversation.

86 For every new word
that sticks to my brain
she gives me
fruit in bite sizes, drowning in sweet, white fluff;
biscuits with drops of chocolate small as rain;
flat, round, pan-fried cakes floating in syrup.

87 My vocabulary grows!

88 She makes me learn rules
I've never noticed,
like *a, an,* and *the,*
which act as little megaphones
to tell the world
whose English
is still secondhand.

89 ***The** house is red.*
But:
*We live in **a** house.*

90 *A, an,* and *the*
do not exist in Vietnamese
and we understand
each other just fine.

91 I pout,
but MiSSSisss WaSShington says
every language has annoyances and illogical rules,
as well as sensible beauty.

92 She has an answer for everything,
just like Mother.

September 16

sensible A sensible rule is one that is simple and shows good judgment.

myNotes

Someone Knows

93 My word for today is delicious,
dì lít-sì-ishss.

94 MiSSSisss WaSShington asks,
Was your lunch delicious?

95 Before speaking,
I have to translate
in my head.

96 She waits.

97 *I eat chocolate in toilet.*

98 MiSSSisss WaSShington
looks panicked.
WHAT?

99 I realize my mistake.
Oh, the *toilet.*

100 She doesn't look
any happier.

101 I add,
Not chocolate all time.

102 *But you* always *eat in the bathroom?*

103 I nod.

104 *Why?*

105 How can I explain
dragonflies do somersaults
in my stomach
whenever I think of
the noisy room
full of mouths
chewing and laughing?

106 I'm still translating
when her eyes get red.

107 *I'll pack you a lunch*
and you can eat at your desk.

108 *No eat in class.*

109 *I'll fix that.*

110 *Things will get better,*
just you wait.

111 I don't believe her
but it feels good
that someone knows.

October 13

Most Relieved Day

112 At lunch the next day
I stay in class.

113 MiSSS SScott nods.

114 Can it be this easy?

115 Inside my first
brown paper bag:
a white meat sandwich,
an apple,
crunchy curly things
sprinkled with salt,
and a biscuit dotted
with chocolate raindrops.

116 Something salty,
something sweet,
perfect.

117 I hear pounding footsteps
in the long hall.

118 I stop chewing.

119 Two students
run into class,
giggling.

120 I firm my muscles,
ready for the giggles
to explode into laughter
thrown at me.

121 But smiles appear instead.

122 The girl has
red hair swaying to her bottom,
a skirt falling to her calves.

123 She says, *Pam*. I hear *Pem*.

124 The boy of coconut-shell skin
is dressed
better than for church,
a purple bow tie,
a white white shirt
that wouldn't wrinkle
even if he rolled down a hill.

125 His shaved head
is so shiny and perfect
I want to touch it.

126 He speaks slowly and loudly,
but I don't mind
because he's still smiling.

127 He says, *Steven*.
I hear *SSsì-Ti-Vân*.

128 I have not
seen them in class.
But then, I mostly
stare at my shoes.

129 I will write in my journal
October 14 is
Most Relieved Day,
as I have noted
April 30 was
Saigon Is Gone Day
and September 2 was
Longest Day *Ever*.

130 Though I was saving
Most Relieved Day
for Father's return,
he can have the title:
My Life's Best Day.

October 14

Respond to the Text

Collaborative Discussion

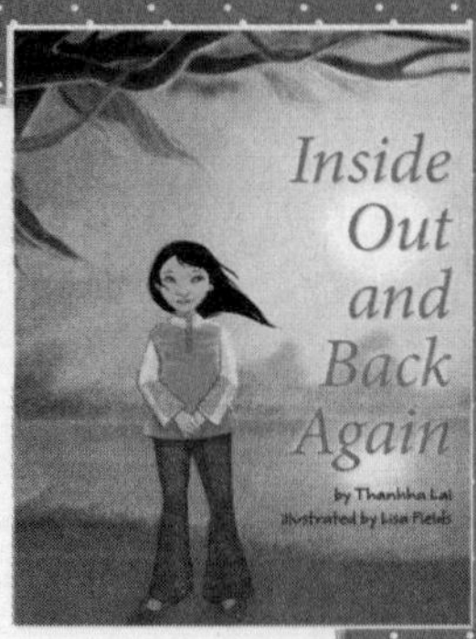

Look back at what you wrote on page 208 and talk with a partner about what you learned during reading. Work with a group to discuss the questions below. Support your answers with examples and details from *Inside Out and Back Again*. Be sure to follow your classroom's rules for good discussion behavior.

1. Review pages 210–213. What do "Our Cowboy" and "American Address" reveal about the speaker's feelings?

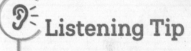

2. Reread page 215. What does the speaker describe in "The Outside"? How will life be different for her family?

3. In what ways is Hà different by the end of the selection? In what ways is she the same?

Listening Tip

Listen politely and look at the person who is speaking. Wait until the speaker is finished before offering to share your ideas.

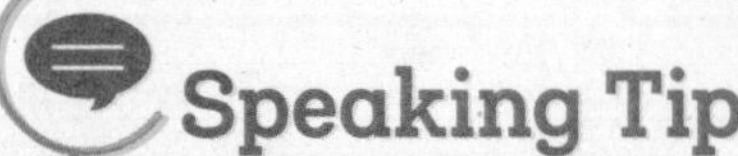

Speaking Tip

When you speak, look at the other members of your group. Speak clearly and loudly enough so that they can hear you.

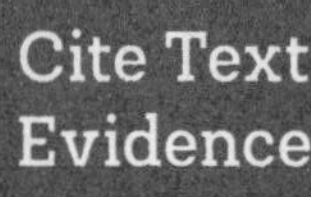

Write a Journal Entry

PROMPT

In *Inside Out and Back Again*, a girl named Hà describes her experiences and feelings after moving to America. At the end of the selection, Hà says she will write in her journal about the "Most Relieved Day" when she makes two friends.

Imagine that you are Hà. Write the journal entry she might write to describe that day. Use first-person point of view and evidence from the text, including imagery, to describe the events of that day. Include some of the Critical Vocabulary words in your writing.

PLAN

Make notes based on the text about the events Hà would describe in her journal entry.

WRITE

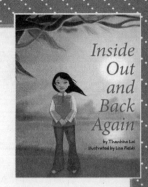

Now write the journal entry for Hà.

Make sure your journal entry

- ☐ is written from Hà's point of view.
- ☐ uses evidence from the text to describe the events of the day.
- ☐ includes imagery.

Inside Out and Back Again

by Thanhha Lai

illustrated by Lisa Fields

Performance Task

Essential Question

How do people adapt to new experiences and make a new place home?

Write a Narrative Poem

PROMPT Think about what you learned in this module about adjusting to a new place.

Imagine that your local or school library has a Poetry Podcast series for students. Write a narrative poem to share on the podcast. Tell a real or made-up story about the events, experiences, and feelings involved in moving to a new place. Use examples from the texts for ideas.

I will write about ____.

Make sure your narrative poem

- ☐ tells a story with a beginning, middle, and ending.
- ☐ describes events, experiences, and feelings.
- ☐ is organized into stanzas.
- ☐ uses concrete words and sensory language.
- ☐ sends a strong message about the meaning of home.

PLAN .... **Map your ideas.**

Will your poem tell a true story, a made-up one, or a combination of both? Look back at your notes and revisit the texts for ideas and examples.

Use the web below to plan your narrative poem. In the center circle, identify your main character or speaker and his or her problem. Then, in the surrounding circles, write events you want to include in your poem. Include notes about the speaker's feelings and other descriptive details about the experience. Add more circles if you need them.

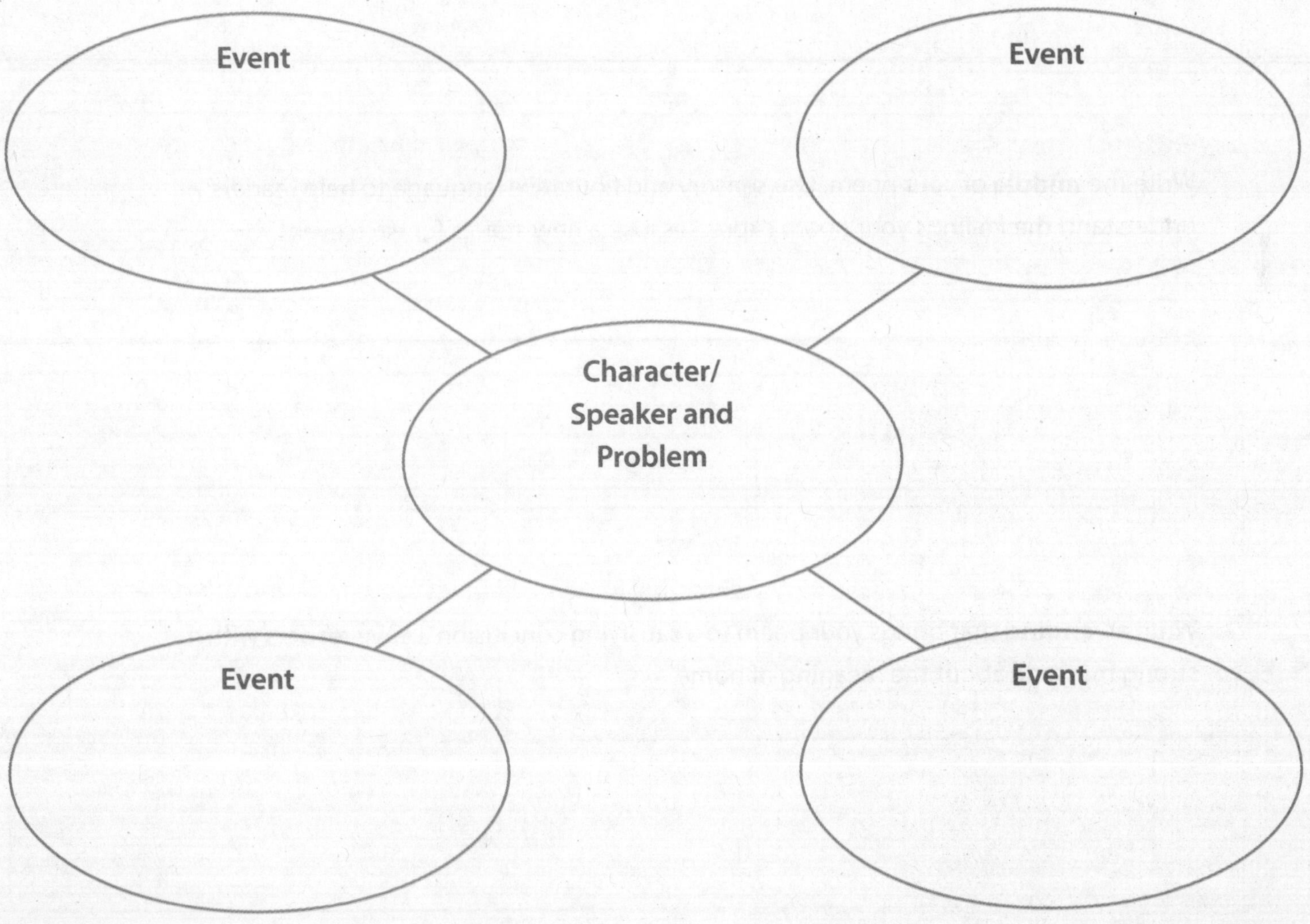

Performance Task

DRAFT .... **Write your poem.**

Write a **beginning** that introduces the main character or speaker. Tell what problem or challenge the person faces. Remember to organize your draft into stanzas rather than paragraphs.

Write the **middle** of your poem. Use sensory and figurative language to help readers understand the feelings your poem expresses. Use a new stanza for each event.

Write an **ending** that brings your poem to a satisfying conclusion. Leave readers with a strong message about the meaning of home.

REVISE AND EDIT .... Review your draft.

In this step, you have a chance to review and improve your draft. Read your poem aloud to a partner. Ask for feedback on the language you used and the feelings you expressed. Use these questions to help you focus on ways to improve your poem.

PURPOSE/ FOCUS	ORGANIZATION	EVIDENCE	LANGUAGE/ VOCABULARY	CONVENTIONS
☐ Does my poem tell a story about adjusting to a new home? ☐ Does the poem leave readers with a thought-provoking message?	☐ Does my poem have a clear beginning, middle, and ending? ☐ Are the lines organized into stanzas, with a new stanza for each event?	☐ Did I support my ideas with details or examples from the texts?	☐ Did I use sensory words and figurative language? ☐ Did I use concrete words and vivid language?	☐ Have I spelled all words correctly?

PUBLISH .... Share your work.

Create a Finished Copy. Use your best cursive handwriting to create a final copy of your narrative poem. You may want to include illustrations or photos. Consider these options for sharing your poem:

1. Bind your poem together with those of your classmates in a class poetry anthology.
2. Make an audio recording of your poem and create a podcast.
3. Perform a dramatic reading of your poem for your class or a small group.

MODULE 9

Unexpected, Unexplained

"The true mystery of the world is the visible, not the invisible."

—Oscar Wilde

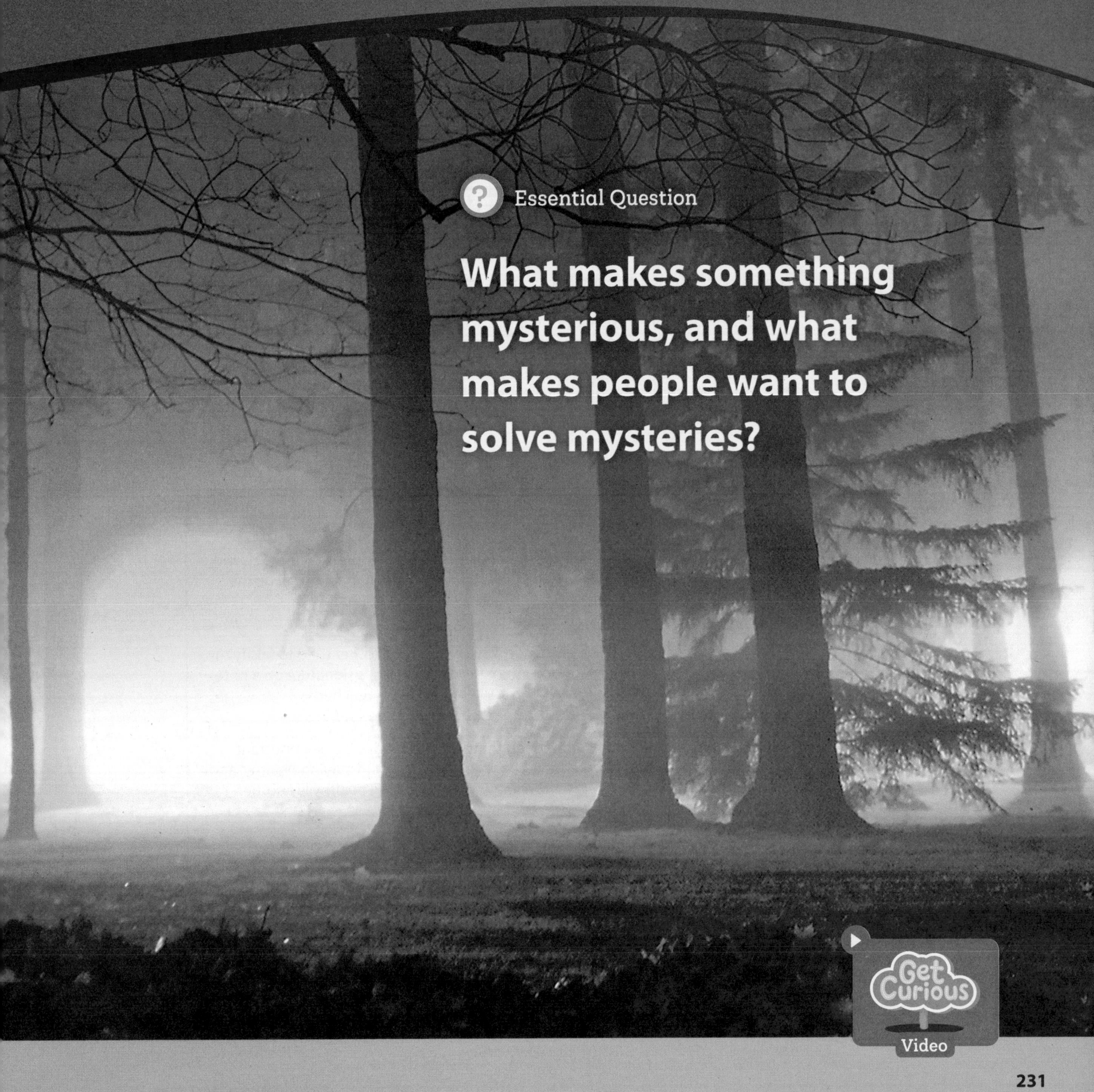

Essential Question

What makes something mysterious, and what makes people want to solve mysteries?

Big Idea Words

Words About Mysteries

The words in the chart will help you talk and write about the selections in this module. Which words about mysteries have you seen before? Which words are new to you?

Add to the Vocabulary Network on page 233 by writing synonyms, antonyms, and related words and phrases for each word about mysteries.

After you read each selection in this module, come back to the Vocabulary Network and keep building it. Add more boxes if you need to.

WORD	MEANING	CONTEXT SENTENCE
suspense (noun)	Suspense is excitement or anxiety due to an uncertain situation.	The suspense of not knowing what happened made me feel nervous.
falsify (verb)	To falsify is to change a statement or document in order to make it untrue.	My brother tried to falsify my parent's signature on a note to his teacher.
factor (noun)	A factor is something that affects a situation.	Exercise is one important factor in staying healthy, and eating healthy is another.
effect (noun)	An effect in a piece of writing or other art is a deliberately created feeling or impression.	In the mystery movie, the director used lighting to create a spooky effect.

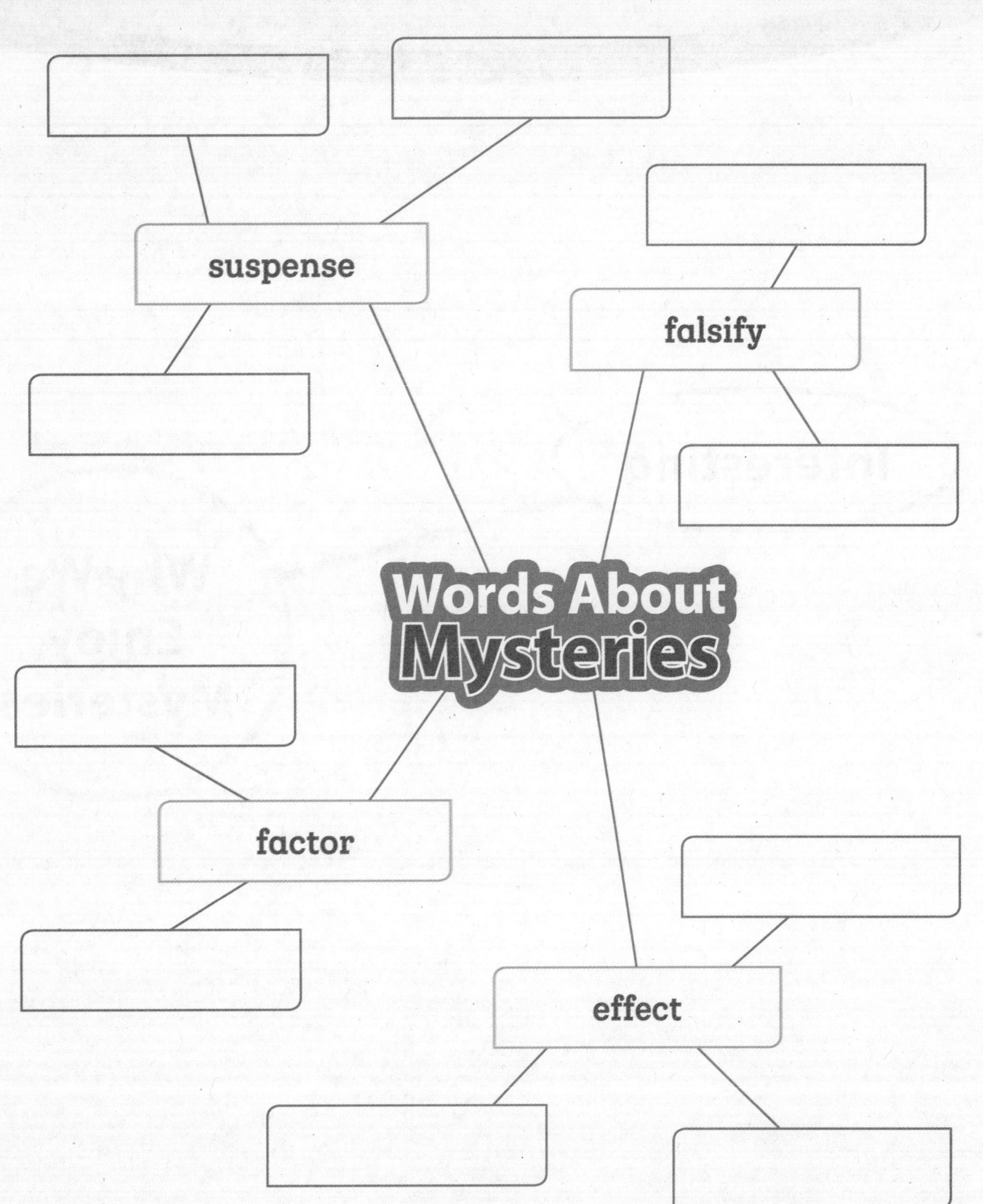
suspense
falsify
Words About
Mysteries
factor
effect

Knowledge Map

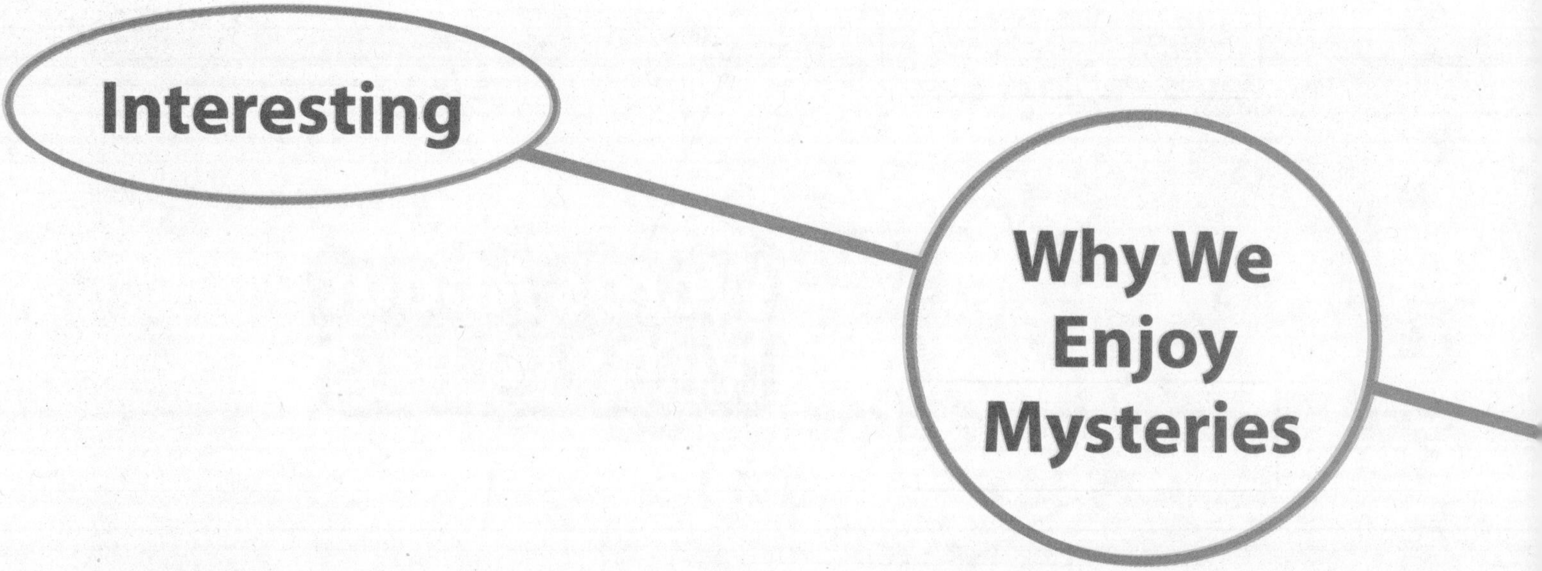

Interesting

Why We Enjoy Mysteries

Educational

Short Read

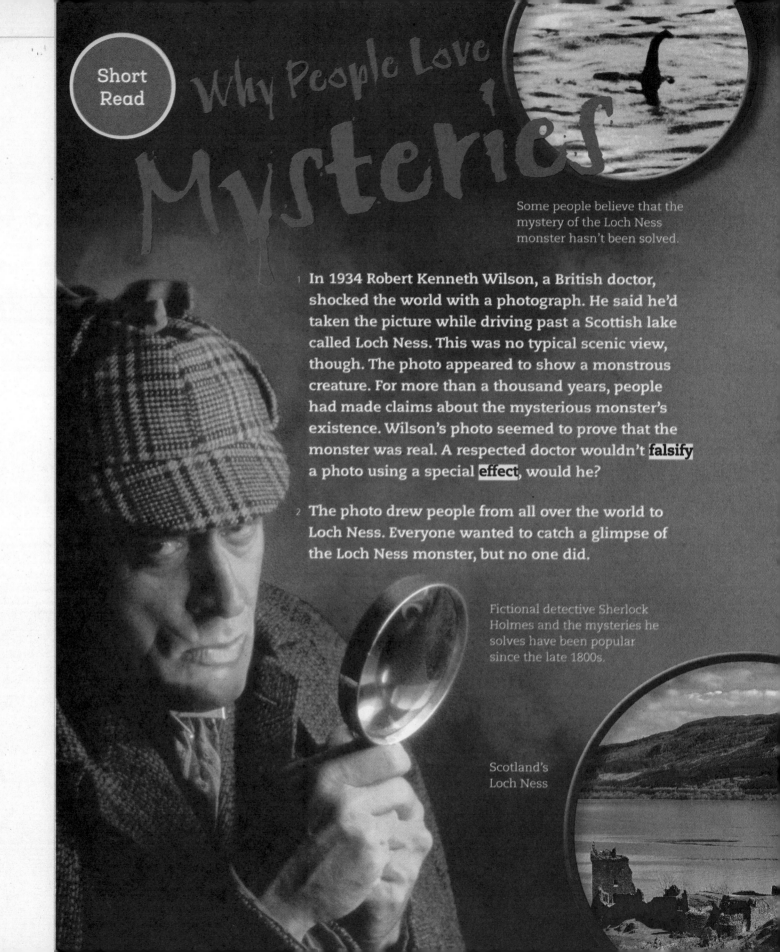

Why People Love Mysteries

Some people believe that the mystery of the Loch Ness monster hasn't been solved.

1 In 1934 Robert Kenneth Wilson, a British doctor, shocked the world with a photograph. He said he'd taken the picture while driving past a Scottish lake called Loch Ness. This was no typical scenic view, though. The photo appeared to show a monstrous creature. For more than a thousand years, people had made claims about the mysterious monster's existence. Wilson's photo seemed to prove that the monster was real. A respected doctor wouldn't **falsify** a photo using a special **effect**, would he?

2 The photo drew people from all over the world to Loch Ness. Everyone wanted to catch a glimpse of the Loch Ness monster, but no one did.

Fictional detective Sherlock Holmes and the mysteries he solves have been popular since the late 1800s.

Scotland's Loch Ness

myNotes

3 Finally, sixty years after the famous photo appeared, a man named Christian Spurling confessed that the picture was indeed fake. He and his stepfather had created the "Loch Ness monster" by attaching a fake sea serpent head and neck to a toy submarine, and the doctor had gone along with their scheme. Despite Spurling's confession, people still come to Loch Ness in search of "Nessie." They want to believe the mysterious Loch Ness monster exists—and that they'll be the ones to prove it!

A Safe Kind of Danger

4 Mysteries are a classic form of entertainment, too. Countless books, movies, and TV shows have centered on Sherlock Holmes, a detective who never met a case he couldn't solve. Holmes's adventures let us follow along in a state of mounting suspense until the great detective cleverly solves the mystery and catches the criminal.

5 While reading or watching a mystery, audiences match wits with criminals, studying clues and trying to figure out the solution before the story's detective, police, or very smart kid next door (who's not supposed to be nosing around the case). It's a fun game, and mystery fans play it again and again.

Figuring Things Out

6 Most people find mysteries like this irresistible, partly because we have a natural instinct for solving puzzles and figuring out how things work. Here's one big factor contributing to this behavior: solving mysteries can help us improve our lives. Over the years, curiosity has helped humans do everything from cure deadly diseases to develop new sources of energy.

7 For example, for thousands of years, people have puzzled over the mystery of lightning and what causes it. Many scientists, including Benjamin Franklin and Nikola Tesla, have studied it. Much has been learned about lightning that has had a positive effect on our lives, including ways to protect ourselves from it. But scientists still haven't fully solved the puzzle.

Big Challenges

8 Scientists could be called professional mystery solvers. They often tackle mysteries that consume a lifetime. For example, anthropologists often try to figure out how people lived long ago, studying ancient buildings, old documents, and artifacts, from weapons to clothing and tools, to uncover the mysteries of ancient life. Learning more about the past helps us better understand how we got to the present.

9 Mysteries are all around us, from murky Scottish lakes to the fiction section of your local library. Which mystery will you solve?

Notice & Note
Contrasts and Contradictions

Prepare to Read

GENRE STUDY **Mysteries** are stories in which the main character sets out to solve a mystery, crime, or other puzzle.

- Mysteries might include foreshadowing, or hints at future events, which may give readers clues.
- Mysteries use dialogue to help develop the story. Authors may also include detailed descriptions of characters' observations and feelings.
- Mysteries might be told in third-person point of view, by an outside observer.

SET A PURPOSE **Think about** the title and genre of this text. What could be mysterious about a library or a book? Write your ideas below.

CRITICAL VOCABULARY

- formidable
- relentlessly
- musings
- sentimental
- prefer
- engulfed
- audible
- will
- keepsake

Meet the Author and Illustrator: Walter Dean Myers and Ivan Kravetz

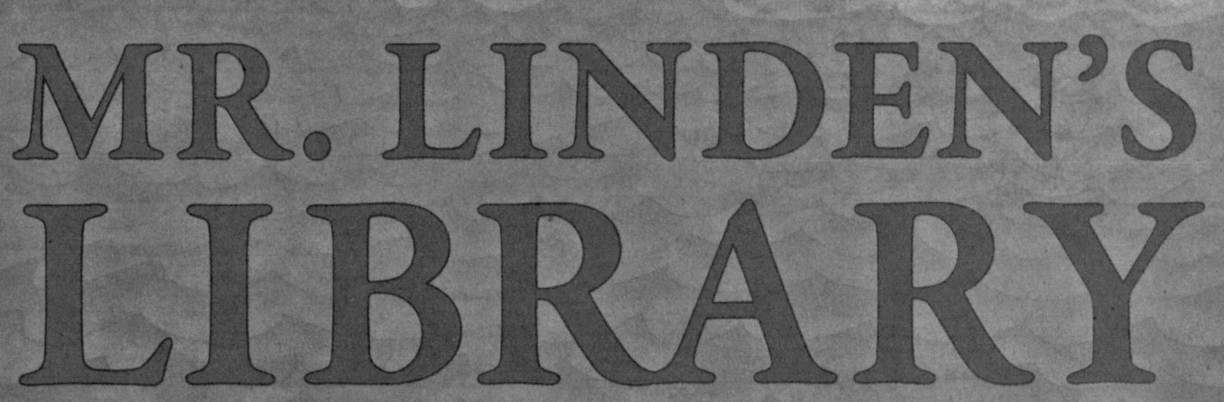

MR. LINDEN'S LIBRARY

BY WALTER DEAN MYERS ILLUSTRATED BY IVAN KRAVETZ

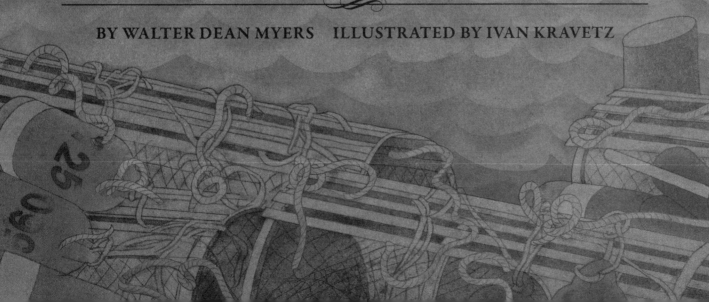

myNotes

1 You wouldn't see anything special about Josiah Linden's house if you passed it on the road, which ran from town up to the small bluff that overlooked Allen's Bay. A scrawny oak tree, gnarled and twisted from years of catching the wind off the bay, sat in front, spoiling what symmetry the old house ever had. The back side of the house looked fairly formidable, especially the rounded corner that seemed for all the world like the turret of a small castle. There were some nights, however, when the moon was full or nearly so, that the corner of the house would glow white against the darkness of the trees and shrubbery behind it and take on an eerie glow.

2 Carol Jenkins didn't know much about Mr. Linden, except that he was one of the few black people in that area of Nova Scotia. The story about him, mostly gathered from the lips of people curious about the old man, or from American Revolutionary War buffs who knew that his ancestors could have been among the ex-slaves who had sided with British, was that Mr. Linden had been a merchant seaman most of his life. He wasn't a big man, and when he walked he shifted his weight more from side to side than straight forward. He was lively, though, and always had a smile for whoever was passing, and a slight wave of the hand. The first time Carol remembered having seen Mr. Linden was in the hardware store, talking to a group of young men about weather conditions in the Arctic.

3 "The cold can catch you when you're not even thinking about it. It caught me about thirty years ago and I lost a bit of my finger to frostbite," he had said, holding up his hand so that the small crowd could see where the tip of the second finger of his left hand had been amputated.

4 "You must have been all over the world," one of the onlookers had remarked.

5 "The lure of seeing new places, different ways of life, has been almost irresistible," Mr. Linden had replied. "Now I collect stories about those places. Pictures and books about the places I've been and places I'd still like to go someday. I have more than two thousand books in my collection."

6 Carol mentioned this story to her friend Peter, who dismissed the idea at once.

formidable If something is formidable, it is a bit frightening but also impressive because of its size or another special quality.

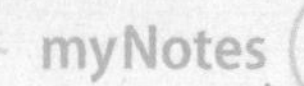

7 "John Altman was up to his place doing some repairs on the window frames, and he said it looked like the old guy read the same page of the same book every day. I bet he doesn't even know how to read."

8 Carol didn't believe Peter but decided not to make a big deal of it, and the matter would have gone completely from her mind if she and her mother hadn't run into Mr. Linden the following April.

9 It was one of those days that the wind, swirling relentlessly from the north, found every opening a poorly buttoned coat offered up and rattled the windows of Brendel's General Store ominously against their frames. Mr. Linden was waiting while the clerk measured out a pound of coffee beans.

10 "Just the thought of a good hot cup of coffee makes me feel warmer," he said in the direction of Carol and her mother.

11 "Mr. Linden, do you think I could borrow one of your books one day?"

12 Carol's request surprised even her.

relentlessly If something happens relentlessly, it never stops.

13 Mr. Linden looked toward Carol's mother, his brows arched questioningly.

14 "Oh, that would be too much of a bother to you, sir," her mother said quickly.

15 "Books are meant to be read," Mr. Linden said. "If you bring the young lady around she can have her pick. I'm sure she'll be careful with them."

16 The Glace Bay Library was small and didn't carry many of the adventure books that Carol liked. After she promised her mother that she did really want to expand her reading and would absolutely take care of the books, Carol and her mother made the short trek up the hill to Mr. Linden's house on a Wednesday afternoon.

17 The interior of Mr. Linden's home was bright with sunlight that streamed through the starched patterned curtains. In the library itself there were dark green bookcases along the wall, and a small writing desk was in the middle of the rectangular room. The surface of the writing desk was covered with dark leather, and in one corner there was a wooden box that contained a sextant. The window seat that looked out over the bay was just wide enough to sit in and, if you were a twelve-year-old girl with a small frame, put your feet up as you read.

18 "You must really love books," Carol said when she saw just how many books the old sailor had.

19 "Books have always been among my most trusted of friends," Mr. Linden replied. "The best of them allow the mind to wander wherever the author's musings lead. I'm reading the book that's lying there, but the rest are yours to borrow."

20 "One book will do," Carol's mom said.

21 Mr. Linden said that he would make tea and started down the stairs, and her mom went with him.

22 Carol began to read the titles on the spines of the books. Many seemed interesting. She looked again at the window seat where the book Mr. Linden was reading was lying. Like the others, it was old, its marbled binding fitting perfectly with the dark colors of the room. She picked up the book and read its title: *Tales From a Dark Sea.* There was no author listed. She opened the book where Mr. Linden had placed the flat bookmark. It was page 201 and contained one short paragraph, which, out of curiosity about Mr. Linden, she read.

musings A person's musings are his or her thoughts.

23 *When Esteban grew tired, when his weak leg was harder and harder to kick in the choppy waters, the dolphin would swim ahead of him, slightly to his left, and almost draw him along. He realized how far he was from the shore and how far away the small island in the mouth of the bay still seemed. And yet Esteban had never managed to swim so far before, and the accomplishment filled him with pride and made him try even harder. He wondered if the dolphin knew how proud he was.*

24 A sentimental story, she thought, one that an older person would find enjoyable. The thought came to her that Mr. Linden must indeed be lonely and that's why he spent his evenings reading. She placed the book carefully down where it had lain before and quickly picked another from the shelf to borrow. When she brought it downstairs, Mr. Linden took it in his hands carefully, almost lovingly, and read the title.

25 *"Dahomey and the Dahomians?"* he asked, turning the book over in his hands. "A surprising choice, but that is the pleasure of reading, isn't it? Books have the ability to take the mind to strange places and in strange ways. Well, enjoy it, young lady."

26 That evening, over dinner, Carol mentioned that she had expected Mr. Linden's library to be stranger.

27 "You mean with little ivory carvings of mermaids?" her mom asked, smiling.

28 "I don't know, just the way he goes on about books. He kind of glows when he talks about them. And did you see the way he handled the book I borrowed?"

29 "Book lovers love books!" her mother announced. "There's a romance about the books—even having them seems to have a kind of excitement."

30 The book on Dahomey, especially the story about the little African girl brought to England, had been quite interesting, and Carol was eager not only to find another interesting story but also to see what other kinds of books Mr. Linden liked.

31 It took four calls to Mr. Linden before they found him in.

"He seemed pleased that you liked the book," Carol's mother said. "He asked if we would prefer tea or coffee. I insisted that we didn't need either, of course."

32 "Oh, I wouldn't mind discussing books over a cup of tea," Carol said. "It fits my image."

33 "Today's image," her mother teased. "Tomorrow we'll go see Mr. Linden, you'll make a selection, and we'll be out of his hair. Agreed?"

34 Carol agreed.

35 During the night she wondered if Mr. Linden missed going to sea, and by the time she and her mother started off for his place she was convinced that he did miss the adventures of his youth.

sentimental If something is sentimental, it has to do with feelings, often about the past.
prefer If you prefer something, you like it better than something else.

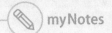

36 The rain had pushed the tide up the shore somewhat and had left a residue of tiny, crablike creatures and kelp along its edges, as well as the familiar scent of the sea, which Carol had always liked. As they approached the house her mother nudged her, telling her to look toward the library window. There was Mr. Linden, his dark frame nearly doubled, sitting in the window seat, completely absorbed in his reading.

37 "The Dahomians seem a bit strange," Carol told him after he invited them in. "But colorful."

38 "It was the author's opinion of them," Mr. Linden said. "I've met a lot of them in my travels, and they're not very strange these days."

39 Mr. Linden gestured toward the stairs that led to his library and went to the fireplace, where he began to straighten the logs with a poker. Carol went up the stairs, past the ancient yellowed wallpaper and the corner table, where a pipe smoldered in an onyx ashtray.

40 She opened several books to see if they contained pictures and found one, *A Narrative of the Cruise of the Yacht Maria Among the Faroe Islands.* The book looked interesting, although at first glance she could see that there were a number of words she would have to look up. She was about to start downstairs when she noted the same book from her previous visit on the seat in the window where Mr. Linden had left it.

41 Carol picked up the book and opened it to the bookmark. It was still on page 201, but the text now ended farther down the page than she had remembered.

42 *For a while Esteban's mind had wandered as the dolphin circled about him, sometimes lifting its sleek body from the water so that it was merely a dark silhouette against the distant sky. The rhythm of the sea, of the waves brushing across his body, had lulled him into a pattern that made time seem to slow to the easy pace of the tide. When Esteban stopped and lifted his head, he saw for the first time that there were trees growing on the island. But when he turned back toward the shore a sense of panic filled his chest and his heart began to beat quickly. Could he make it back? The dolphin swam around him, the late-afternoon sun sparkling on the water dripping from its body. Its mouth wide open, it appeared to be smiling. Esteban was worried, and his leg began to ache again as he turned for the shore.*

 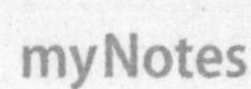

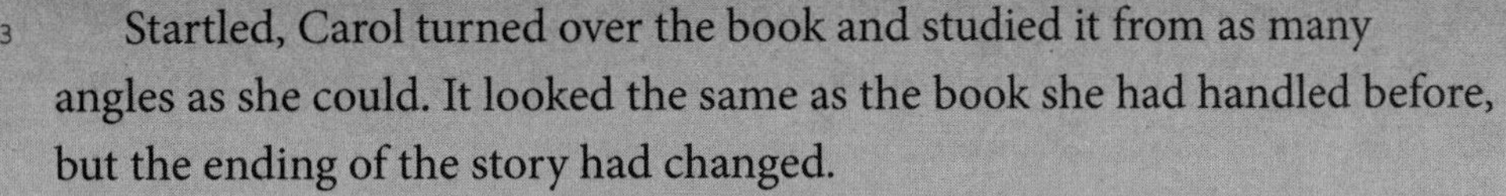

43 Startled, Carol turned over the book and studied it from as many angles as she could. It looked the same as the book she had handled before, but the ending of the story had changed.

44 Taking a deep breath, she calmed down. There had to be a logical explanation. It was as if she had remembered a previous day but had mixed that day with another.

45 "I'm glad to discover another reader," Mr. Linden said downstairs in the kitchen. He cradled a cup of tea in his hands. "We are a dying breed, I'm afraid."

46 That night Carol's sleep was disturbed by troubled dreams. Carol dreamt of sitting in Mr. Linden's library, questioning him about his life and all the books in his library. Then she awoke and lay in the darkness of her room, thinking of the book on the window seat and how she must have allowed her imagination or some random thought to change the way she remembered the page.

47 All things made sense. There were no mysteries in the real world. She thought of mentioning the book to her mother but decided against it. It was her mystery, and she rather enjoyed the curiousness of it all.

48 The next time they were supposed to visit Mr. Linden, Carol's mother wasn't feeling well. She had one of the headaches that plagued her when the weather grew heavier, just before the late fall and temperatures plummeted the town into its annual winter doldrums. Now that her mother knew more about Mr. Linden, she was fine to let Carol go by herself.

49 As she made her first trip alone to Mr. Linden's house, turning aside from the wind that rippled the bay, Carol thought about asking him directly about the book. Perhaps she would start by talking about the last book she had borrowed. But not at first, of course. First she had to get her hands on his book and check it out.

50 She hoped he would allow her to go into the library alone, and he did. She held her breath and walked more softly, almost sneaking up on the books that awaited her.

51 She glanced at the window seat. The book was still there, angled so that the sun cast a shadow diagonally across the title. She turned away from it, allowing her glance to capture it now and again as she read the titles of the shelved books.

52 She found a book with small drawings of ships and islands, *The Traveler's Guide to Madeira and the West Indies,* and leafed casually through it, all the time listening for sounds from below. When she heard the clinking of the metal teakettle against the stove, she moved quickly to Mr. Linden's book.

53 *Esteban told himself that he had been swimming long enough. He had already gone much farther than anyone he knew, even farther than men with strong legs. No one swam all the way to the island. Now he was nearer than he had ever been, but it no longer seemed important to him. It was as if he were swimming not for himself but for the dolphin that went before him most of the time but sometimes behind him, nudging him forward.*

54 *He began breathing hard, showing the dolphin how tired he was, how afraid he was to keep going when he wasn't at all sure of himself. He was not that strong and had already done more than he had ever done in his life. He stopped and treaded water for a while, with the dolphin only a few feet away. Esteban felt that he and the dolphin were on a mission together, that they were proving something. But what were they proving, and where would it lead?*

55 Again Carol checked the number on the page, even looking at the numbers of the pages before and after the one she was reading. She was right; the story had changed. It was changing from day to day! The boy in the story was swimming out farther each time, and the dolphin swam with him, as if it knew something special about the boy's mission. But how could the story be different each time she read it?

56 She grabbed the book she would borrow, holding it with both hands, and carried it down to Mr. Linden.

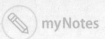

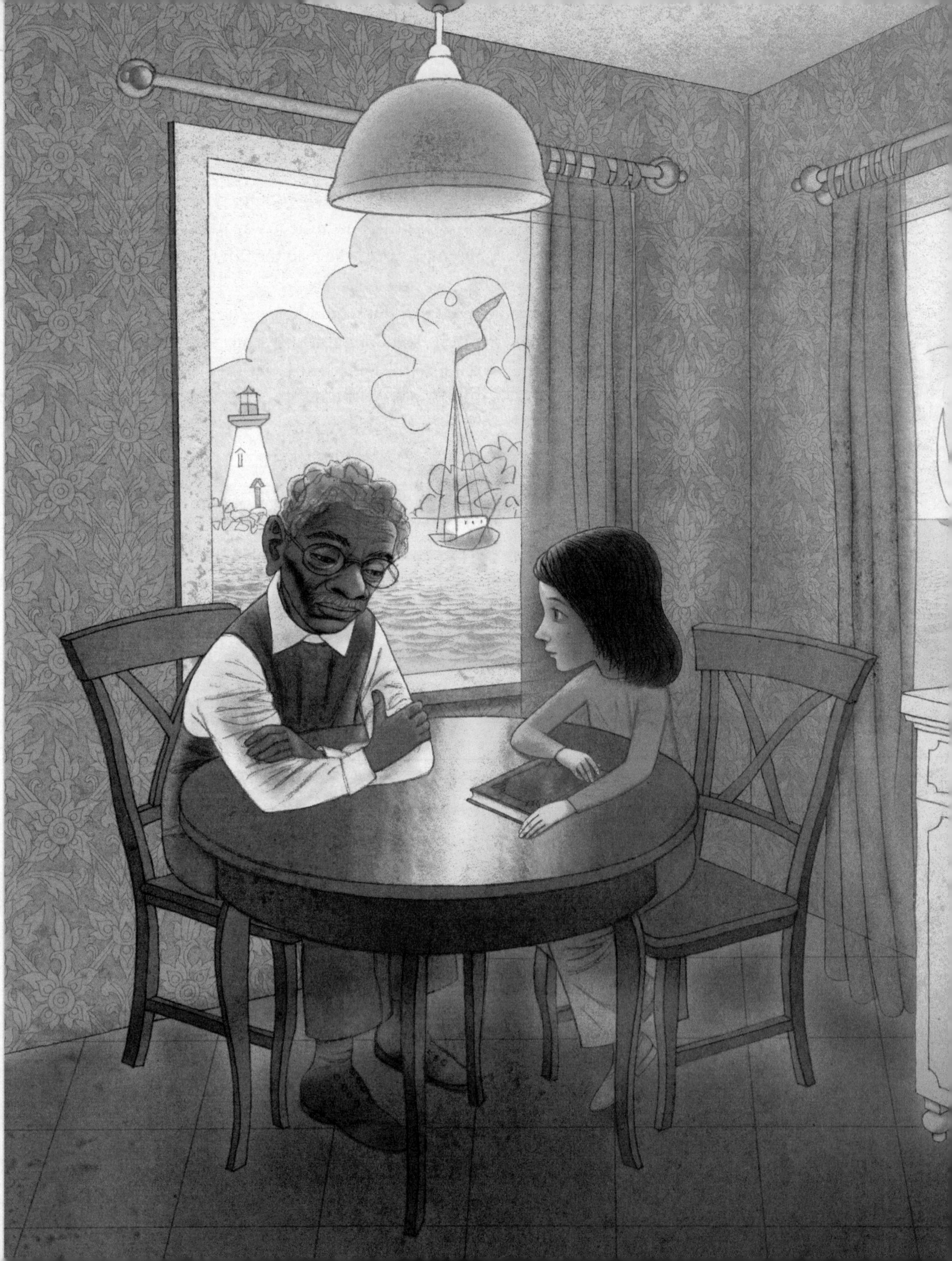

57 "Ah, George Miller's travel adventure from the age of sail." Mr. Linden examined the book over the rimless glasses he wore. "Excellent choice."

58 "What are you reading?" Carol asked. "Something about dolphins, I think."

59 The old black man looked quickly away. For a long moment the room was engulfed in silence. In the distance, barely audible, the gentle lapping of the low tide on the graveled shore came rhythmically.

60 "It's not a very good book." His voice was lower than it had been. "You wouldn't be interested."

61 "I am," she said, resolutely. "I am interested."

62 "Yes, I hear it in your voice, child. I hear it clearly. But let me tell you—warn you, even—that there are books like frigates, that carry the mind gloriously across oceans of ideas," he said. "And then there are books—a few books, I would say—that capture more of the mind than one would want to surrender, books that are better off never read, never opened."

63 "That doesn't make sense!" Carol said.

64 "Sense? No, I suppose it doesn't," Mr. Linden said. "But it doesn't make sense to reach my age and discover that everything doesn't make sense, either.

65 "You can keep that book you're holding," he went on. "It's a fun book. He made drawings of the ships he encountered and the places he visited. Words and pictures. You can't ask for more than that, can you?"

66 Carol felt as if she were being dismissed and was angry with herself for not being more careful with Mr. Linden. She thought of not taking the book she held, but finally managed a smile, put on her jacket, and started home.

engulfed If one thing is engulfed by another, it is surrounded or completely covered by it.
audible If a sound is audible, it is loud enough to hear.

myNotes

67 Josiah Linden died on a bitterly cold winter's day. His funeral was held at the Baptist Church on York Street, and more people came than anyone imagined could have possibly known him. Many were sailors and others were just townspeople who remembered him from the time when the town was busier.

68 The house was sold, and the proceeds, according to the old man's will, went to a charity for aged seamen. A dealer from Westport made an offer for the books. Carol told the dealer that she had been a friend of Josiah Linden's. "I would love to buy one of his books as a keepsake," she said.

69 "Well, you're welcome to take any book you'd like," he replied. "I always like to encourage young people to read."

70 She searched for the book, checking every title and even behind the rows of books that still stood, waiting as if they expected Mr. Linden to return and reach a dark hand to take one of them down from the shelves. When she didn't find the book, she was very disappointed and for a brief moment thought of taking another book just as a keepsake, as she had suggested.

71 But then she thought about the book and her fascination with it. She had heard that he had died in bed, and she went into the small room in which he had slept. She looked around quickly and spotted a corner of the book sticking out from under the pillow.

72 "It's about dolphins," she said to the man that now owned Mr. Linden's library.

73 The man glanced at the book and nodded approvingly.

74 "You should try *National Geographic,*" he said. "I think I remember a series on dolphins."

75 Carol smiled.

76 At home she put the book under her own pillow and waited until that night before turning to the page 201, the bookmark still in place.

will A will is a legal document that tells what someone wants done with his or her belongings after that person dies.
keepsake A keepsake is something you save to remember a person or an event.

77 *The late-evening sun, spreading across the bay and behind the island, lay before him. Esteban had already turned and saw that the shore he had left, his shoes and the sandwich he had brought to the water's edge, were too far away for him to reach. The dolphin sensed it as well, and the two of them swam, Esteban with some difficulty as his arms tired, the dolphin with ease, through the dark waters, toward whatever was on the island. Esteban had heard stories about treasures being buried there, about exotic birds, wildflowers, and even the graves of hermits who had lived there. He didn't know for sure, but he did know that he would reach the island after so many times trying. And even if no one believed him, he would know that the dolphin would have seen him and that maybe, just maybe, all the dolphins in the ocean would know as well.*

78 *In the morning, if all went well, he would try to return to the shore from which he started.*

79 *In the waning light he could still see the shadow of the dolphin as it swam ahead. Would it be there in the morning to help him back?*

80 Carol put the book down and closed her eyes. Then she opened them again and began to read slowly. The story went on about how the boy awoke in the morning, cold and alone and hungry, and how he had seen not one but two dolphins in the bay, but neither was very close to where he stood on the island's edge. Carol wanted Esteban to be safe, and to make it back to the shore. She wanted the dolphins to help him, but she wasn't at all sure they would.

81 Mysteries were about finding out how they ended, not new and more difficult mysteries that kept going on and on. She looked at the book and then threw it down on her bed, telling herself that she would never pick it up again. Now she knew why Mr. Linden read the same book every day. He had warned her about the book. Now it was too late.

82 She lay quietly in the darkness of her room. Now and again her hand would reach out from under the covers toward the light by the side of her bed.

83 "Don't open the book again," she pleaded with herself. "Please."

84 From the far side of the bay, the town had grown dark. Occasionally a truck made its way along the winding road or the reflection from the lighthouse through the fog could be seen. Other than that, all was dark, the occasional flicker of a small bedroom light hardly noticeable.

Respond to the Text

Collaborative Discussion

Look back at what you wrote on page 238. Tell a partner two things you learned during reading. Then work with a group to discuss the questions below. Look for details and examples in *Mr. Linden's Library* to support your ideas. Before you begin talking, work together to decide on the discussion rules your group will follow.

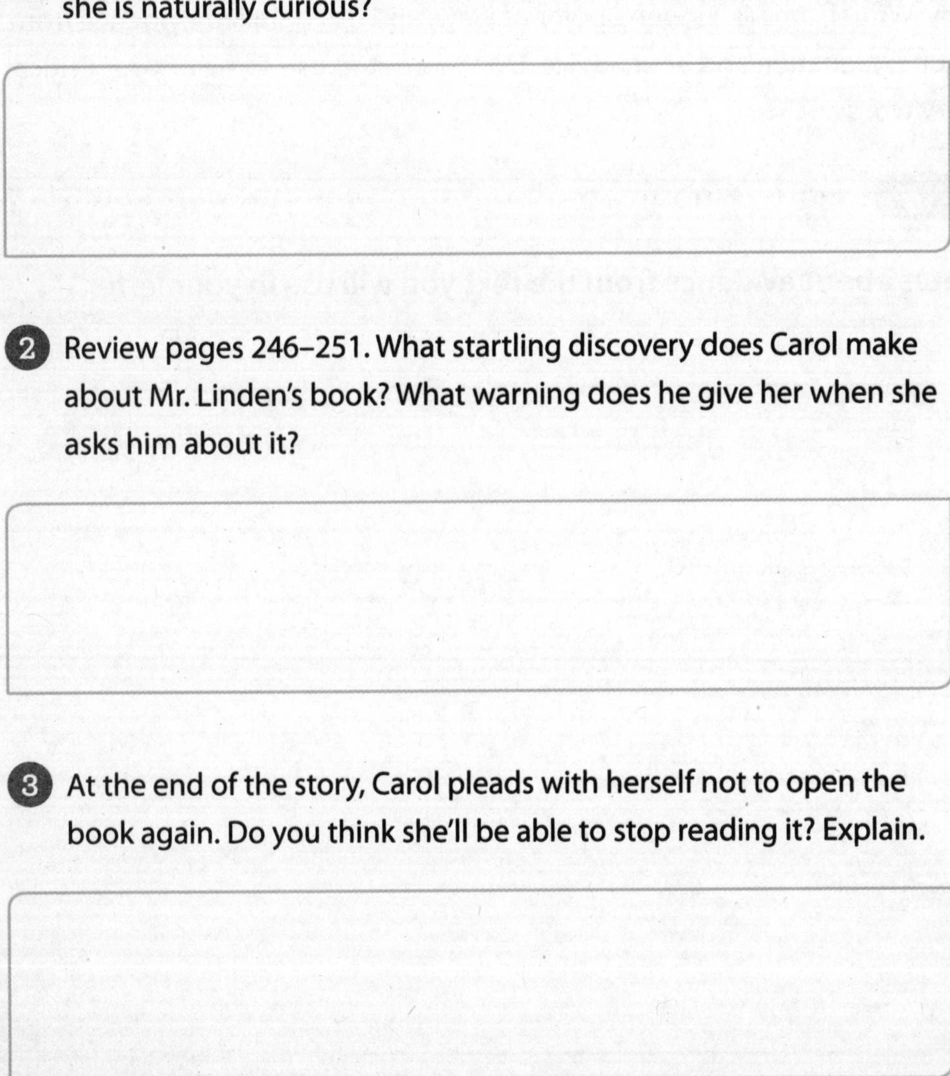

1. Reread pages 240–242. Which of Carol's thoughts and actions show she is naturally curious?

2. Review pages 246–251. What startling discovery does Carol make about Mr. Linden's book? What warning does he give her when she asks him about it?

3. At the end of the story, Carol pleads with herself not to open the book again. Do you think she'll be able to stop reading it? Explain.

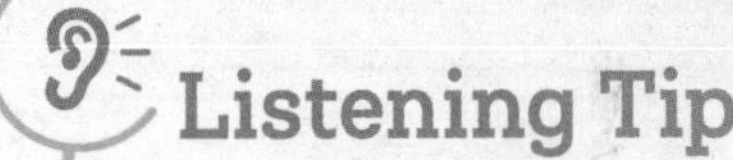

Listening Tip

Listen carefully to what each person has to say. Look at the person who is speaking.

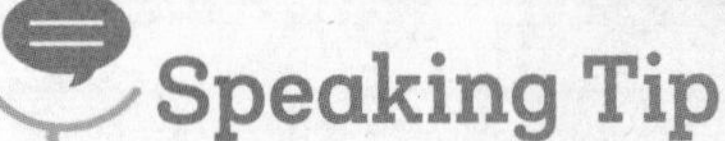

Speaking Tip

Wait patiently for your turn to speak. Don't interrupt!

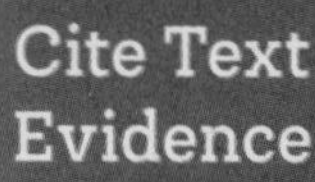

Write a Letter

PROMPT

In *Mr. Linden's Library,* Carol begins reading a story from *Tales From a Dark Sea*, and soon discovers that this story is like no other she has read before.

Imagine that you are Mr. Linden and that you noticed Carol's interest in the book when she visited your library. Write a fictional letter to Carol that you will leave inside *Tales From a Dark Sea* for her to find after you are gone. Explain why you warned her not to begin reading the book, and offer her some advice now that she has become captured by its story. Write from Mr. Linden's point of view, and use detailed evidence from the text in your explanation and your advice. Don't forget to use some of your Critical Vocabulary words.

PLAN

Make notes about evidence from the text you will use in your letter.

WRITE

Now write your letter of advice to Carol.

Make sure your letter

- ☐ is written in the voice of Mr. Linden.
- ☐ uses evidence from the text to explain the book.
- ☐ gives advice to Carol that shows understanding of the characters.
- ☐ uses a friendly letter format.

Prepare to View

GENRE STUDY **Documentary videos** present facts about a topic or an event in visual and audio form.

- A narrator gives information supported by footage or images.
- Sound effects and background music may be included to engage viewers and appeal to their emotions.
- Real people and sources are used in the video to help viewers understand the topic or event.

SET A PURPOSE **As you watch**, think about how the Loch Ness monster legend was created. What do you already know? What do you want to learn? Write your ideas below.

CRITICAL VOCABULARY

- chastised
- sightings
- earnest
- desperately
- convinced

myNotes 

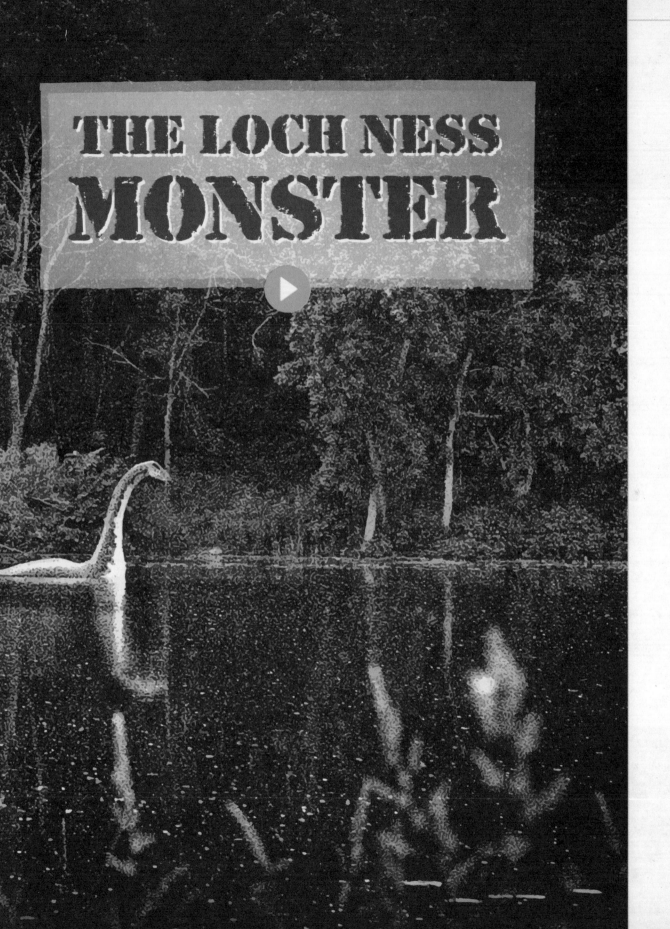

THE LOCH NESS MONSTER

As you watch *Loch Ness Monster,* think about how the video uses sound and visual elements to explain events and experiences. How do the narration and reenactment of the Spurling/Wilson photograph help you understand the creation of the Loch Ness Monster legend? Take notes in the space below.

Listen for the Critical Vocabulary words *chastised, sightings, earnest, desperately,* and *convinced*, and for clues to the meaning of each word. Take notes in the space below about how the words are used in the video.

chastised If you are chastised, you are scolded severely.

sightings If there are sightings of something, people have seen it with their own eyes.

earnest If you say something in earnest, you are very serious and believe it to be true.

desperately If you are trying desperately, you are trying as hard as you can.

convinced If you are convinced of something, you are certain that it happened.

Respond to the Video

Collaborative Discussion

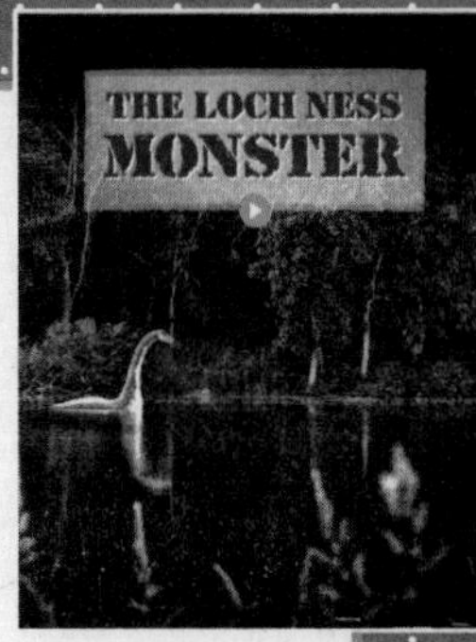

Look back at what you wrote on page 258 and tell a partner two things you learned from the video. Then work with a group to discuss the questions below. Provide details and examples from *The Loch Ness Monster* to support your thoughts. In your discussion, respond to others by asking questions and making comments that build on their ideas.

1. When was Kenneth Wilson's photo of the monster published? What "stunning revelation" did Christian Spurling later make about it?

2. How did Duke Wetherell create the famous photo?

3. Why do you think the Loch Ness legend has held people's attention for so long?

Listening Tip

Give your full attention to other speakers in the group. Ask thoughtful questions to clarify their answers.

Speaking Tip

Build on others' responses by adding support from the video or by connecting their responses to your own.

Cite Evidence

Write a Video Review

PROMPT

In *The Loch Ness Monster* you learned about the legend of the Loch Ness Monster and the origin of a well-known photograph of "Nessie."

Imagine that you've been asked to write a video review. Summarize the video's main ideas and important details. Then give your opinion of the video and support it with reasons. Is the video informative and entertaining? In what ways? Do its reenactments and other visuals help viewers understand the topic? Use some of the Critical Vocabulary words in your writing.

PLAN

Make notes about the video's main ideas and details and your opinion of it as a whole.

WRITE

Now write your video review.

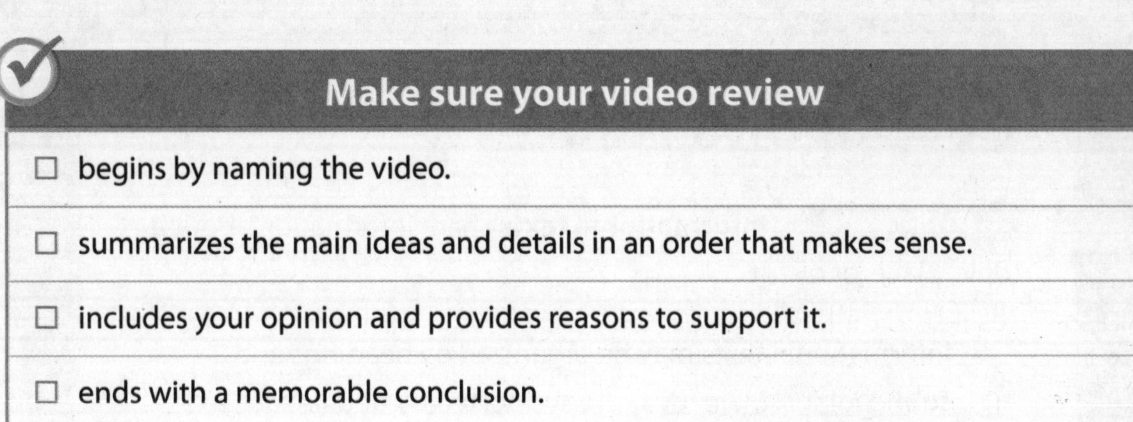

Make sure your video review
☐ begins by naming the video.
☐ summarizes the main ideas and details in an order that makes sense.
☐ includes your opinion and provides reasons to support it.
☐ ends with a memorable conclusion.

Notice & Note
Contrasts and Contradictions

Prepare to Read

GENRE STUDY **Informational texts** share information about a topic, place, or event.

- Informational texts may be organized by headings and subheadings. Main ideas are supported by details such as facts, definitions, examples, or quotations.
- Authors of informational texts may include science or social studies words that are specific to the topic.
- Visuals and text features, such as sidebars, enhance the text and provide additional information.

SET A PURPOSE **Think about** the title and genre of this text. What do you know about the Bigfoot mystery? What do you want to learn? Write your ideas below.

CRITICAL VOCABULARY

- misperception
- hoaxes
- elusive
- theoretical
- encounters

Meet the Author:
Martha Brockenbrough

FINDING BIGFOOT: Everything You Need to Know

by Martha Brockenbrough

myNotes

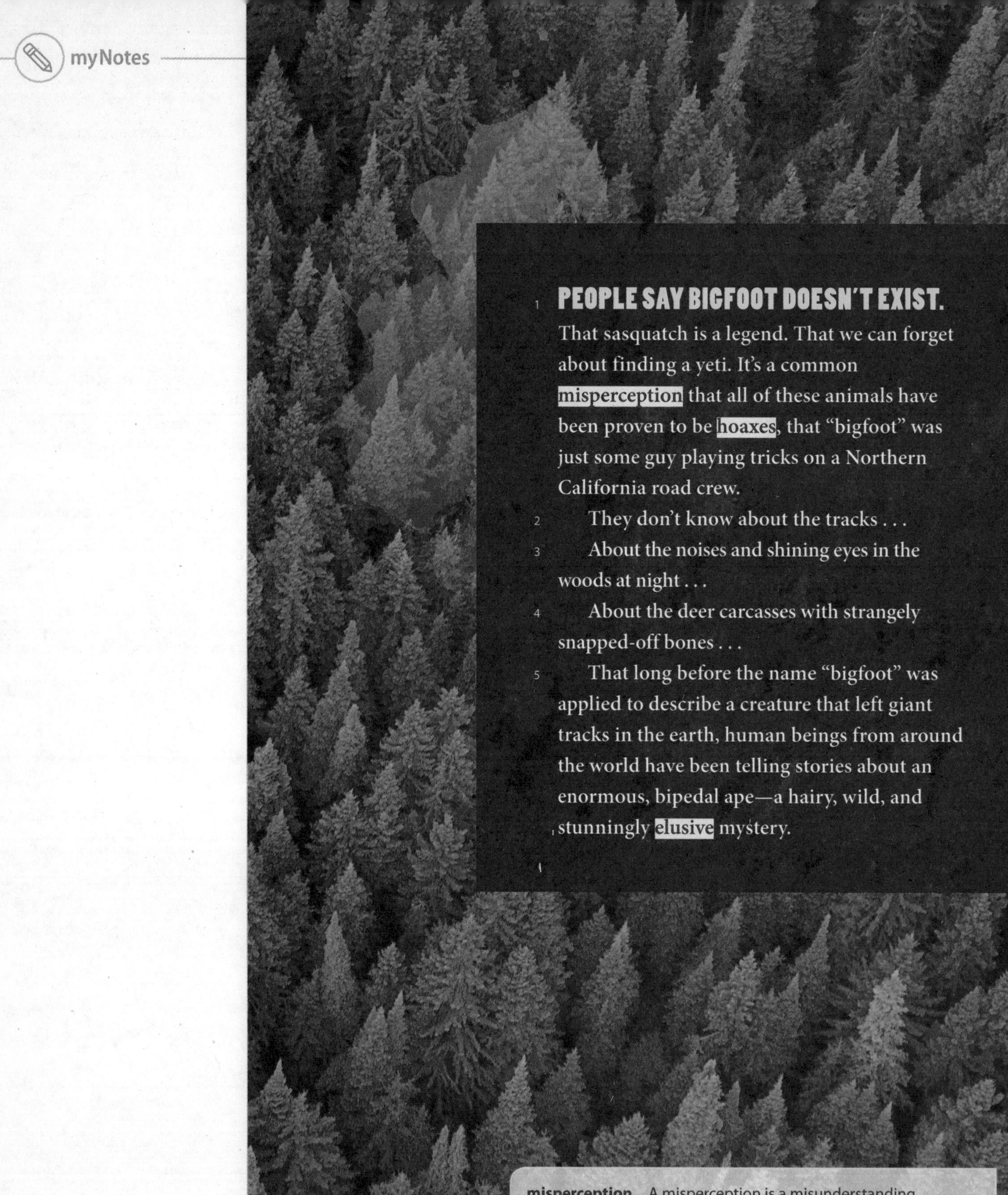

1 **PEOPLE SAY BIGFOOT DOESN'T EXIST.** That sasquatch is a legend. That we can forget about finding a yeti. It's a common misperception that all of these animals have been proven to be hoaxes, that "bigfoot" was just some guy playing tricks on a Northern California road crew.

2 They don't know about the tracks . . .

3 About the noises and shining eyes in the woods at night . . .

4 About the deer carcasses with strangely snapped-off bones . . .

5 That long before the name "bigfoot" was applied to describe a creature that left giant tracks in the earth, human beings from around the world have been telling stories about an enormous, bipedal ape—a hairy, wild, and stunningly elusive mystery.

misperception A misperception is a misunderstanding.
hoaxes Hoaxes are acts that involve tricking and lying to people.
elusive Something that is elusive is hard to find or understand.

myNotes

The Case for CRYPTIDS

6 Some people believe we know everything there is to know about this world. People who believe every inch of land has been conquered, every drop of ocean explored. And while it's true that adventurers have made their way around the globe, mapping the edges of oceans and continents, the heights of the mountains, the depths of the rivers and lakes, it's also true that scientists learn new things every day. What's more, we find new animals all the time.

7 Since 2012, for example, we have discovered all sorts of previously unknown creatures, including monkeys, frogs, sharks, and lizards—even primates. Would you believe there is such a thing as a poisonous spider with hook-like claws on each of its legs? A group of people exploring a cave in bigfoot country—southern Oregon—stumbled across this family of spiders deep in the throat of a cave in 2012. The *Trogloraptor marchingtoni* was the first family of native North American spiders to be found in more than a century.

8 That same year, a Louisiana State University snake expert named Christopher Austin followed strange chirping noises while he was inside a Papua New Guinea forest. It turns out a frog the size of a housefly, the world's tiniest vertebrate, was responsible for the singing. (The same professor has found several other species that hadn't yet been recognized by science, including other frogs, lizards, and parasites.)

9 There was a new primate recognized around the same time: the lesula monkey, a wise-looking creature with a grayish brown beard. This one was found in 2007 living as a school administrator's pet in the Democratic Republic of the Congo. Researchers studied its DNA to conclude it was an unrecognized species. It's already endangered because it's being hunted for its meat. It's only the second new kind of African monkey to be recognized in twenty-eight years, and it might have died out before scientists learned of its existence.

10 While most of these newly discovered creatures are small or live in remote places, history is full of animals once called legend that turned out to be real. The list of animals known by reputation first and recognized by science later includes gorillas, giant pandas, Komodo dragons, bonobos, megamouth sharks, giant geckos, and the okapi, a short-necked giraffe relative.

11 There's a controversial field of science that specializes in the study of "hidden" animals. It's called "cryptozoology," a word invented in the late 1950s by Bernard Heuvelmans, a zoologist. The word itself sounds pretty out there, but its meaning is straightforward: *crypto* means "hidden" and *zoology* means "the study of animals." It's related to paleontology, the study of prehistoric life, and both use reconstructions and evidence to build pictures of animals that haven't been seen or are no more. In addition to bigfoot, another famous cryptid, or hidden animal, is the Loch Ness Monster.

In this image, an illustrator imagines what the Loch Ness Monster might look like, based on witness descriptions.

SPOTTED!

"It Was Kind of Creepy"

Howie Dagg lives in Hydaburg on Prince of Wales Island in Alaska. He and a neighbor had taken his truck out into the woods for a hike, hoping to relax and unwind after school. At first, they didn't even notice the tracks.

But then he got a closer look.

"I stopped and one of the tracks had toes, big toes in it," he said. "I stopped and we took some pictures . . . it was kind of creepy."

What's more, he and his friend felt as if they were being watched. Still, he felt skeptical, so he pushed on. Were they really bigfoot prints? He followed the trail all the way up the mountain. At the top, where the road was choked with trees, he noticed a lot of branches had been snapped off about seven feet off the ground—a classic bigfoot sign.

The sun dipped behind the hill and it started to get dark, and that's when Howie's neighbor got scared, calling the creature a Gogit, which is a term used to describe a hairy giant in parts of Prince of Wales. Howie also had the willies, so they left.

The photos they took that day show prints 17.3 inches long and about 6.5 inches wide, the sort that might belong to a large sasquatch.

Although black holes are real, they are invisible. In this image, an illustrator imagines what a black hole might look like.

Is Bigfoot REAL?

12 The truth is, no one knows for sure, although many people have strong opinions on the matter. We can only be absolutely certain there is such a creature as bigfoot when we have found one.

13 Otherwise, bigfoot remains a theoretical possibility. A theory is an explanation of something based on observations, experiments, and reasoning. When formed with care, theories are scientifically valid—even if they are not proven, and even when they apply to things we haven't seen.

14 Take black holes, for example. These are spots in space, big and small, where matter has been compressed (this can happen when a star dies). The compression of matter makes for an incredibly strong gravitational pull—a pull so strong nothing can escape it, not even light.

15 No one has ever seen a black hole (they're invisible!). No one has ever been inside one. But we can form theories about their existence because of careful, repeatable observations that have been made. As we learn more about physics, we might someday adjust our understanding and definition of black holes. But no one calls scientists crazy for believing such a thing exists because there is enough evidence to make it a reasonable thing to believe in.

16 Scientists ask questions, make observations, come up with smart guesses, devise experiments to test them, and consider the results thoughtfully. And that's exactly what you can do when it comes to bigfoot. There's nothing wrong with a healthy dose of skepticism. That's how scientists get smarter. And open minds are the only ones that can learn new things.

theoretical Something that is theoretical is based on a guess rather than truth.

myNotes

The Arguments FOR Bigfoot

17 Plenty of smart people believe bigfoot is alive and well and hiding from humanity. What makes them so sure there's a bigfoot when others say there's no such creature? It comes down to four things:

18 **Folklore.** One of the oldest surviving works of literature, *The Epic of Gilgamesh*, describes a hairy wild man named Enkidu. Similar tales of a hairy wild man who lives in the forest are part of many cultures around the world. Ancient cave paintings in California depict a hairy man and his family, and stories that go along with them sound very much like bigfoot tales. If no such animal exists, why would these stories be so common?

19 **Eyewitness Accounts.** Thousands of people in the United States have reported seeing bigfoot. People in Canada have sasquatch sightings. In Nepal, people claim to have seen yetis. In Indonesia, a smaller version of a hairy man-like creature that walks on two feet is known as the Orang Pendek. There's also the Australian yowie. Many people who've had encounters are respected community members, including police officers and judges, who have a lot to lose by lying. If they're not lying, what did they see?

"Thousands of people in the United States have reported seeing bigfoot."

encounters Encounters are meetings, especially those that are unplanned.

20 **Physical Evidence.** Although no one has found the body of a bigfoot, people have seen what they consider to be physical evidence. Footprints are among the best-known forms of evidence. The Bigfoot Field Research Organization (BFRO), for example, has collected more than seven hundred suspected bigfoot prints. Many that come from different areas are strikingly similar in size and overall proportions.

21 Other physical evidence includes hair samples, some of which have not been identified as belonging to other known animals. Does it belong to bigfoot? We can only know for sure when there is a known specimen of bigfoot to test against. Bigfooters have also gathered what they believe are blood and stool samples.

22 And finally there are twisted-off branches, animal carcasses with cleanly broken bones, and clumps of sticks arranged into sleeping nests, all of which are considered evidence of the creature's presence in the woods.

23 **Photos, Videos, and Audio Recordings.** There are photographs, a famous film, thermal video recordings, and audio recordings said to be multiple bigfoots communicating with one another.

24 When you combine all of this evidence, believers say, you have a compelling picture of a large, hairy, bipedal animal that lives in remote forests and swamps.

Thermal image of a human hand ▸

Some people believe broken-off branches are evidence of a bigfoot creature. ▾

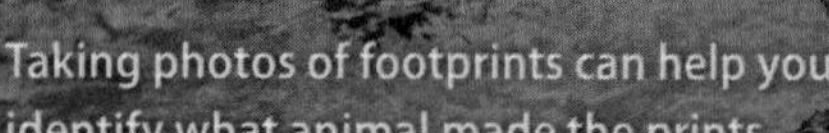

Taking photos of footprints can help you identify what animal made the prints.

SPOTTED!
A Flying Piece of Wood from "Out of Nowhere"

Nyna Heury drives a cab in Alaska's Prince of Wales Island, making regular trips back and forth during the night. On one of those wee-hours trips, she had a passenger with her.

"Out of nowhere, this piece of wood comes flying at us," she said. "It hit the front end of the car and cracked my windshield all the way across."

Something big had to have thrown it because the impact shook her entire van. Nyna wanted to stop, but her frightened passenger urged her on.

She returned to investigate the next day and found the piece of wood. It smelled putrid. She looked up into a nearby tree and saw a pair of big green eyes looking at her from inside a "humongous" body.

"There's no way it was a bear," she said.

Building a Bigfoot from a Track: ZADIG'S METHOD

25 In many ways, bigfoot hunters have to think like detectives, taking bits of information they have to make a picture of the animal as a whole. When you go through a process like this with the natural world, you use something called Zadig's Method, taking signs that are visible and deducing as much information as possible.

26 Baron Georges Cuvier, who created the modern field of paleontology, observed that if you saw a cloven hoof print, you could project a lot of information about the animal. For example, it would be a ruminant, meaning it is a mammal that chews plant material, softens it in the first part of its stomach, and then regurgitates it for a bit more chewing. But that's not all.

27 "This single track therefore tells the observer about the kind of teeth, the kind of jaws, the haunches, the shoulder, and the pelvis of the animal which has passed," he wrote in 1834.

28 This is what bigfoot believers are trying to do, and many people believe the evidence of bigfoot that has been gathered to date justifies the continued search.

The Arguments AGAINST Bigfoot

29 Bigfoot has an army of doubters. Their best argument is that people have been looking unsuccessfully for bigfoot for decades and, lately, even using sophisticated equipment such as cameras that can detect heat. If there really were such a creature, all those dedicated searchers using that great technology would have found proof.

30 That's a hard argument to counter, although die-hard "squatchers" will tell you the evidence they have gathered is proof. But if we define proof of bigfoot as an actual bigfoot, dead or alive (preferably alive, for the sake of the bigfoot), then we are about eight hairy feet and six hundred fifty pounds shy of certainty. Likewise, a DNA sequence confirmed by independent laboratories would also work as proof. Unless scientific standards relax, which isn't likely, you'd certainly need a holotype—a physical example of a bigfoot, a bigfoot body part, or DNA—for an official species to be named.

"In many ways, bigfoot hunters have to think like detectives . . ."

myNotes

Bringing SCIENCE to the Search

31 For bigfoot to become an official species, we need concrete evidence that can be examined systematically and thoroughly. We also need a theory that explains why, despite a lot of searching, no one has ever found bigfoot, a skeleton, or even a few remaining bones that once belonged to the creature.

32 Bigfoot researcher Cliff Barackman has advice for bigfooters about how to take a scientific approach to the search: Follow the scientific method. Here's how that model of thinking works:

1. Ask a question.
2. Research. Look for evidence and other clues that could point to an answer.
3. Take a guess at an answer. This guess is called a hypothesis.
4. Create an experiment to see if your hypothesis could be right.
5. Execute the experiment. Were you right? Repeat the experiment to verify. If you're not, start again at step 2.
6. Write about your experiment and results, and share them with other researchers to see if they find the same thing.

33 The goal of these observations—or any scientific observations, really—is to establish a set of reliable facts. Using those, we can then conduct further research. It's sort of like building with toy blocks. You start with a foundation and keep adding to that, replacing blocks or theories that have been disproved with additional observations and experiments.

34 Many people in traditional science are so skeptical of bigfoot they don't even bother to consider new evidence. But this doesn't mean scientists are jerks. Science can be a bigfooter's best friend. Many kinds of science can potentially come into play: paleontology, the study of prehistoric life; anthropology, the study of human behavior and cultures; kinesiology, the study of human movement; primatology, the study of primates; and of course genetics and wildlife biology.

35 Generally speaking, the more you know about science, the more opportunities and insight you will have in life. When it comes to bigfoot specifically, the more you know about what sort of animal bigfoot might be, the more you know about how and where a bigfoot might live. That insight gives you a better chance at encountering a bigfoot at last.

Respond to the Text

Collaborative Discussion

Look back at what you wrote on page 264 and talk with a partner about two things you learned during reading. Then work with a group to discuss the questions below. Support your answers with ideas and details from *Finding Bigfoot*. During your discussion, point out how your ideas connect to those of others.

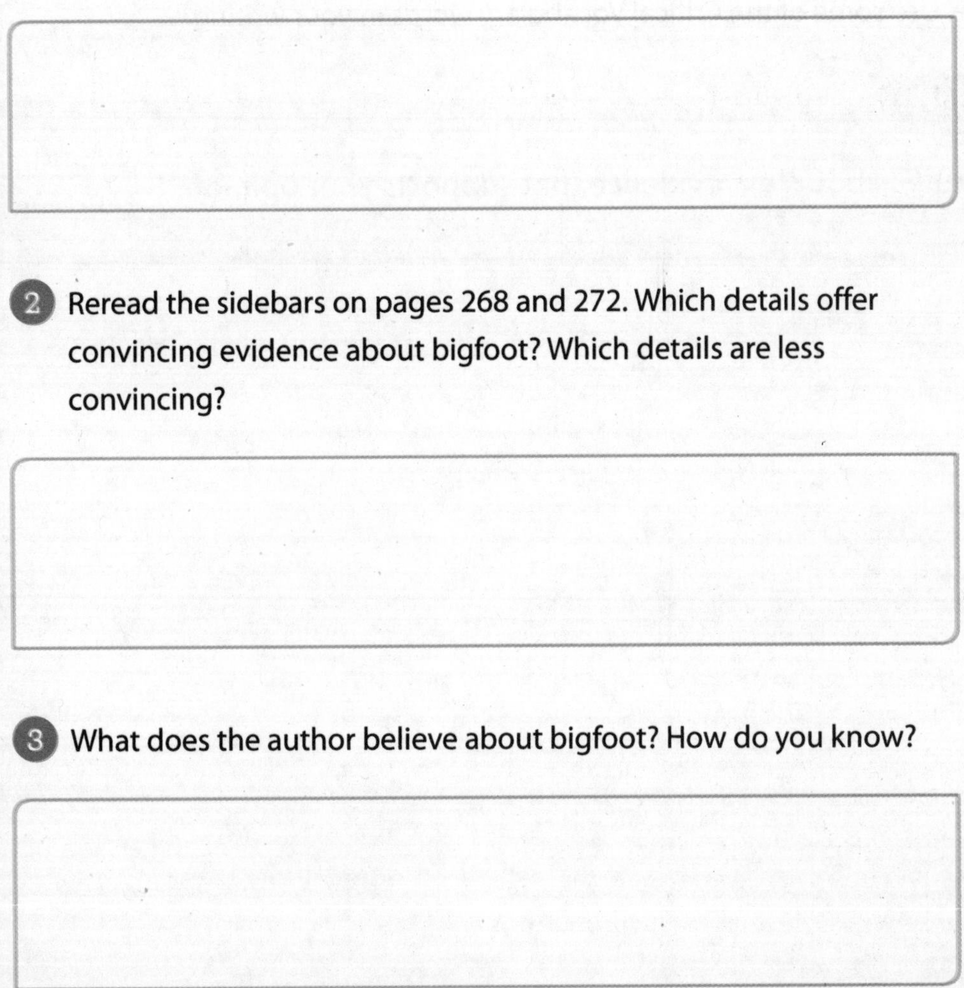

1. Review pages 266–267. Why does the author begin by describing recently discovered creatures?

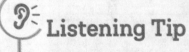

2. Reread the sidebars on pages 268 and 272. Which details offer convincing evidence about bigfoot? Which details are less convincing?

3. What does the author believe about bigfoot? How do you know?

Listening Tip

Listen closely to each speaker's ideas. Think about how you can connect your own ideas to them.

Speaking Tip

Connect your ideas to what other speakers say by using phrases such as *another reason* or *a different way to think about it.*

Write an Online Comment

PROMPT

In *Finding Bigfoot*, you read that some people believe "bigfoot" creatures exist and some do not. The author presents facts and opinions for both sides of the argument. A section titled "Spotted! A Flying Piece of Wood from 'Out of Nowhere'" tells about a woman's claim that she encountered a bigfoot creature.

Imagine this story of her encounter appeared in a newspaper's online edition. Write an online comment in response to that story. Begin by stating an opinion, and then support your opinion with text evidence. Be respectful of other opinions in your response. Use some of the Critical Vocabulary words in your writing.

PLAN

Makes notes about text evidence that supports your opinion.

WRITE

Now write your online comment about the woman's "bigfoot" enounter.

Make sure your online comment

- ☐ clearly states your opinion.
- ☐ includes evidence from the text to support your opinion.
- ☐ is respectful of others who have different opinions.

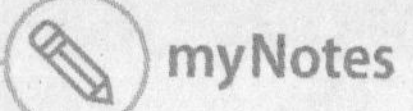

Prepare to Read

GENRE STUDY **Mysteries** are stories in which the main character sets out to solve a mystery, crime, or other puzzle.

- Mysteries tell the story through the plot. Events often appear in chronological order, or the order in which they happened.
- Mysteries might include illustrations that help create a mood, or emphasize the characters and setting.
- Mysteries might tell the story in third-person point of view, by an outside observer.

SET A PURPOSE **Think about** the title and genre of this text. How could a watch behave mysteriously or have a secret? Write your ideas below.

CRITICAL VOCABULARY

- hastily
- muffled
- gaping
- beckoned
- feeble
- shudder
- conviction
- faltering
- extinguished

Meet the Author: Trenton Lee Stewart

THE SECRET KEEPERS

by Trenton Lee Stewart illustrated by Chris King

1 *While exploring an alley in his neighborhood, 11-year-old Reuben Pedley has found an unusual-looking pocket watch and an old key carefully hidden long ago in a brick wall. Inside the watch's case is the inscription "Property of P. Wm. Light." Reuben has shown it to a watch expert named Mrs. Genevieve, who believes that this is not an ordinary watch for telling time. She's told Reuben that a mysterious figure known as The Smoke, who secretly rules the city, has been trying to find this watch for many years.*

2 SO THE WATCH HAD A SECRET.

3 All the way home Reuben could think of nothing else. Except, of course, The Smoke, thoughts of whom kept him glancing over his shoulder and quickening his pace. He took the stairs in his building at such a rate he was left gasping for breath as he staggered down the hallway to his apartment. Never had its musty, dusky interior felt so welcoming, nor had he ever been so quick to lock the door behind him.

4 After wolfing down a hastily constructed sandwich and gulping milk from the carton (it was well past lunchtime now), Reuben hurried into his bedroom and opened his backpack. He was going to figure this out.

5 In moments he had the watch in his hand and an eye on his alarm clock. He wound up the watch. After fifteen minutes, it stopped ticking. He tried again, with the same result. A watch that had to be wound every fifteen minutes was ridiculously impractical, so of course Mrs. Genevieve was right. The spring must have been designed for some other purpose—a secret purpose. But what? And did The Smoke know the secret? Was that why he wanted the watch so badly?

6 Reuben felt a sudden need to double-check the lock on the apartment door.

hastily If something happens hastily, it happens with great speed.

7 He came back and dragged the old cardboard box of toys from his closet. He hadn't opened it even once since they moved here, but he was pretty sure he still had a windup toy robot. Sure enough, he found it at the bottom of the box, among a jumble of action figures. He wound it up and set it on the threadbare carpet. The robot managed a couple of awkward steps with its block-like feet before toppling over. Reuben remembered why he'd never been fond of this toy. It always ended up that way, with its feet churning uselessly, like a beetle on its back.

8 His plan had been to pry it open and study how its spring mechanism worked. But as he dug through the box looking for something to use as a prying tool, he came upon an old jack-in-the-box and had a sudden inspiration. Mrs. Genevieve had seen no way to open the watch from the outside, but what if something made it open up from the *inside*? What if it was like the jack-in-the-box, which opened unpredictably when you turned its crank?

9 Maybe there was something valuable inside the watchcase, and the only way to get to it was to set the watch to a certain time and then wind it up—rather like the combination lock on a safe. Why not? The more Reuben thought about it, the more convinced he felt he was right. He jammed the cardboard box into the closet and sat down on his bed.

10 Taking a breath to steady himself—his heart was racing now—Reuben eased the watch's winding key back up into its setting position and turned the hour hand from one o'clock to two o'clock. He pushed the key all the way in again and wound the watch. Then, tense with expectation, he pulled the key back up to allow the spring to unwind. Nothing happened. He held the watch to his ear and confirmed that it was ticking. Perhaps the secret mechanism would be triggered at some unpredictable point during the unwinding.

11 And so Reuben stared at the watch in his hand, waiting. A minute passed, then two. He found himself growing more and more excited. He couldn't tear his eyes away. He hated even to blink for fear he'd miss something, and he began to feel jittery and hot. The purpose of a jack-in-the-box, after all, is to fill you with mounting anticipation, the tension increasing second by second as you wait for that startling moment when the hidden figure pops up—and Reuben was waiting for something far more dramatic than a little clown puppet. By the time ten minutes had passed, the tension had grown almost unbearable. After fifteen he felt ready to collapse. And indeed, when the watch stopped ticking, he sank back onto the bed with an exhausted and disappointed sigh.

12 Ten more positions to try. What if nothing happened until the last attempt? He would have to endure over two hours of nerve-wracking waiting. And of course it was possible that nothing would happen at all. Reuben didn't choose to believe that, however.

13 He turned his head toward the wooden box sitting open on the bed. He gazed at the inscription inside the lid. "Hey, Mr. Light," he mumbled, "what's the secret?" For he felt sure now that P. William Light had known it, whatever it was. But if the man's ghost was hanging around the watch, it certainly wasn't whispering any hints to Reuben. He was going to have to do this the hard way.

14 He rolled onto his belly, set the watch to three o'clock, and tried again. Again nothing happened. Fifteen minutes of pointless ticking, that was it. Reuben groaned and pressed his face into the mattress.

15 By the time he'd tested all the positions through eleven o'clock, Reuben's eyes were bleary from staring, his entire body ached from the tension, and his hand was cramped from squeezing the watch too tightly. He hated to stop with only one position left to try, but he desperately needed a break.

16 Returning the watch and key to their box, Reuben flopped over onto his back. Despite the mounting disappointments, he still felt strangely confident that he was right about the watch's secret, and he wondered what might be hidden inside it. He closed his eyes and imagined a tiny velvet pouch stuffed with diamonds. Or rubies. Something small but precious. Something he could sell. His dream of riches wasn't over, he thought, not by a long shot.

17 He woke to the sound of someone at the apartment door. A muffled thump, the scrape of a key. Reuben sat up with a gasp. He hadn't meant to fall asleep. What time was it? How long had he slept? His eyes shot to the alarm clock. Almost six. But it couldn't be his mom at the door—she had to work that evening. And yet there was no mistaking the familiar squeak of the lock turning.

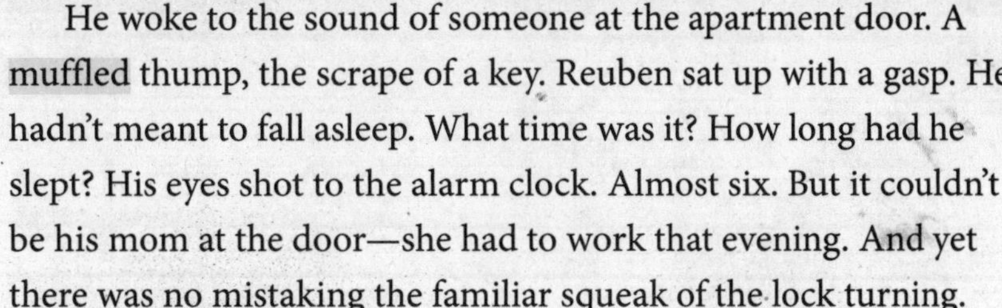

18 Reuben leaped up, snatched the wooden box, and shoved it under his bed. He was groggy, disoriented, wondering if he should hide. He was still trying to decide, watching with dread through his bedroom doorway, when the apartment door swung open.

19 "Hey, kid, guess who's home?" called a familiar voice, and Reuben almost collapsed with relief.

20 His mom stepped in, closing the door with her foot. She had her purse slung over one shoulder, a larger handbag with her change of clothes in it over the other, and grocery sacks in both hands. She turned and saw him gaping at her. "Oh, hey! Change of plans. I'm off tonight." She cocked her head to the side. "Reuben? Are you okay? Hello?"

21 Reuben snapped to and rushed to help her. Her forehead was beaded with sweat. She thanked him as he carried the grocery sacks into the kitchen. "Whew," she breathed, letting her purse and handbag drop to the floor. She kicked her shoes off to complete the pile. "Were you wondering why I didn't call from the market?"

22 "Sorry, no, I just woke up," he said, hurrying back to lock the door. "I guess I fell asleep. I mean, I know I did—I just didn't mean to." He shook his head. He still felt rattled from waking up in such a fright.

muffled A muffled sound is quiet and hard to hear.
gaping If you are gaping at something, you are staring at it.

23 “I’m sure you needed it,” said his mom, with a tired smile. As usual, she looked as if she could use a long nap herself. “Well, I was afraid you’d worry when you didn’t hear from me, but I was rushing to make the first bus. Otherwise it would’ve been another half hour.” She beckoned him over for a hug. “I got asked to trade shifts. I’ll have to work Saturday, but it’s nice for tonight, anyway, right?” She kissed his head and walked into the kitchen.

24 “Sure,” said Reuben, after a pause; he tried not to sound disappointed, but it had just occurred to him that now he was going to have to put off testing the watch.

beckoned If someone beckoned you, she made a gesture for you to come near or follow.

25 After dinner his mom glanced at the clock and said that an old movie was about to come on. "Looks straight-up silly," she said, "but it might be fun. What do you think?"

26 Reuben's scalp tingled. Just like that, he had his opportunity!

27 "Do you care if I miss the start?" Reuben asked. "I kind of want to finish a book I'm reading. I only have a few pages left." It was a thin excuse but plausible. He usually did have a book going.

28 His mom patted his cheek. "Go read. I'll fill you in."

29 Reuben retreated to his room and closed the door. He found a library book he'd already finished, opened it to the last chapter, and laid it on his bed. Beyond the door he could hear his mom switching on the television, then moving about the kitchen, pouring popcorn kernels into a pot. He knew he should wait until she went to bed. But it was the last test. He had to know.

30 He got out the watch and key. From the television came the muffled sounds of movie dialogue; he heard his mom groaning at some feeble joke. He set the watch to twelve o'clock. "Midnight," he whispered, and felt a shudder run through him. He had a sudden conviction that he ought to have tried the twelve o'clock setting first. Wasn't midnight always the magical hour?

31 Then he had to laugh at himself. What was he expecting, anyway? Certainly not magic. It wasn't as if he believed in fairy tales. Besides, he was thinking of twelve o'clock as midnight, but of course it could also be noon. Nonetheless, it was with a sense of powerful expectation that Reuben wound the watch.

32 *Moment of truth*, he thought, easing the key out of its winding position.

33 And everything went black.

34 Reuben yelped. He thought he might throw up. He closed his eyes and opened them again and still saw nothing but darkness. He squeezed them tightly, opened them again. Nothing. His skin burned with panic.

35 His mom knocked on the door. "Reuben? Are you okay?"

feeble Something that is feeble is weak.
shudder A shudder is a shiver or trembling caused by fear.
conviction A conviction is a strong belief or certainty.

36 Reuben looked toward the door but saw nothing. He opened his mouth to answer but found himself speechless with horror. The door opened. His mom's voice said, "Reuben? Reuben?"

37 Then, to Reuben's even greater shock, her voice retreated. He heard her walking to the bathroom calling his name, then into her bedroom. He couldn't make sense of it, was still in too much of a panic to think. His thoughts were a terrifying jumble. It took him several seconds to remember the watch in his hand. The watch! He flung it down onto the bed as if it were a burning coal.

38 The instant he did so, he could see again. His relief was so powerful that tears started to his eyes. He bent forward, covering his face with his hands, trying not to weep. For some sliver of awareness in him understood that he needed to protect this terrible secret, to keep it from his mom at all costs.

myNotes

39 "Reuben?" His mom was in the living room again. She sounded half-concerned, half-suspicious. Not alarmed, though. He had hidden from her too many times for her to be truly alarmed. "I swear, if you jump out and scare me, I'm going to scream. You know you hate it when I scream."

40 Reuben tossed a pillow over the watch, which he dared not touch, and in a faltering voice he called out, "In here." If he'd been thinking clearly, he would have waited until he'd composed himself, but he was too shaken up. All he knew was that he desperately wanted his mom to come back.

41 When she appeared in the doorway, he threw his arms around her, burying his face against her chest. She held him tightly. "Oh, honey, what's the matter? Are you okay? What happened?"

42 Reuben shook his head, not looking up. He had no idea what to say.

43 "I heard you cry out—I thought you'd seen a rat or something. Where were you? I looked in here and didn't see you."

faltering Something that is faltering is hesitant and not confident.

44 “You did?” Reuben said, utterly confused. But of course she had. He’d heard her.

45 “Well, I just poked my head in, but you weren’t on your bed.”

46 For a moment Reuben felt as if his brain were out of focus. Then, suddenly, realization thundered inside his head. It crashed and hammered and pounded like a violent storm: *She couldn’t see you! She couldn’t see you! She couldn’t see you!*

47 “I was . . . under it,” he muttered, trying, despite the crazy tumult in his mind, to think of an excuse. “I was . . . getting my book out from under it and then I thought I saw something—or, well, I thought I heard something, and then I looked over and thought I saw a person in my closet. . . .”

48 “You poor thing. Did you bang your head?” his mom asked, gently feeling the crown of his skull for a bump.

49 “No, I’m fine. I just panicked, I guess. It was . . . only my jacket.”

50 She winked. “Just come out when you’re ready, okay?”

51 He closed the door behind her. Then, as quietly as he could, he locked it. He stood with his hand on the doorknob, his mind still whirling. *She hadn’t seen him.* She had looked at his bed and hadn’t seen him sitting right there. He turned to look at the bed, to see what she had seen—what she *hadn’t* seen. It was impossible. But it had happened.

52 He stood there, perfectly still, trying to think of what to do. His heartbeat was galloping. He had an idea and ran to his closet. Once again he pulled out the box of toys. A few years earlier, his mom had given him a toy digital camera for Christmas. He had loved it at the time, though he was pretty sure it was a factory reject she’d gotten on deep discount. It took terrible photos, and you couldn’t print them or anything, only look at them on a miniature screen. But it would serve his purpose now.

53 In a moment Reuben had the camera out. Was there any chance the batteries weren’t dead? He pressed the pale green power button. The camera emitted a barely audible whine. The little display screen flickered on. Yes!

54 Reuben went to the bed and uncovered the watch. A chill of dread ran through him, but he ignored it. He had to know. He held the camera out at arm's length, pointing it back at himself. Then he took a deep breath and reached for the watch. At the last instant, he closed his eyes—he wasn't sure why. Perhaps he felt it would be less frightening if he didn't actually experience that first moment of blindness. But even with his eyes closed, as soon as his fingers touched the watch, Reuben sensed the light beyond his eyelids being extinguished. The imperfect darkness was made perfect. He shuddered and snapped the picture.

55 He opened his eyes onto blackness, then let go of the watch. Instantly the room rematerialized around him, as if he'd thrown a switch.

56 "Wow," he whispered.

57 And then again, "*Wow!*"

58 Bracing himself, Reuben turned the camera around and looked at the display screen. There was his bed. There was his closet door. A little fuzzy, both of them, but clearly there.

59 Reuben, however, was clearly *not*.

extinguished A light that has been extinguished has stopped shining.

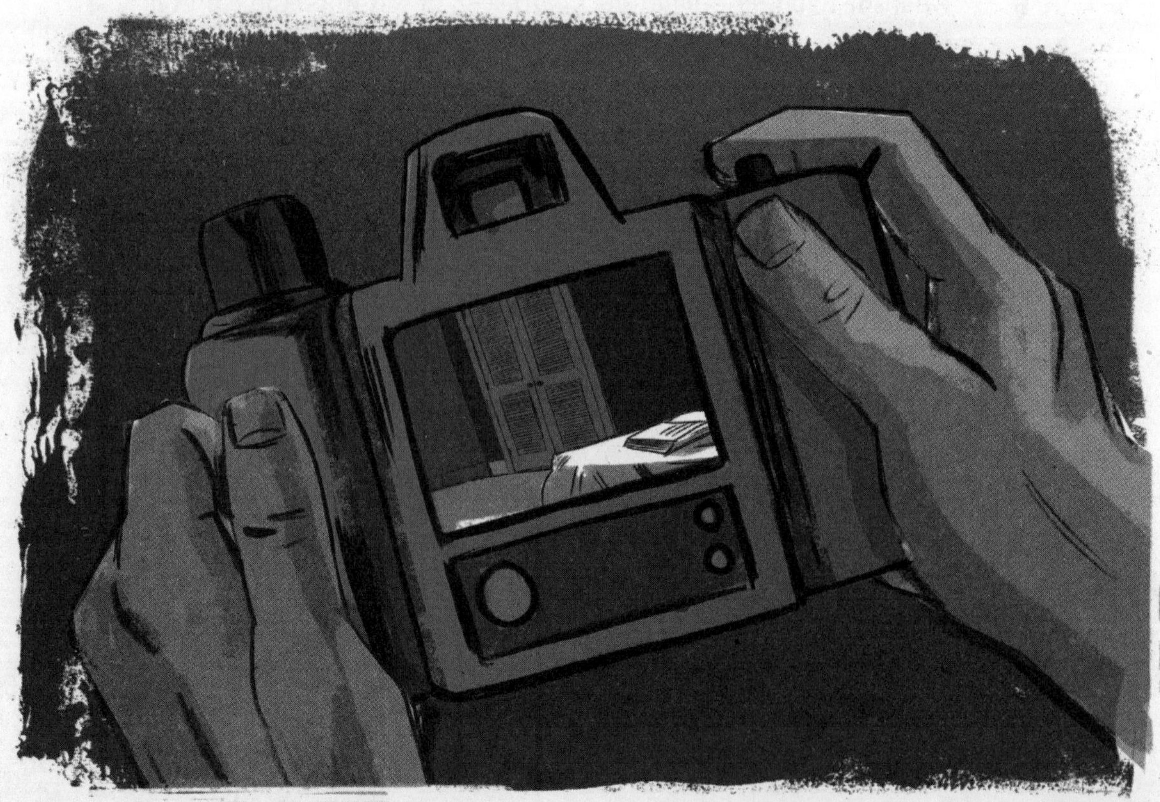

Respond to the Text

Collaborative Discussion

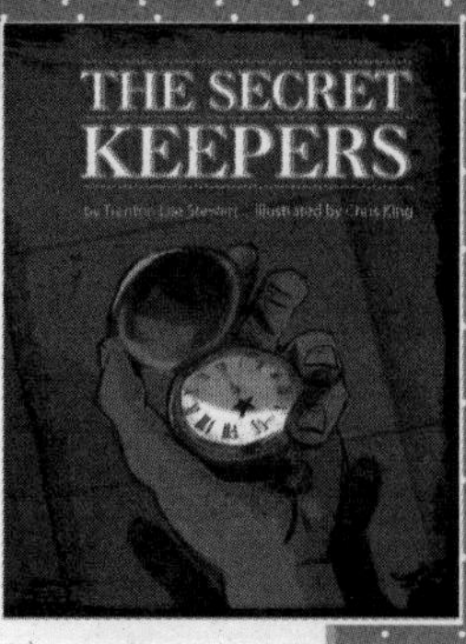

Revisit what you wrote on page 278 and talk with a partner about what happened in the story. Then work with a group to discuss the questions below. Use details and examples from *The Secret Keepers* to show why you answer as you do. Keep an open mind when someone else's answer is different from yours.

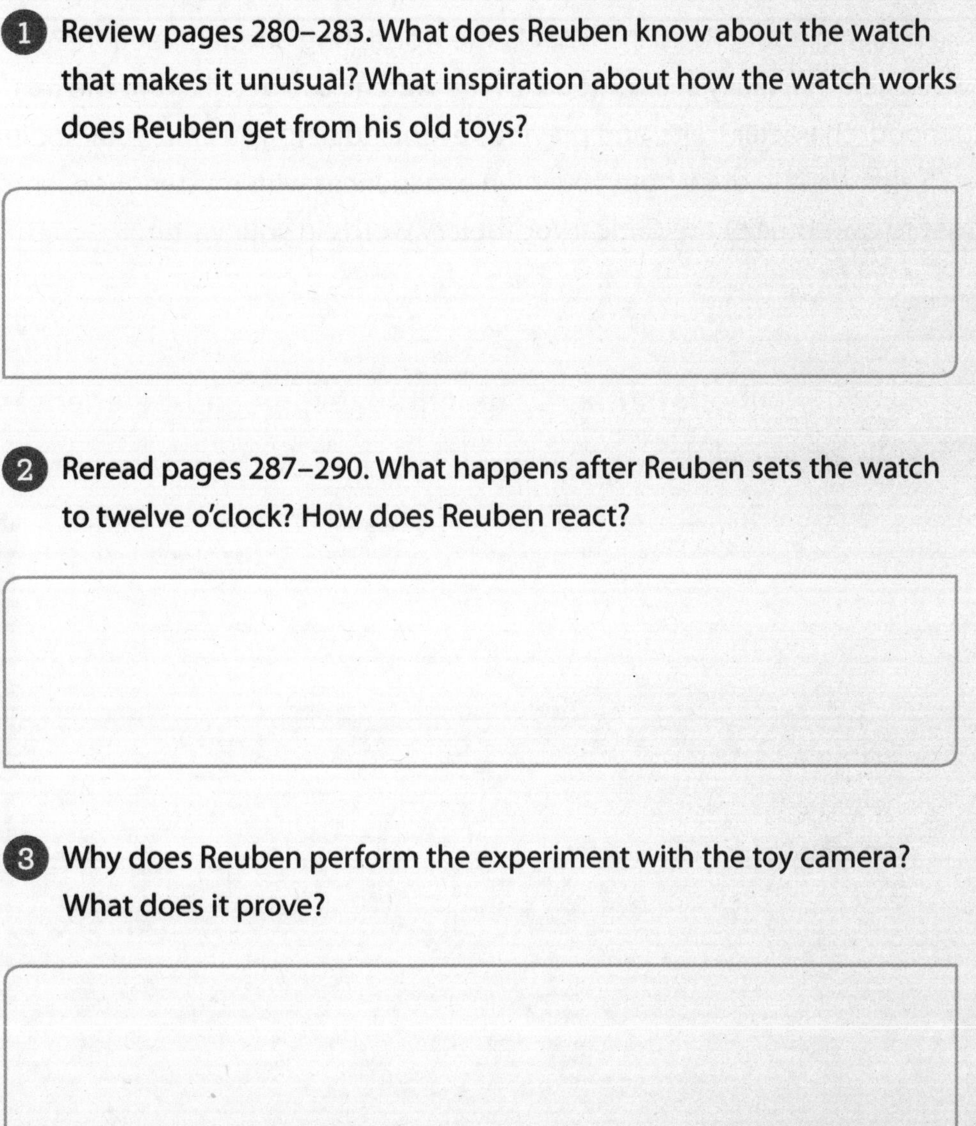

1. Review pages 280–283. What does Reuben know about the watch that makes it unusual? What inspiration about how the watch works does Reuben get from his old toys?

2. Reread pages 287–290. What happens after Reuben sets the watch to twelve o'clock? How does Reuben react?

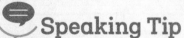

3. Why does Reuben perform the experiment with the toy camera? What does it prove?

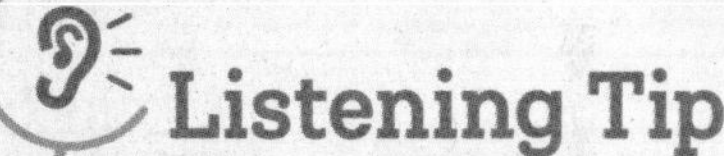

Listening Tip

Listen closely to what others have to say. Think about whether their answers change your mind about the topic of the discussion.

Speaking Tip

Refer back to what other speakers have said. Explain how their ideas supported or changed your answers.

Cite Text Evidence

Write the Next Scene

PROMPT

The Secret Keepers tells about an unusual watch that holds mysterious and frightening power. The reader follows the story through the thoughts, feelings, and experiences of the main character, Reuben.

Use your imagination to create the next scene for the story. Change the point of view, telling this part of the story from Reuben's mother's perspective. How is she feeling? What is she noticing about Reuben? What is she wondering about his actions? What will happen when she finally sees or touches the watch? Use details from the text, including mood, character traits, and previous events to help you craft your ending scene. You'll also want to draw from your own experiences with mysterious events. Don't forget to use some of the Critical Vocabulary words in your writing.

PLAN

Make notes about Reuben's mother's thoughts, feelings, and experiences in the new scene.

WRITE

Now write your scene from Reuben's mother's point of view.

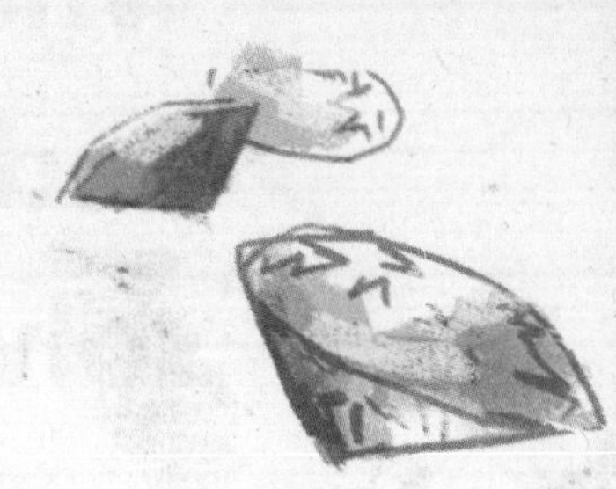

Make sure your new scene

- ☐ describes events from Reuben's mother's point of view.
- ☐ presents all events in an order that makes sense.
- ☐ builds from details in the story.
- ☐ draws from personal experiences.

Performance Task

Essential Question

What makes something mysterious, and what makes people want to solve mysteries?

Write a Persuasive Speech

PROMPT Think about what makes some of the mysteries in this module seem believable.

Imagine that your class will have a debate about those mysteries. Choose one of the mysteries that you feel strongly about. Write a speech to persuade your classmates that the mystery could be real—or that it is fake. State your opinion in a convincing way, and support it with reasons and text evidence.

I will write about ______________________________.

Make sure your persuasive speech

- ☐ begins with an introduction that will grab listeners' attention and clearly states your opinion.
- ☐ presents reasons that support your opinion.
- ☐ uses text evidence to support each reason.
- ☐ contains a strong conclusion that restates your opinion.

PLAN .... **Gather information.**

How will you persuade your classmates to agree with you? What reasons will convince them? Review your notes along with the texts and video for supporting evidence.

The chart below can help you plan your speech. Write your topic and a sentence that states your opinion. Then write your reasons and the evidence that supports each one. Use Critical Vocabulary words where appropriate.

My Topic: ____

My Opinion

Reason 1	**Reason 2**	**Reason 3**

Performance Task

DRAFT

Write your persuasive speech.

Write an **introduction** that states your opinion in a clear and convincing way. A good start will grab your listeners' attention and keep it.

In the **body** of your speech, present your reasons in an order that makes sense. Support each reason with evidence from the text.

Write a **conclusion** that restates your opinion and briefly reminds listeners of why they should agree with you.

REVISE AND EDIT ········ Review your draft.

Make your draft better with a careful review. Start by reading your speech aloud to a partner. What questions does your partner have? Does he or she find the speech convincing? Use these questions to help you find more ways to improve your essay.

PURPOSE/ FOCUS	ORGANIZATION	EVIDENCE	LANGUAGE/ VOCABULARY	CONVENTIONS
☐ Did I state my opinion and grab listeners' interest? ☐ Do my reasons clearly support my opinion?	☐ Are reasons presented in an order that makes sense? ☐ Does the conclusion restate my opinion?	☐ Does my evidence provide strong support for each reason? ☐ Do any of my reasons need additional supporting evidence?	☐ Did I use linking words and phrases to connect the opinion, reasons, and evidence? ☐ Did I use strong persuasive language?	☐ Have I spelled all words correctly? ☐ Do all verbs agree with their subjects?

PUBLISH ········ Share your work.

Create a Finished Copy. Make a final copy of your persuasive speech and create visuals to go with it if you wish. Consider these options for sharing your speech:

1. Deliver your speech to your class or a small group. Practice ahead of time so you can look at your audience rather than at your text. To help your audience understand, read at a rate that is neither too fast nor too slow.
2. Make a recording of your speech. Post it on a school or class website. Invite students who disagree with you to share their opinions and reasons.
3. Hold a debate with classmates who wrote about the same mystery. Present your opinion and reasons. Listen politely to opposing views. Ask each other questions to clarify ideas.

MODULE 10

The Lives of Animals

"We are not just rather like animals; we are animals. Our difference from other species may be striking, but comparisons with them have always been, and must be, crucial to our view of ourselves."

—Mary Midgley

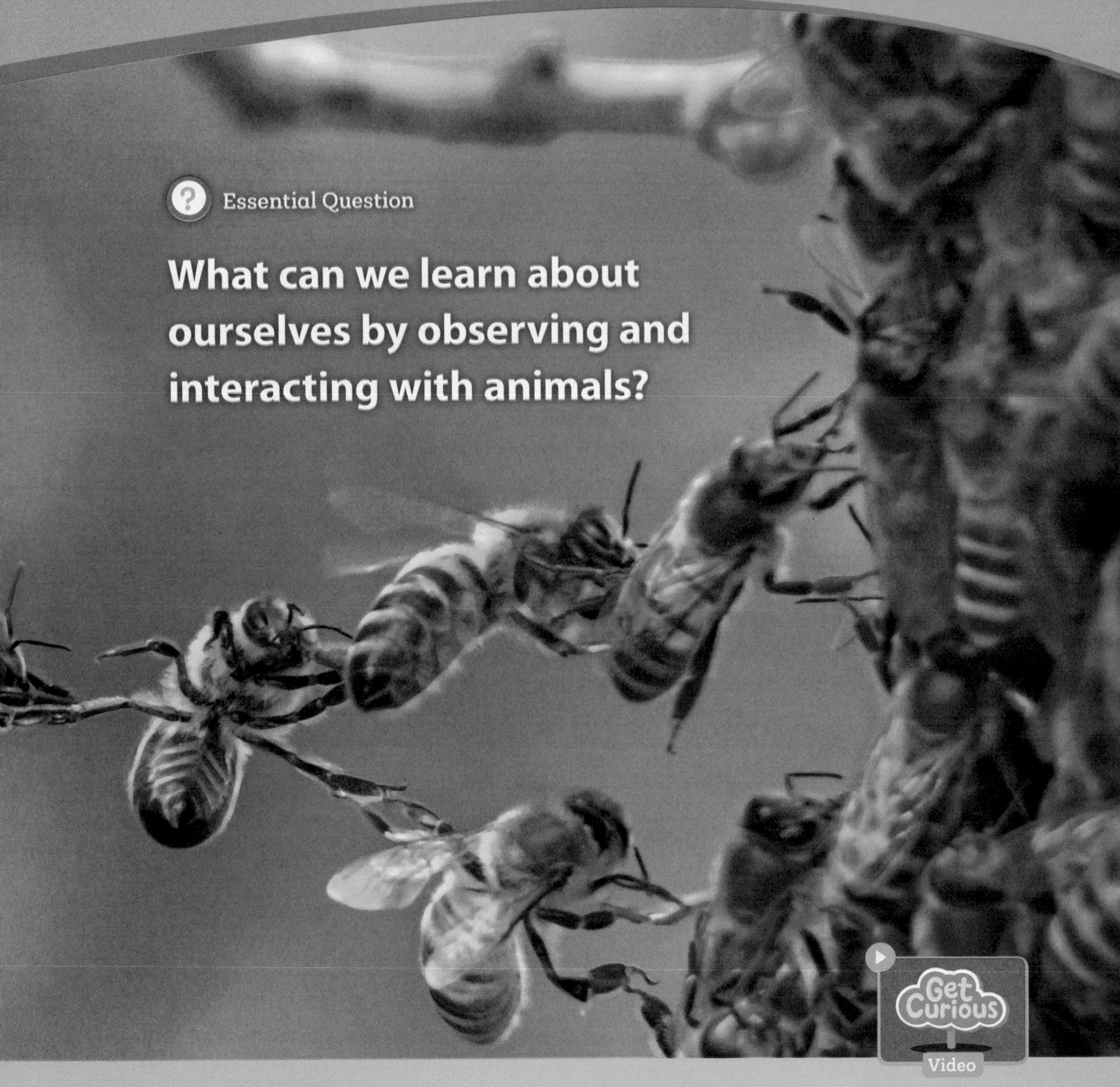
Essential Question
What can we learn about ourselves by observing and interacting with animals?
Get Curious
Video

Big Idea Words

Words About Animal Behavior

The words in the chart will help you talk and write about the selections in this module. Which words about animal behavior have you seen before? Which words are new to you?

Add to the Vocabulary Network on page 303 by writing synonyms, antonyms, and related words and phrases for each word about animal behavior.

After you read each selection in this module, come back to the Vocabulary Network and keep building it. Add more boxes if you need to.

WORD	MEANING	CONTEXT SENTENCE
tension (noun)	A difficult situation can produce a feeling of tension, or stress.	There was a feeling of tension and fear when we heard a noise outside our tent.
antisocial (adjective)	If you're feeling antisocial, you don't feel like being around other people.	Usually my cat is friendly, but today he is being a little antisocial.
bond (noun)	People who feel friendship or love toward each other have a bond that unites them.	The dog and the cat grew up together and formed a close bond of friendship.
relationship (noun)	The way people feel and act toward each other is their relationship.	The relationship between people and their pets can be very affectionate.

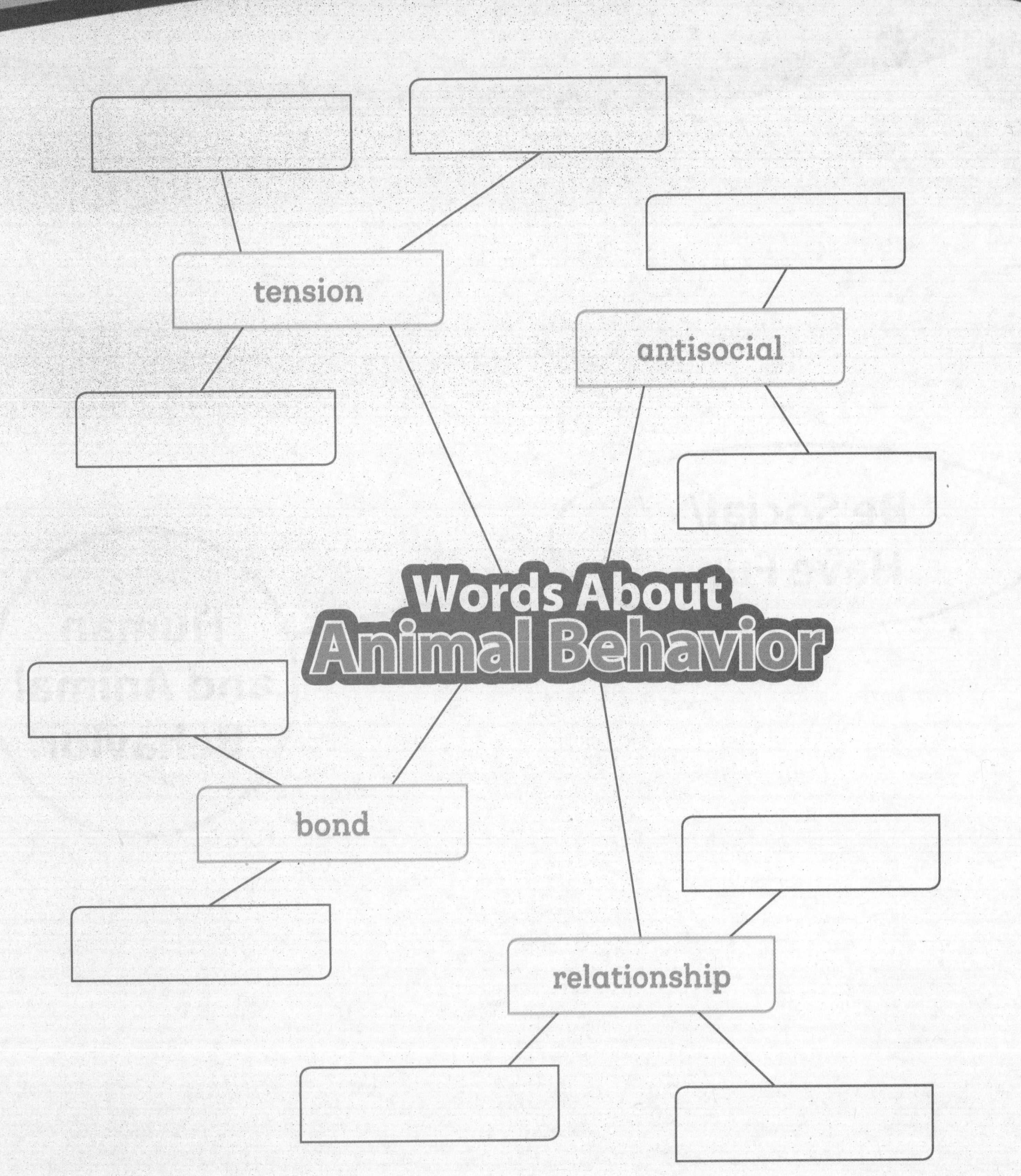

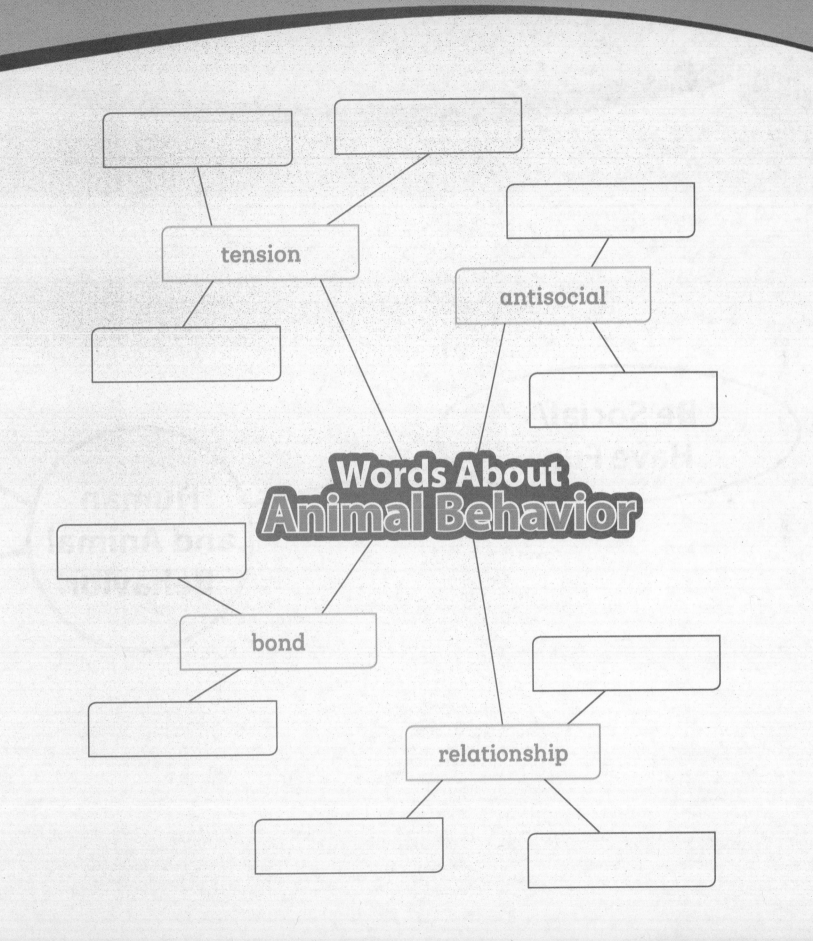

tension
antisocial
Words About
Animal Behavior
bond
relationship

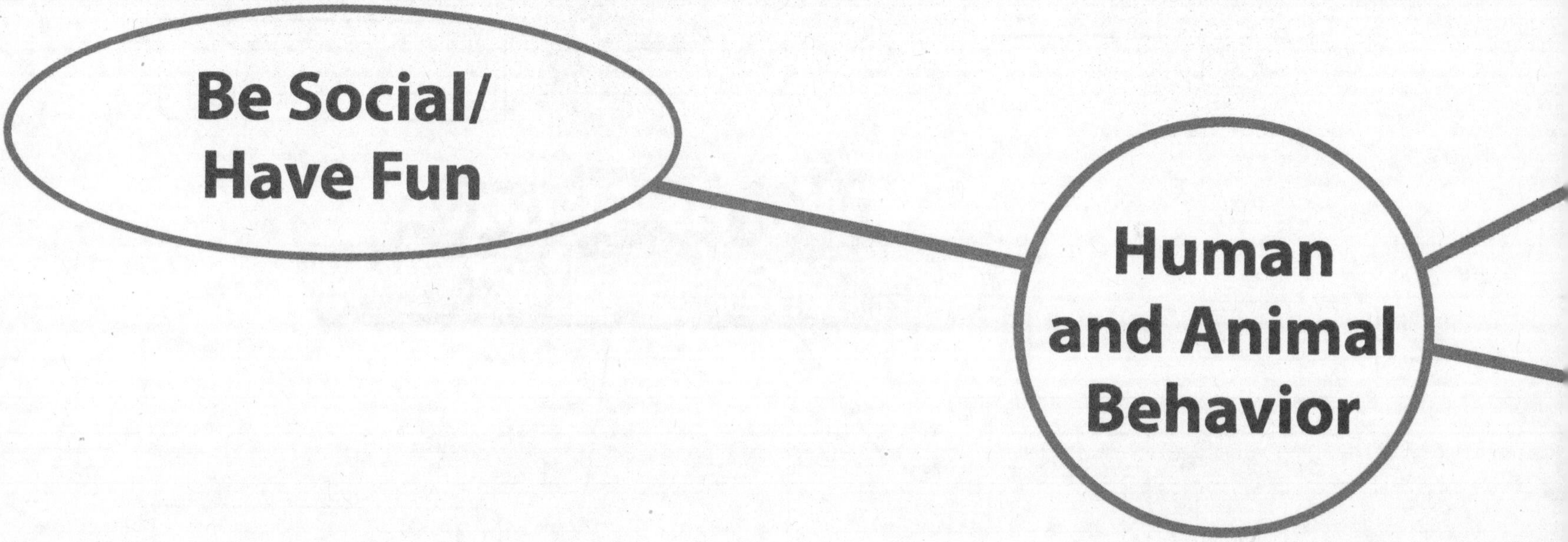

Knowledge Map

Be Social/
Have Fun

Human
and Animal
Behavior

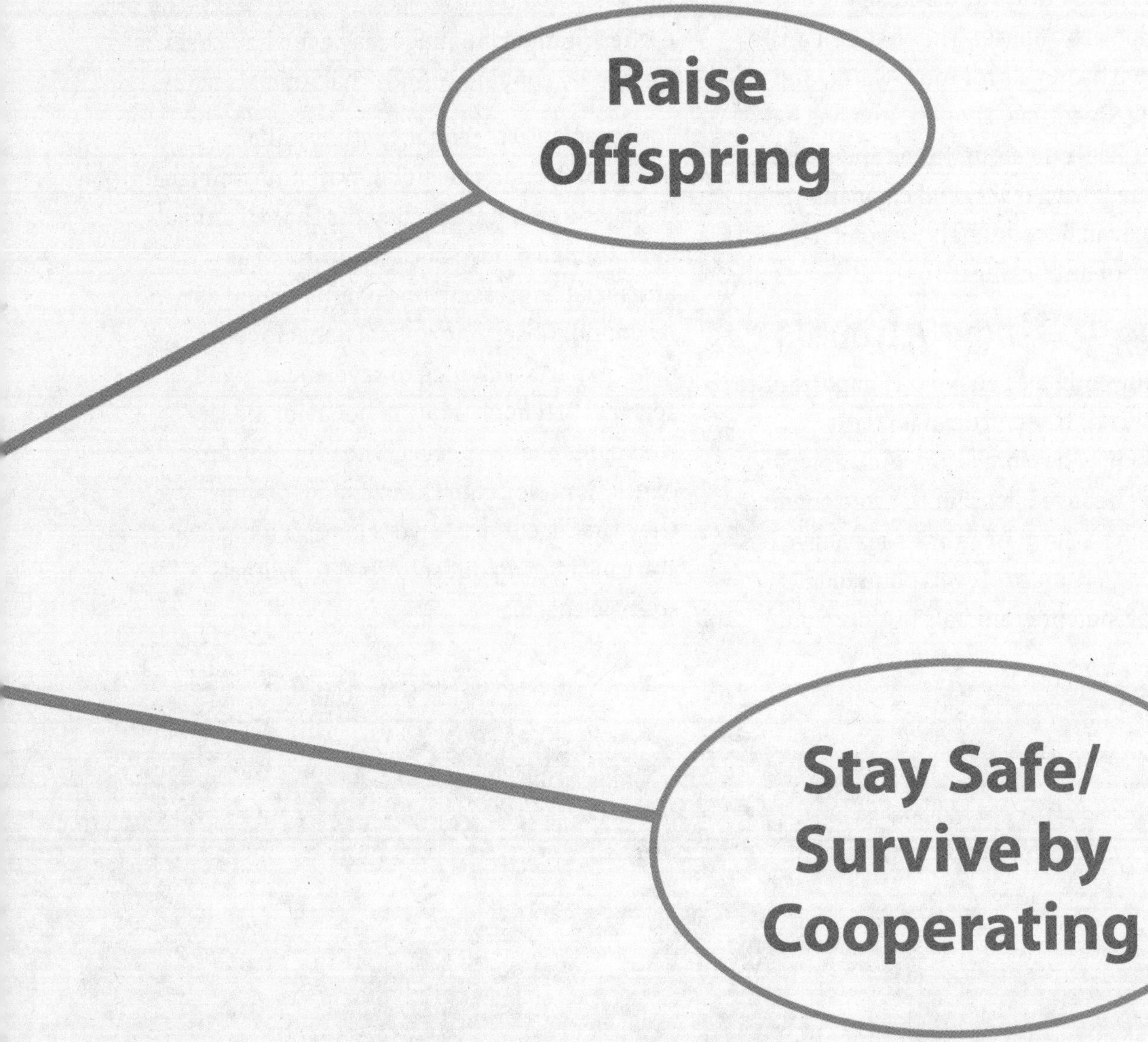

Raise Offspring

Stay Safe/ Survive by Cooperating

myNotes

Short Read

Why We Watch Animals

1 We humans have always had a close relationship with animals. The first humans competed with animals for food, water, and living space. Over time, though, humans have learned to raise animals on farms and use them for travel, help with tasks, and companionship. Many of us even have animals we consider to be members of our families!

Getting to Know Animals

2 Knowing how animals behave was important to human survival. It was crucial for early humans to know how predators such as wolves and big cats behaved in order to avoid them. The traveling patterns of animals may have led early people to sources of water and food. Hunters watched prey animals to figure out the easiest and safest ways to catch them. The earliest human language may even have been formed by copying sounds that animals made!

3 Today, scientists regularly study animal behavior around the globe. Watching animals helps us understand behaviors that all animals, even humans, have in common, such as antisocial aggression or a parent's bond with its young. Observing animal behavior also gives experts a chance to save endangered species. Often, changes in behavior are the first clues that a species is heading toward extinction. Noticing these changes when they first occur may give scientists a head start in figuring out solutions to protect specific species.

A water buffalo pulls a farmer's plow.

A wolf pack hunts.

A mother gorilla carries her young.

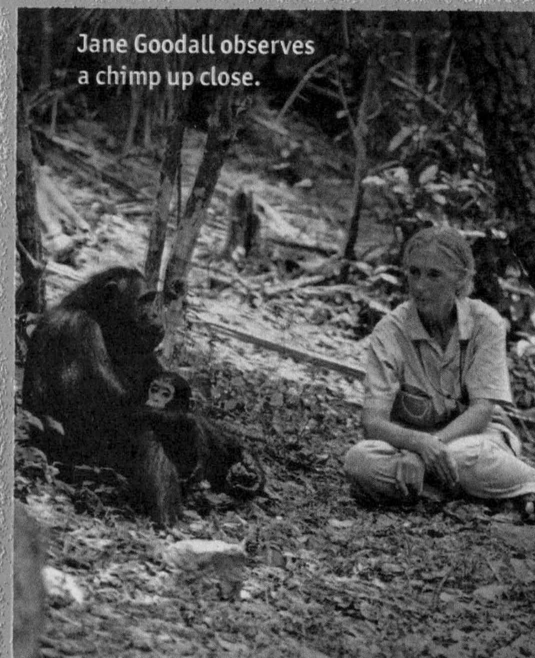
Jane Goodall observes a chimp up close.

Animals in the Wild

4 Jane Goodall began studying chimpanzees in the Gombe Stream Game Reserve in Africa in the 1960s. Her methods were simple. She sat in the forest among the chimps and watched them. Over time, she made a number of important discoveries about chimp diets, tool use, and social interaction. Now, these chimpanzees are endangered, and Goodall is using her knowledge to help save them from extinction.

Animal Spies

5 These days, scientists have come up with some pretty ingenious ways to study animals in the wild. Dr. Yvon Le Maho (ee-VON luh-MOWE) of France has been studying penguins for almost fifty years. He noted that human interaction with penguins in the wild causes stress and tension for the birds. So Dr. Le Maho teamed up with a documentary film company to create a remote-controlled camera that looked like a penguin chick. The penguin robot could approach penguins in the wild without disturbing them. For the first time ever, an Emperor penguin in Antarctica was filmed laying an egg.

6 The same company now uses similar spy cams all over the world. Off the coast of Antarctica, a spy puffer fish recorded an unusual game of catch that dolphins play. They actually use a real puffer fish as the "ball." Another spy cam that looks like a crocodile egg caught the unusual relationship between Nile crocodiles and a water bird called a dikkop (DIK-cup). Dikkops build their nests right next to crocodile nests. The birds help protect both nests from predators.

Our Animal Fascination

7 Probably the biggest reason why people study animals is that animals just fascinate us. We love to read about them, watch them, and care for them. In fact, there are over 163 million pet cats and dogs in the United States alone. There is even a cable television channel dedicated to animals, their behavior, and their relationships with humans. When it comes to animals, it seems we humans just can't get enough of them!

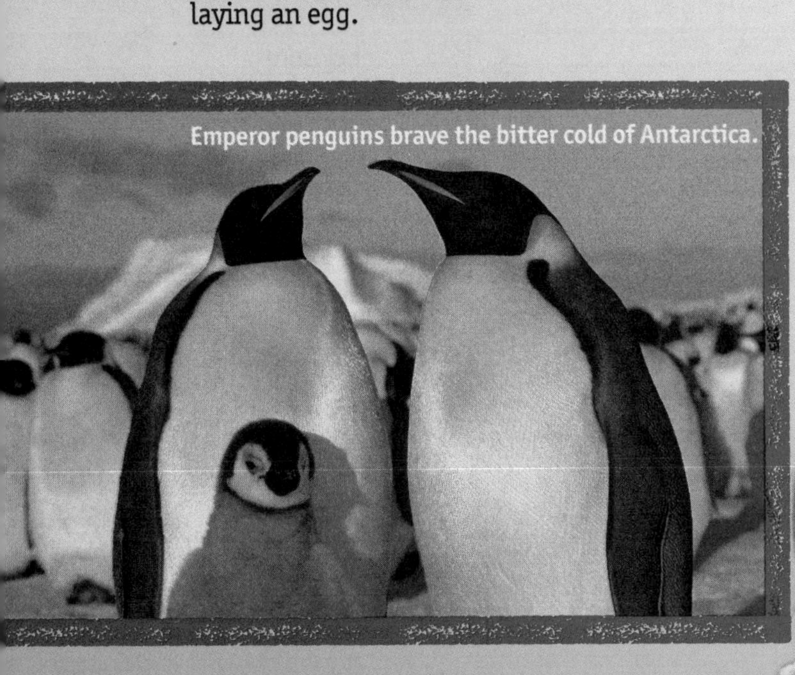

Emperor penguins brave the bitter cold of Antarctica.

Notice & Note
Again and Again

Prepare to Read

GENRE STUDY **Narrative nonfiction** tells factual information in a way that reads like a story.

- Narrative nonfiction texts present events in chronological order, like plot events in a story.
- Narrative nonfiction usually focuses on the true-life experiences of people and animals.
- Vivid descriptions help readers picture and relate to the places, events, and people in the text.

SET A PURPOSE **Think about** the title and genre of this text. What do you know about gorilla behavior? What do you want to learn? Write your ideas below.

CRITICAL VOCABULARY

- enclosure
- anticipation
- possession
- inhumane
- solitary
- territory
- coaxing
- generation
- dominated

Meet the Author:
Nancy Roe Pimm

WILLIE B. A STORY OF HOPE

by Nancy Roe Pimm

In August 1959, James Morgan, mayor of Birmingham, Alabama, holds young Willie while Atlanta's mayor, William B. Hartsfield, looks on.

1 **CAPTURED IN THE JUNGLES OF AFRICA IN 1961,** a three-year-old western lowland gorilla was on his way to the United States. His days of playing among the trees in Cameroon were over. Named after the then-mayor of Atlanta, William Berry Hartsfield, "Willie B." found himself in a new home: a twenty-five-by-forty-foot enclosure of concrete and glass at the Grant Park Zoo in Atlanta, Georgia.

2 In the early days, Willie B.'s zookeepers went into his cage to wrestle and play with him. Just as gorillas in the wild play with one another, the keepers tickled and chased him. But when they left after each play session, Willie B. tried to follow them out the door. As he grew older and stronger, the gorilla nearly tore his playmates' clothes off in an attempt to keep them from leaving. Obviously, it was no longer safe for the keepers to be inside the cage with the gorilla. From then on, the only thing Willie B. had to play with was a rubber tire hanging by a chain in the middle of his cage. And every night, when the keepers locked up the zoo, Willie B. was sent to his night pen, all alone.

3 Soon Willie B. grew to be a potbellied, barrel-chested, full-grown silverback gorilla. At six-feet-tall and weighing more than four hundred pounds, Willie towered over most of his keepers. His massive head sat upon his forty-inch-round neck. All day long visitors came to stare at the huge gorilla—and, unlike gorillas in the wild, Willie B. stared right back.

The only thing Willie B. had to play with was a rubber tire hanging by a chain.

enclosure An enclosure is an area that is surrounded by a fence or walls.

4 He passed the time people-watching. If he found visitors who particularly interested him, the great gorilla invited them to play with him. He walked toward the spectators, hitting the bars with his elbows and encouraging them to play chase.

5 When the visitors left each night, Willie B. gathered up anything he could find: sticks, rope, hair, fruit peels, pieces of tile he had removed from his cage, and sometimes bits of trash. Then the giant silverback carried his fistfuls of treasure into his night room, set them down, and fell asleep with them beside his head.

6 Sometimes Willie B. would offer one of these objects to a zookeeper, usually as a trade for his favorite snack: fruit treats. Another favorite of Willie B.'s was his daily cup of milk. As the keepers poured the milk into a cup, Willie B. would raise his arms above his head and bark in excitement. In anticipation of the treat, the heavyweight gorilla would run around his pen, causing the walls and floors to shake!

anticipation If you are in anticipation of something, you are expecting it to happen and are excited or anxious about it.

Fruit was a favorite treat for Willie.

"Willie B. loved the sweet taste of gum. If he noticed someone was chewing gum, he would sit directly in front of that person."

7 Day after day, Willie watched the people who were watching him. He particularly liked the gum chewers, because Willie B. loved the sweet taste of gum. If he noticed someone was chewing gum, he would sit directly in front of that person. Holding a steel bar of the cage in each hand, he'd push his nose in between the bars and stare. While he stared, he pretended to be chewing gum himself. The zoo visitors often asked zookeeper Charles Horton if Willie had gum in his mouth. As soon as Charles explained that it was Willie's way of communicating that he would like some gum, the visitors almost always began to search through their pockets or purses to find a piece for Willie B. Charles always removed the wrapper and handed the gum to Willie, and then everyone watched the gum-chewing gorilla.

8 Although Charles never went into the cage with Willie, the two still played many games together. One activity they both enjoyed was a kind of a game of "boo." When Charles walked down the aisle between the glass and the bars, Willie would sit in the back corner of his cage, looking up and down, and acting generally uninterested. Then, once the keeper got closer, Willie B. would jump up and charge him, as silverbacks do in the wild, but in a playful way. Charles always ran away, acting more afraid than he really was. As Charles ran, he could hear Willie B. chuckling with satisfaction. Willie B. and Charles also liked to play chasing games and tug-of-war. They even pretended to wrestle by mimicking each other's actions through the glass partition.

myNotes

9 One of Willie B.'s favorite activities was to play in a tub of water. He would hop into the tub and splash around like a little kid. With his legs hanging over one end, he would lie back, raking the water over himself. When the tile floors became wet, it was "slip-and-slide" time. Willie would run across the wet floor, plop down on his rear end, and start spinning until he crashed into a wall. Then he would get up, race to the other side of the cage, and do it all over again.

10 He didn't have a playmate, so Willie B. sometimes entertained himself with something as simple as a paper towel. First, he got a paper towel good and wet, and then he wrung it out. Next, he carefully straightened it, held his head up, and laid the towel across his face. He sat like that for a while, and then he wiped his face. When he finished using the towel as a washcloth, he blew his nose in it. Finally, Willie B. simply opened wide and ate his well-used (and slightly gross) paper towel!

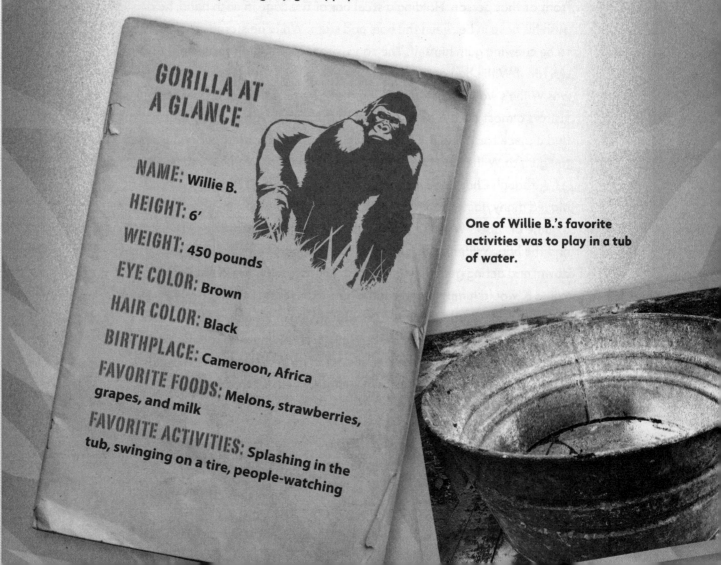

GORILLA AT A GLANCE

NAME: Willie B.

HEIGHT: 6′

WEIGHT: 450 pounds

EYE COLOR: Brown

HAIR COLOR: Black

BIRTHPLACE: Cameroon, Africa

FAVORITE FOODS: Melons, strawberries, grapes, and milk

FAVORITE ACTIVITIES: Splashing in the tub, swinging on a tire, people-watching

One of Willie B.'s favorite activities was to play in a tub of water.

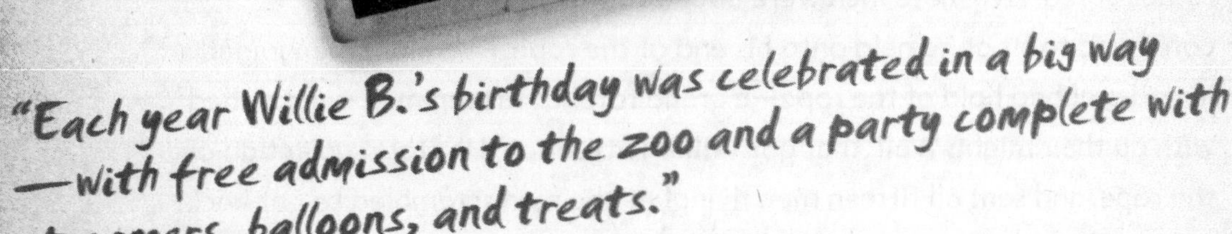
"Each year Willie B.'s birthday was celebrated in a big way
—with free admission to the zoo and a party complete with
streamers, balloons, and treats."

11 Willie was also quite the party animal—but because he was born in the wild, his actual birthday was unknown. The zoo recorded his birthday as May 8, 1958, a combination of his estimated age (which is probably accurate to within a few months) and the date of his arrival at the zoo (May 8, 1961). Each year Willie B.'s birthday was celebrated in a big way —with free admission to the zoo and a party complete with streamers, balloons, and treats. Willie B. usually received a birthday basket filled with his favorite fruits: melons, grapes, kiwis, and strawberries. The zoo staff and visitors sang "Happy Birthday" and blew out the candles on his birthday cake. They served a bakery cake to the public and a special gorilla cake to the "birthday gorilla."

12 On his twenty-fifth birthday, a local company donated a colored television set, which hung from the ceiling outside his enclosure. People asked which television show Willie preferred. Did the big gorilla enjoy the drama of soap operas, the action of a football game, or a good movie? A test was set up in hopes of finding the answer. Three television sets were placed in his viewing area, each with a different channel on. Supplied with snacks, a man sat behind the middle television set observing Willie B. Instead of watching any of the shows, the gorilla simply stared at the man eating his food. Clearly Willie B. preferred people-watching—so perhaps at the zoo, we are the most entertaining show of all.

myNotes

"He held onto his new prized possession night and day for three months, playing with it during the day and coiling it up to sleep on at night."

13 On another birthday, the zookeepers staged a tug-of-war with a three-inch-thick, forty-foot-long nautical rope that had once been attached to a ship's anchor. The men put a big knot in the middle of the rope so if Willie won, he wouldn't be able to pull the rope through the bars and into his cage. When the game began, five partygoers held onto one end of the rope, and Willie B. sat in his enclosure, holding onto the other. Willie held the rope effortlessly, looking rather bored. Five more men were added to the other side. Willie continued to sit as he held onto his end of the rope. Five more men joined in and grabbed hold of the rope—a grand total of fifteen men—and pulled with all their might. Well, that got Willie's attention. He stood up, let go of the rope, and sent all fifteen men flying! As the men scrambled to get back on their feet, Willie B. yanked the rope, knot and all, into his cage. He must have decided that the rope would make a fine birthday present. He held onto his new prized possession night and day for three months, playing with it during the day and coiling it up to sleep on at night.

Big Changes for Willie B.

14 In 1984, the Grant Park Zoo, where Willie B. lived, was considered by the Humane Society of the United States to be one of the worst zoos in the country. The animals were housed in cramped, dirty, and inhumane conditions. When some animals died and some went missing, a grand jury began an investigation into the zoo. According to former mayor Andrew Young, if it weren't for the zoo's star attraction—Willie B.—the whole operation might have been shut down. In 1985, Mayor Young appointed Dr. Terry Maple as the zoo's new director. Maple took charge and made some big changes, including giving the place a new name: Zoo Atlanta.

15 Dr. Maple knew that Willie B. drew a big crowd, but he also knew that Willie's life of solitary confinement was all wrong.

possession A possession is something you own.
inhumane To be inhumane is to be cruel and unfeeling.
solitary Someone who is solitary is alone.

"I felt sorry for Willie B.," Maple said. "He was a big, handsome fellow, and he had to be the loneliest gorilla in the world." Soon after taking the job as director, Dr. Maple took an expedition to the Congo to see how gorillas lived in the wild. He returned from Africa on a mission, eager to make changes for Willie B.'s sake.

16 Dr. Maple convinced a corporate sponsor to build an African rain forest at Zoo Atlanta. The new exhibit would house up to twenty-five gorillas in four areas separated by transparent walls and include an outdoor area for them. Just as in the wild, the gorillas would live in groups with one silverback, a few females, and hopefully some youngsters. On May 13, 1988, for the first time in twenty-seven years, Willie B. was ready to make his grand entrance into the outside world—in the newly finished outdoor exhibit. Zoo staff, visitors, and the media excitedly waited for the big moment when Willie B. would leave his home of concrete and bars for one of grass and sky.

17 Willie B. stayed in the doorway of his cage for a while, cautiously peering out. He touched the ground a few times before he gained the confidence to explore the new territory. With his friend Charles Horton close by, coaxing him and telling him not to be afraid, Willie B. took a few steps forward into the rain-forest exhibit. His head remained statue-like on his massive neck, while he looked cautiously to the right and to the left. For the first time in almost three decades, Willie B. got to see the blue sky and the green grass and to inhale a breath of fresh, springtime air. (And yes, gorillas do see in color.)

Even in his new outdoor enclosure, Willie B. spent most of his time watching people.

territory Territory is an area of land.

coaxing If you were coaxing someone, you were gently trying to convince that person to do something.

18 Shutters clicked and cameras flashed, startling the already apprehensive gorilla. Charles noticed a strong odor coming from Willie B., which a silverback emits when he is alarmed or nervous. “It’s okay, Willie,” Charles told him. Then the clouds opened up, and rain began to fall. When Willie B. felt the strange sensation of raindrops, he ran back to the safety of his concrete box.

19 Later in the day, after the press and the public had left, Charles once again coaxed Willie out into his new home. This time Willie ran to a big oak tree and snapped off one of its branches. He dashed about the habitat. Then he went to the top of the hill and looked down at all of the land around him. It seemed to the keepers that he was claiming the land as his own, posturing as male gorillas do in the wild. The echo of clanking metal doors and the hum of fluorescent lights were now a part of Willie’s past.

20 After exploring his new land for some time, he walked down to the glass and sat, staring at his keepers. Although he was still alone, plans were being made to introduce Willie to a couple of female gorillas in the hopes that they would breed a new generation of gorillas. He had lots of land on which to roam, but he still sat by the glass most of the time, watching his visitors. After spending six months alone in his new habitat, the day came for Willie to meet two female gorillas, Katie and Kinyani. Their “first date” didn’t go as well as some had hoped.

21 The smaller, but more socially experienced Katie dominated Willie from the start. She ran around the enclosure and chased him for a few laps, with Kinyani quickly joining in. In his attempt to run away, Willie stumbled and fell over backwards. Willie clearly had some lessons to learn about standing his ground—and these two females were going to teach him.

generation A generation is a group of people or animals who are about the same age.

dominated If someone dominated another, he or she was more powerful and controlled what the other did.

22 After Willie learned some life lessons from Katie and Kinyani, he was introduced to the gorillas who would become his lifelong mates: Choomba, Machi, Mia Moja (MOH-jah), and Kuchi. Six years later, Willie fathered his first baby with Choomba, a female named Kudzoo. "I feel like crying," said Zoo Atlanta Director Dr. Terry Maple, watching Choomba cradle the baby she had given birth to late on a Tuesday night. Over the years, Willie B. fathered four more babies—Willie B. Jr., Olympia, Lulu, and Sukari.

23 Daddy Willie liked to spend time with the little ones, letting them slide down his big belly. When his mate Mia Moja became ill, Willie B. completely took over the care of their baby Olympia for a day or two. Olympia followed her big daddy around until her mother was well enough to join the troop again.

Willie B. spends quality time with his first mate, Kinyani, at Zoo Atlanta.

And when Willie B. Jr. fell into the moat around the gorilla enclosure, Willie B. Sr. took charge. The keepers tried to put all of the gorillas in the building so they could rescue the baby in distress without the distraction of the curious other apes, but Willie B. would not hear of it. He insisted on staying in the habitat above his trapped little one and even helped with the rescue effort. Sure enough, Willie pulled Willie Jr. to safety. The once-lone gorilla proved to be quite the "family guy." Charles Horton says Willie has taught him a valuable lesson: "It's never too late for things to happen for you."

Willie's mate, Mia Moja, holds her newborn as two-year-old Kudzu looks on.

Respond to the Text

Collaborative Discussion

Look back at your response on page 308 and talk with a partner about what you learned during reading. Then work with a group to discuss the questions below. Support your answers with information and details from *Willie B.* During the discussion, look for ways to build on what others have said.

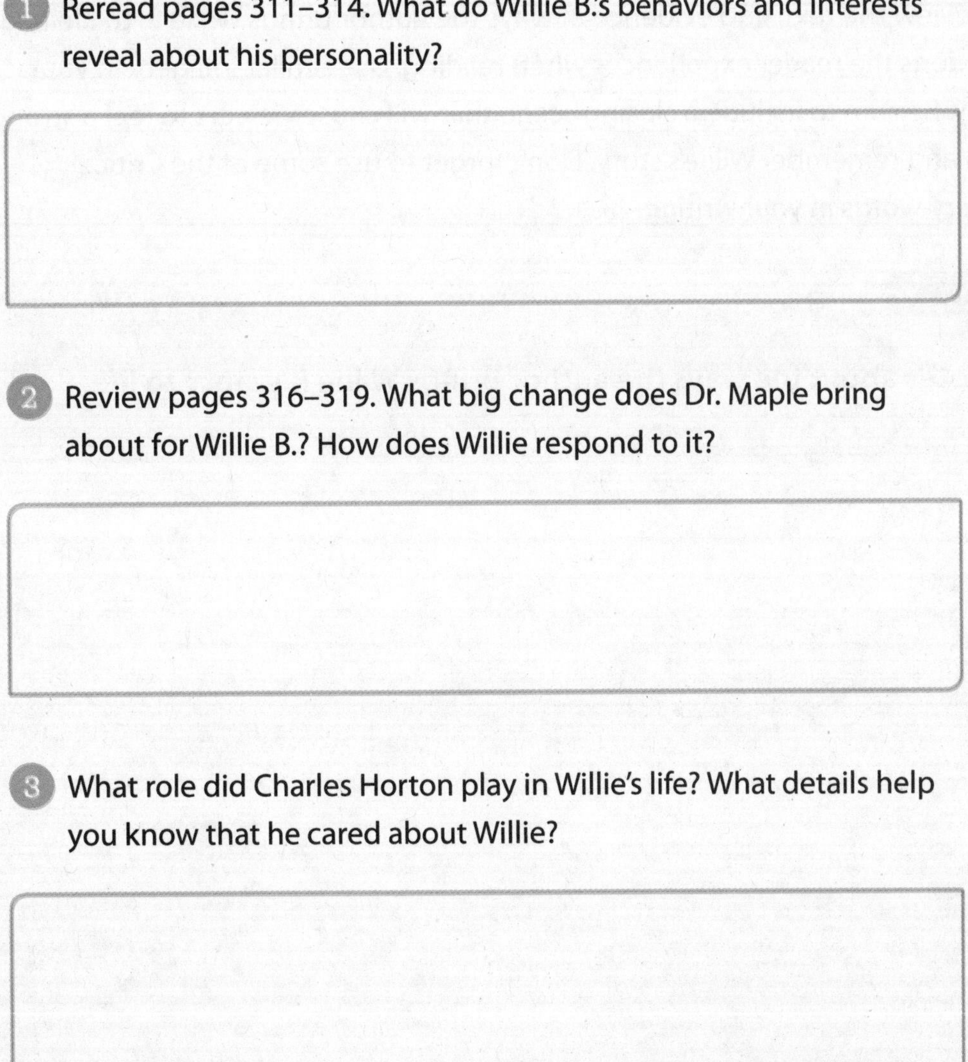

1. Reread pages 311–314. What do Willie B.'s behaviors and interests reveal about his personality?

2. Review pages 316–319. What big change does Dr. Maple bring about for Willie B.? How does Willie respond to it?

3. What role did Charles Horton play in Willie's life? What details help you know that he cared about Willie?

Listening Tip

Listen carefully to the ideas others share, and think about how you can add to what they have said.

Speaking Tip

Point out an idea you agree with, and build on it by adding another example or detail.

Cite Text Evidence

Write a Movie Summary

PROMPT

Willie B.: A Story of Hope tells about the life of a silverback gorilla in an Atlanta, Georgia, zoo. The author uses strong imagery to help make a strong connection between the reader and the events in Willie B.'s life.

Imagine that the zoo is planning to make a movie about Willie B. Decide which parts of his life should be included, and write a summary for each scene or section of the film. As you review the text, find evidence of ways the author brings Willie B. to life and note the emotions the reader experiences when reading. Use similar imagery in your summary. Be sure to include a closing scene that will cause viewers to feel a strong emotion and remember Willie's story. Don't forget to use some of the Critical Vocabulary words in your writing.

PLAN

Make notes about the ways the author brings Willie B.'s story to life.

WRITE

Now write your movie summary about Willie B.'s life.

Make sure your movie summary

- ☐ introduces Willie B. in the opening scene.
- ☐ describes the events of Willie's life in sequence.
- ☐ includes strong imagery that helps the viewer feel a connection.
- ☐ includes an ending scene that causes an emotional response.

Prepare to View

GENRE STUDY **Science videos** present facts and information in visual and audio form.

- Science videos include words that are specific to the topic.
- Key ideas are explained by a narrator and supported by images, clips, or animations.
- Footage of nature or of animals in the wild is often used to illustrate the topic.
- Sound effects and background music may be used to engage viewers.

SET A PURPOSE **As you watch,** think about the ways animal parents teach their young. What do you already know? What do you want to learn? Write your ideas below.

CRITICAL VOCABULARY

- posture
- master
- technique
- utilize
- fend
- status

Dolphin Parenting

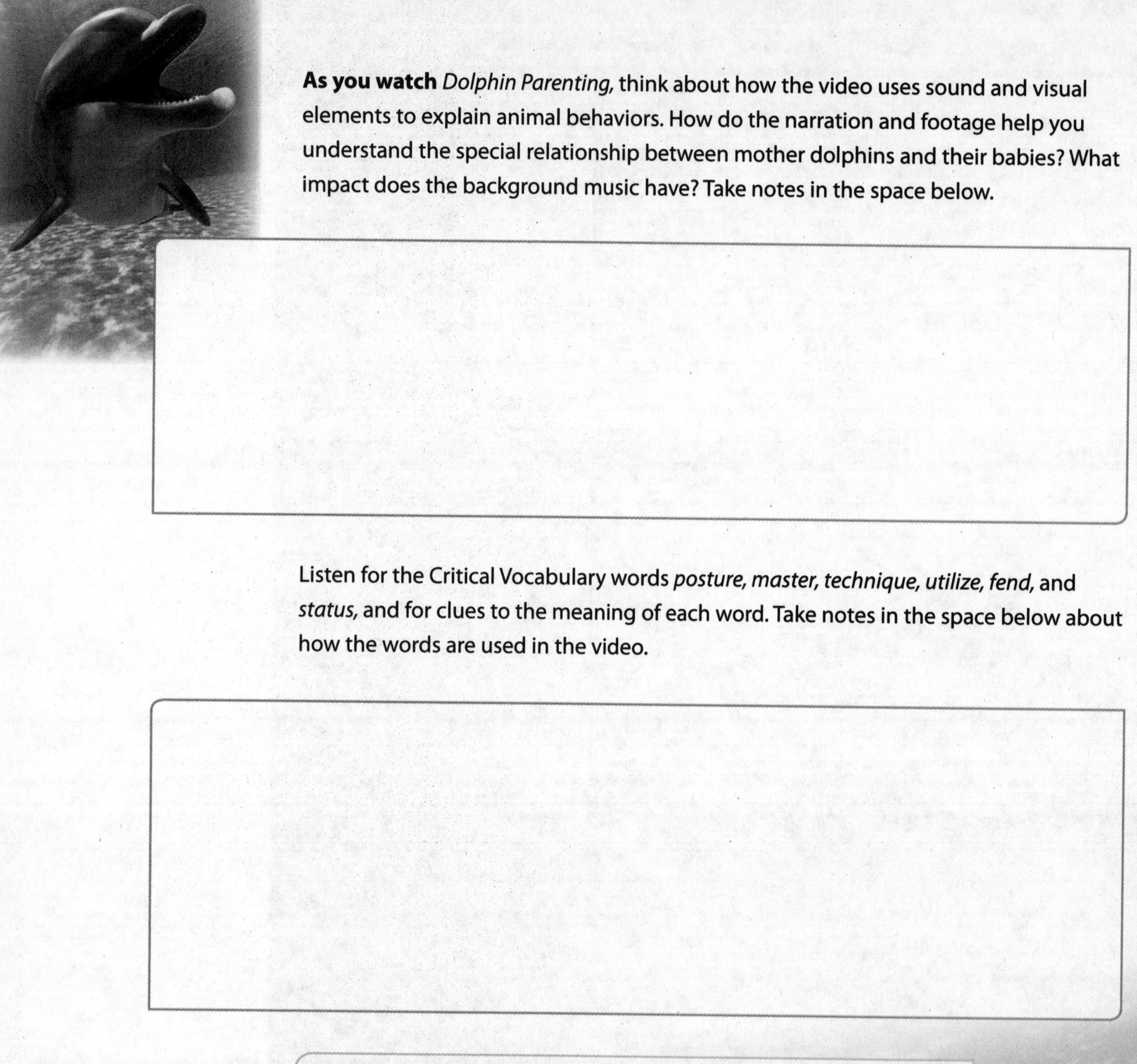

As you watch *Dolphin Parenting,* think about how the video uses sound and visual elements to explain animal behaviors. How do the narration and footage help you understand the special relationship between mother dolphins and their babies? What impact does the background music have? Take notes in the space below.

Listen for the Critical Vocabulary words *posture, master, technique, utilize, fend,* and *status,* and for clues to the meaning of each word. Take notes in the space below about how the words are used in the video.

posture Posture is the position of a person's or animal's body.
master To master an activity is to learn to do it well.
technique A technique is a way of making or doing something.
utilize To utilize something is to use it.
fend People and animals that fend for themselves survive without help.
status Status is the level of importance a person or animal has within its social group.

Respond to the Video

Collaborative Discussion

Look back at what you wrote on page 324. Tell a partner two things you learned from the video. Then work with a group to discuss the questions below. Use information from *Dolphin Parenting* to support your answers. Note whether your thinking changes as a result of others' comments.

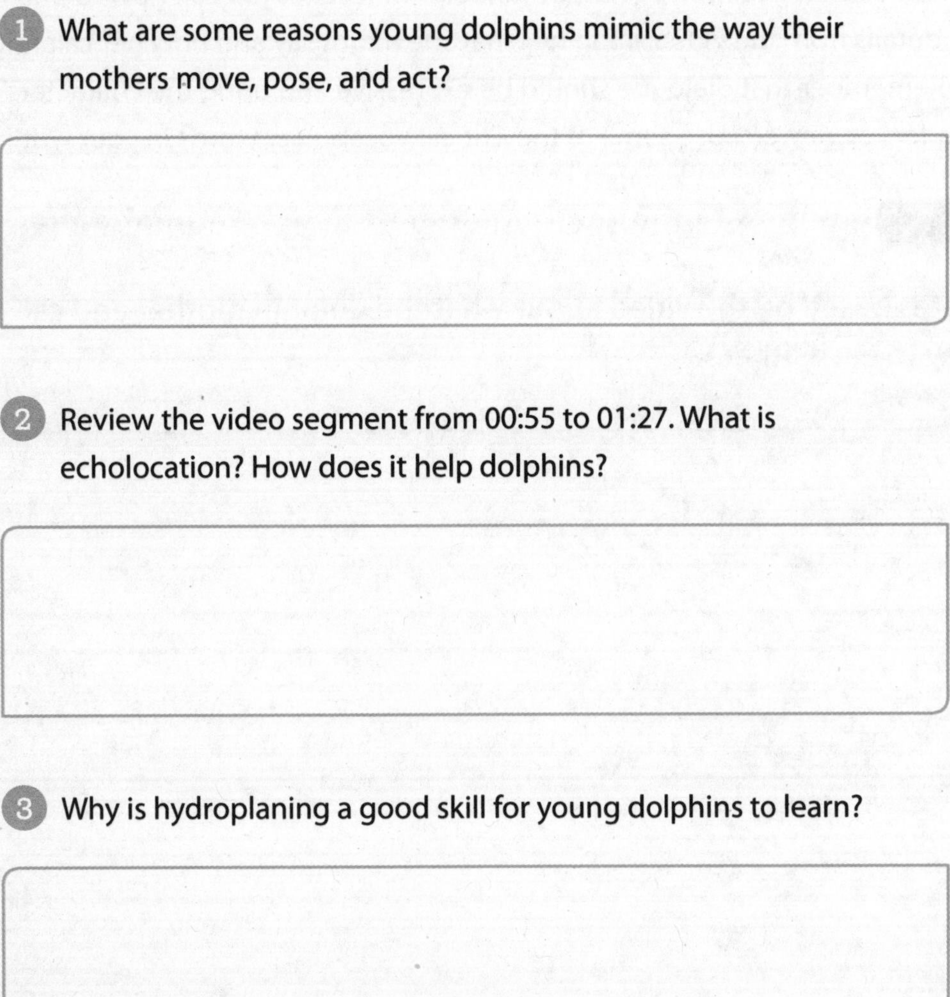

1. What are some reasons young dolphins mimic the way their mothers move, pose, and act?

2. Review the video segment from 00:55 to 01:27. What is echolocation? How does it help dolphins?

3. Why is hydroplaning a good skill for young dolphins to learn?

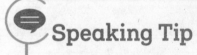

Listening Tip

Listen closely to each speaker's ideas and think about the conclusions you draw from those ideas.

Speaking Tip

When you comment on what someone has said, begin by reviewing that person's statement or idea. Then explain the conclusion you have drawn from the discussion.

Cite Evidence

Write Dialogue for a Movie Script

PROMPT

In *Dolphin Parenting,* you learned how a mother dolphin teaches her calf to survive. The video notes that the mother communicates with her calf using dolphin "language."

Imagine that you're writing a script for an animated movie about dolphins. Write a short section of dialogue in which a mother dolphin teaches her calf how to find food. Based on details from the video, imagine what she might say and how her calf might respond. Remember that dialogue should be expressive and bring the characters to life for readers or viewers. Use some of the Critical Vocabulary words in your writing.

PLAN

Make notes based on the video about what the dolphin mother and calf might say to each other.

WRITE

Now write your movie script dialogue for the dolphin mother and calf.

Make sure your script

- ☐ starts each dolphin character's dialogue on a new line.
- ☐ identifies the character at the start of the line, followed by a colon.
- ☐ is based on facts you learned from the video.

Notice & Note
3 Big Questions

Prepare to Read

GENRE STUDY **Magazine articles** give information about a topic, person, place, or event.

- Authors of magazine articles may organize their ideas using headings and subheadings. Main ideas are supported by details, such as facts and quotations from experts.
- Magazine articles may include words that are specific to science or social studies.
- Visuals, such as photos and illustrations, may be used to enhance or help clarify key concepts.

SET A PURPOSE **Think about** the title and genre of this text. What do you know about animal relationships? What do you want to learn? Write your ideas below.

CRITICAL VOCABULARY

- cowered
- benefit
- clan
- restore
- reconcile
- enabled

Build Background: Animal Communication

Can We Be Friends?

by Ellen R. Braaf

myNotes 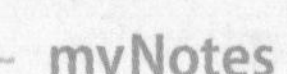 

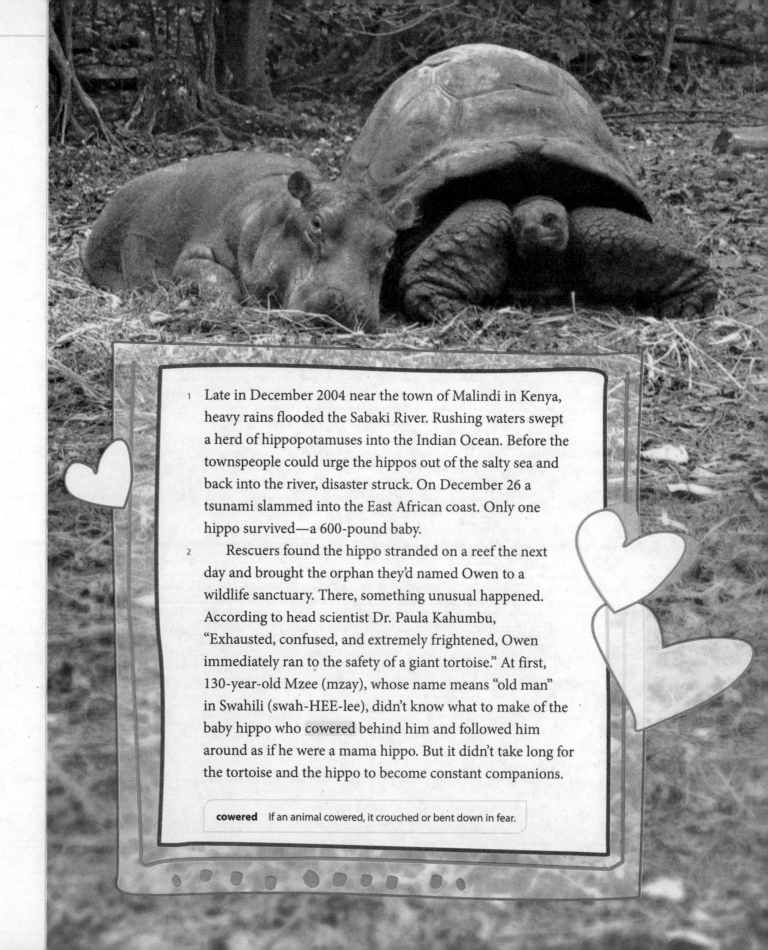

1 Late in December 2004 near the town of Malindi in Kenya, heavy rains flooded the Sabaki River. Rushing waters swept a herd of hippopotamuses into the Indian Ocean. Before the townspeople could urge the hippos out of the salty sea and back into the river, disaster struck. On December 26 a tsunami slammed into the East African coast. Only one hippo survived—a 600-pound baby.

2 Rescuers found the hippo stranded on a reef the next day and brought the orphan they'd named Owen to a wildlife sanctuary. There, something unusual happened. According to head scientist Dr. Paula Kahumbu, "Exhausted, confused, and extremely frightened, Owen immediately ran to the safety of a giant tortoise." At first, 130-year-old Mzee (mzay), whose name means "old man" in Swahili (swah-HEE-lee), didn't know what to make of the baby hippo who cowered behind him and followed him around as if he were a mama hippo. But it didn't take long for the tortoise and the hippo to become constant companions.

cowered If an animal cowered, it crouched or bent down in fear.

"Owen and Mzee continue to spend their days together in the pond, feeding and patrolling," Kahumbu says. "Owen nudges Mzee to come for walks, and Mzee sometimes even follows Owen."

3 Are Owen and Mzee friends? You might answer yes, but many scientists hesitate to use the word "friend" to describe a relationship between nonhuman animals. As Dr. Lee Dugatkin, a biologist at the University of Louisville in Kentucky, cautions, "You see all sorts of cooperation in the animal kingdom, and you see some things we might call 'friendship.' But we have to remember we're not quite sure animals feel or think like we do when they're doing these things. We shouldn't automatically think they're friends with each other in the same sense you're friends with your buddy down the street."

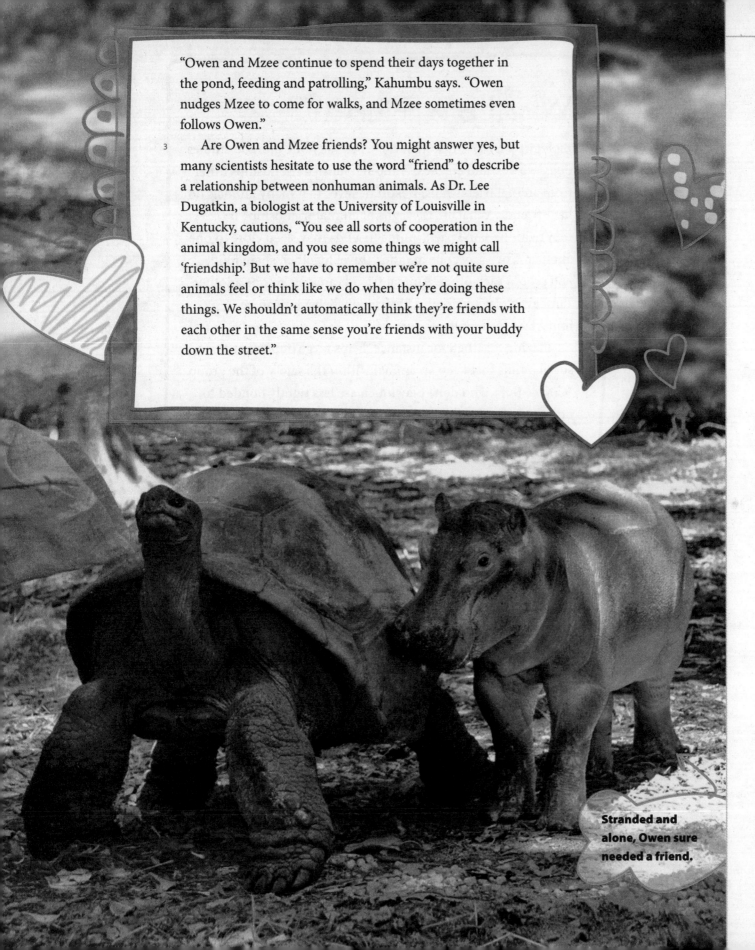

Stranded and alone, Owen sure needed a friend.

What Is a Friend?

4 Biologist Dr. Marc Bekoff at the University of Colorado studies dogs, wolves, and coyotes. Although human friendships differ from animal friendships, Bekoff believes that many animals do have friends. What are the signs of animal friendship? If they're in the same pack, animal friends may sleep close to one another. They greet one another, travel together, share food, and groom each other. Animal friends are nice to one another. They even play together. This friendly behavior can be important to an animal's survival.

5 Playing together, for instance, helps forge important social bonds that keep an animal within the safety of the group. "Coyote pups who don't play much are less tightly bonded to other members of their group and are more likely to strike out on their own," says Bekoff. Leaving the protection of the group is dangerous. In his seven-year study of coyotes in Wyoming's Grand Teton National Park, Bekoff found that 60 percent of the youngsters who left the group failed to survive.

6 For more than 35 years, Dr. Frans de Waal (VAHL) at Emory University in Atlanta, Georgia, has studied primates—animals such as apes and monkeys. He, too, believes friendship plays a role in understanding how these animals interact.

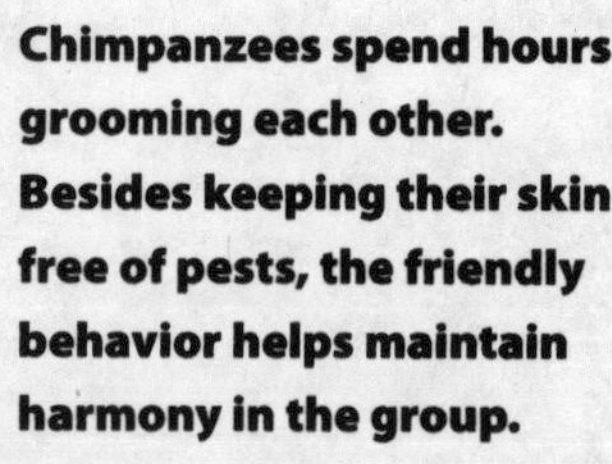

Chimpanzees spend hours grooming each other. Besides keeping their skin free of pests, the friendly behavior helps maintain harmony in the group.

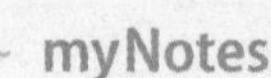

7 How does de Waal define friendship? "Friendship involves liking, loyalty, and common purpose," he says. "I know two female chimpanzees who 30 years ago were already close friends. They lived in a zoo group in the Netherlands with more than 25 chimpanzees. Last year I visited and noticed that they were still friends, still grooming each other, helping each other in fights, and so on. Loyalty!"

8 Why do animals have friends? "Mainly because in the long run they benefit from friendships," de Waal says. "It is all give and take. Sometimes one gives more, the other takes more, but in the end both parties gain."

benefit If you benefit from something, it makes your life better in some way.

Kiss and Make Up

9 Many kinds of animals, from insects to primates, benefit from living in groups. In fact, their survival often depends upon their cooperation. But members of a group also compete for food and mates—which can lead to fights. We may not be able to tell if two animals are really friends, but we do know that many animals work hard not to stay enemies. Making up after a conflict is essential to the survival of the group.

10 Making up often involves physical contact. People shake hands; dolphins take turns rubbing flippers. They also swim close together—one dolphin leans a flipper against the other's side and gets towed through the water.

11 Spotted hyenas often meet in the clan's den to say, "I'm sorry." Within minutes after a fight, they greet each other with licks, sniffs, and groans. Friendly reunions help restore relationships and ease tension, especially between unrelated animals.

12 Chimpanzees actually kiss when they make up—a behavior some researchers think has roots in mouth-to-mouth food sharing between a mother and child.

clan A clan is a group of animals or people who are usually members of the same family.

restore To restore something is to change it back to the way it used to be.

Spotted hyenas can be fighting one minute and friends the next.

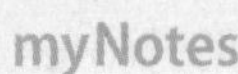

13 Dr. de Waal believes reconciliation is a "learned social skill." For five months, he housed together two groups of young monkeys with very different peacekeeping styles—"bossy" rhesus monkeys that rarely reconcile after a fight and their tolerant stumptail cousins that are masters at making peace. At first, both groups kept to themselves, but in the end, "they did everything together" and the rhesus monkeys reconciled after conflicts as often as the stumptails. When the two groups were separated, the rhesus monkeys kept up the more peaceable ways they had learned.

reconcile If you reconcile with someone, you make up after a disagreement.

myNotes

The Friendliest Animal

14 So, can animals be friends? Like humans, animals cooperate, play together, share resources, and protect and defend each other. Some form strong, long-lasting partnerships. But maybe there's more to friendship than that. Human brains are "wired" for complex emotions and thoughts. And humans can talk. You can share more than food with your friends. You can share ideas, dreams, secrets, sorrows, joys, worries, and hopes. Some scientists think that our ability to form friendships, to trust each other, share, and cooperate—and especially to help one another when we get nothing in return—has enabled humans to be the most successful animals on earth.

enabled If a situation enabled people or animals, it gave them what they needed in order to do something.

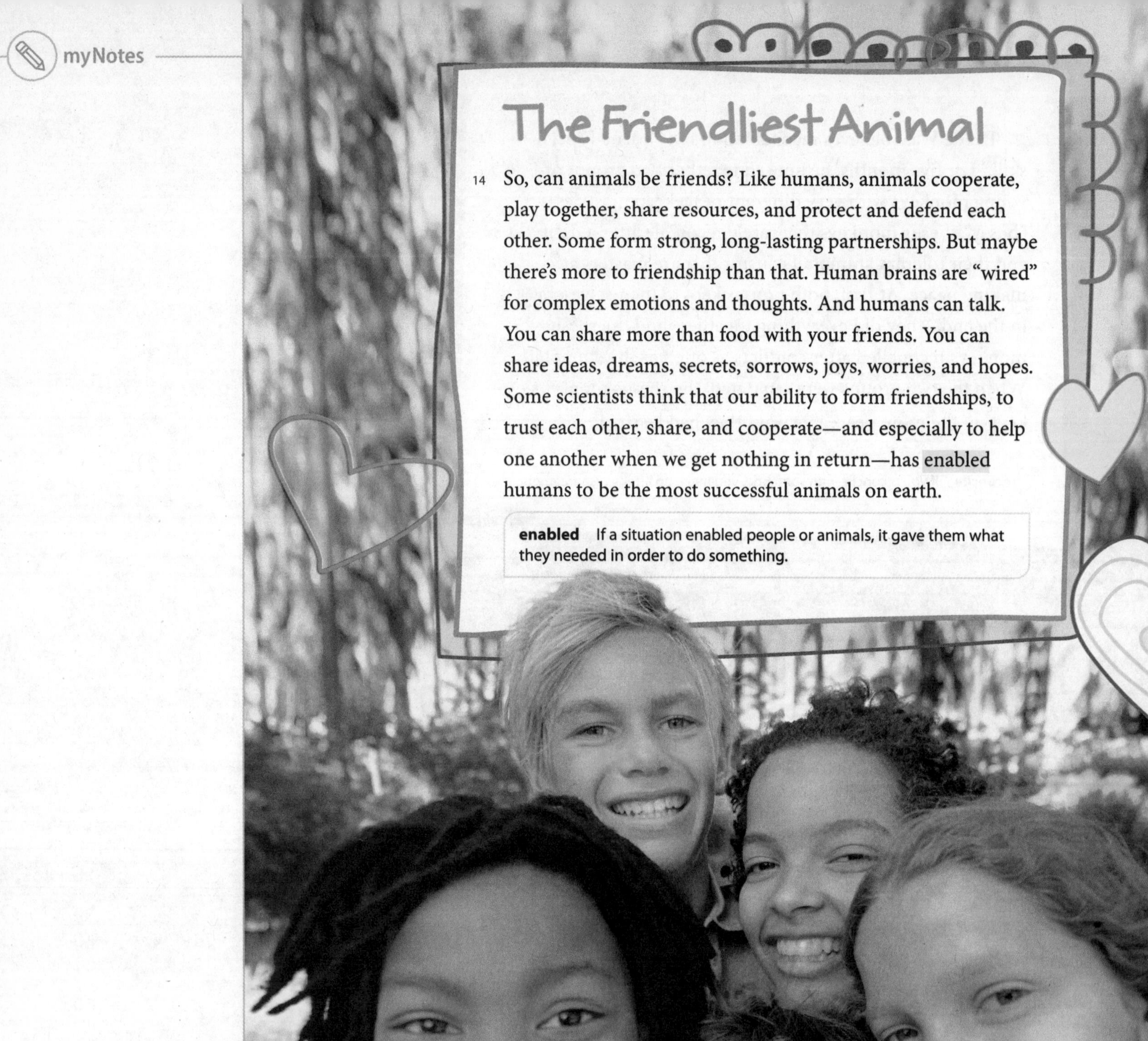

Respond to the Text

Collaborative Discussion

Look back at what you wrote on page 330. Tell a partner two things you learned from the text. Then work with a group to discuss the questions below. To explain why you answer as you do, use details and examples from "Can We Be Friends?" Choose a group leader who will make sure everyone has a chance to share his or her ideas.

1. **Reread pages 332–333. What details in the text support the idea that Owen and Mzee are friends?**

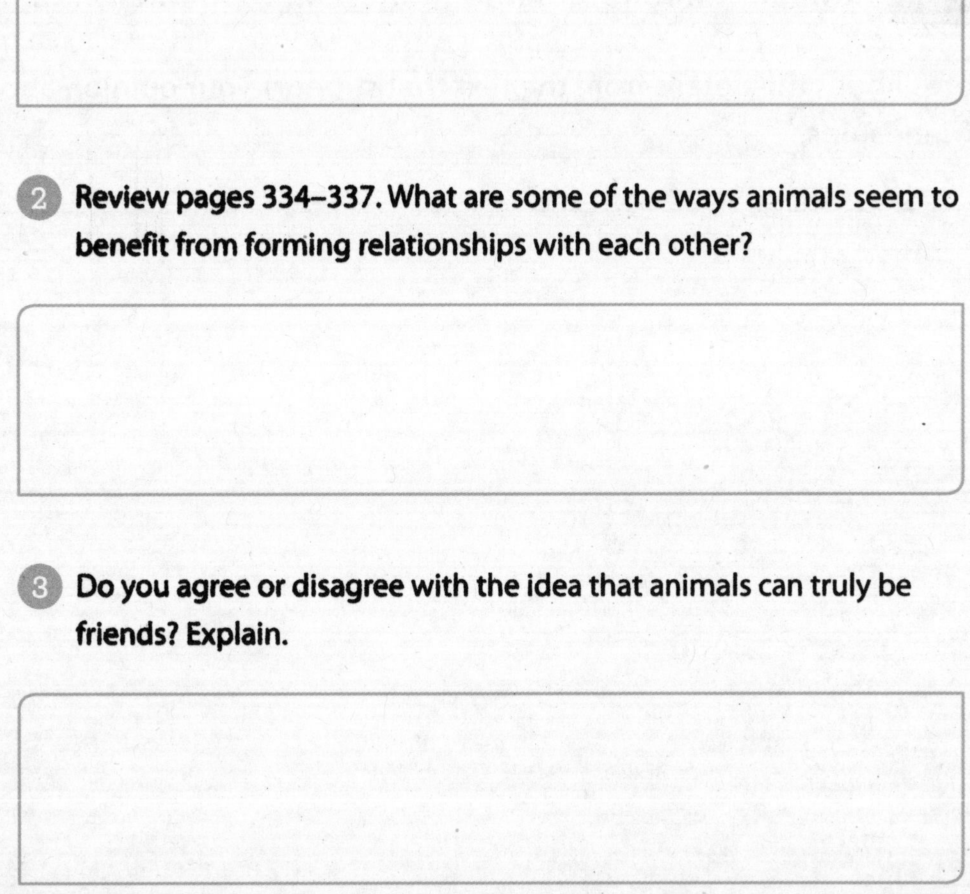

2. **Review pages 334–337. What are some of the ways animals seem to benefit from forming relationships with each other?**

3. **Do you agree or disagree with the idea that animals can truly be friends? Explain.**

Listening Tip

Give each speaker your full attention. Focus on speakers' ideas and answers, rather than on what you will say when it is your turn to speak.

Speaking Tip

Wait for your group's leader to invite you to speak, and be sure to say "Thank you!" as you begin to share your ideas.

Cite Text Evidence

Write a Social Media Post

PROMPT

Can We Be Friends? **describes observations of behavior among different types of animals. It presents scientists' opinions about whether there can be friendships among these animals.**

Imagine that you can contact one of the scientists from the article on social media. Share your opinion about animal friendships with the scientist. In your post, compare details from the article with your own observations about animal behavior. Use evidence from the text to support your opinion. Don't forget to use some of the Critical Vocabulary words in your writing.

PLAN

Make notes about the details from the text that support your opinion about animal friendships.

WRITE

Now write your social media post to share your opinion.

Make sure your social media post
☐ clearly states your opinion on the topic.
☐ compares evidence from the text with your own observations.
☐ cites evidence from the text to support your opinion.

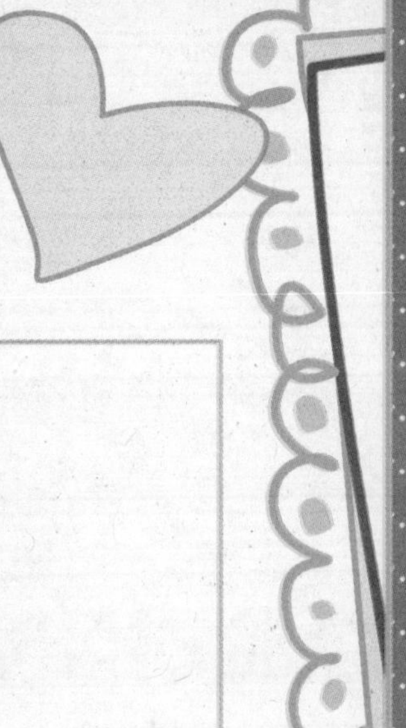

Notice & Note
Again and Again

Prepare to Read

GENRE STUDY **Multi-genre texts** blend two or more genres, such as poetry and informational text, into a single piece of writing.

- Authors of multi-genre texts use creative and fact-based writing to share information or ideas, or to convey feeling.
- A text that includes both poetry and informational text might present an artistic description of a subject and also provide related science or social studies content.
- Authors of multi-genre texts use sensory and concrete language to give readers a more complete understanding of a topic.

SET A PURPOSE **Think about** the title and genre of this text. What do you know about animal behavior in winter? What do you want to learn? Write your ideas below.

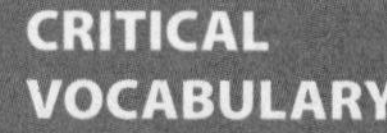

CRITICAL VOCABULARY

- migrate
- aquatic
- formations
- random
- scaled
- resume
- grasp
- resistant

Meet the Author and Illustrator: Joyce Sidman and Rick Allen

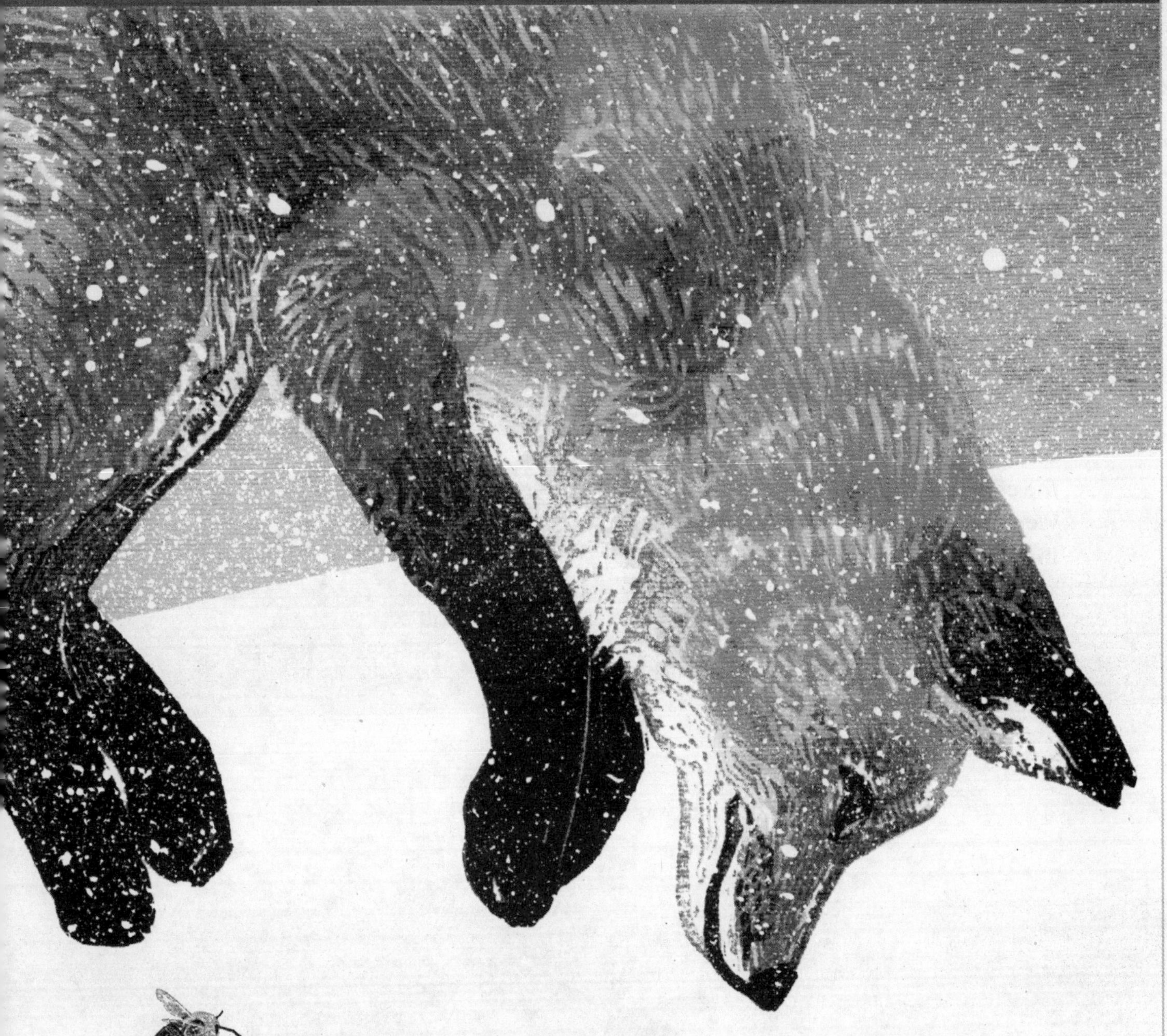

WINTER BEES

and Other Poems of the Cold

by Joyce Sidman illustrated by Rick Allen

DREAM OF THE TUNDRA SWAN

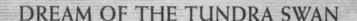

1 **Dusk fell**
and the cold came creeping,
came prickling into our hearts.
As we tucked beaks
into feathers and settled for sleep,
our wings knew.

2 **That night, we dreamed the journey:**
ice-blue sky and the yodel of flight,
the sun's pale wafer,
the crisp drink of clouds.
We dreamed ourselves so far aloft
that the earth curved beneath us
and nothing sang but
a whistling vee of light.

3 **When we woke, we were covered with snow.**
We rose in a billow of white.

4 Why do some birds migrate as winter approaches? Because the best spots for raising chicks are not always the best places to spend the winter. True to their name, **tundra swans** breed in the treeless tundra of far northern Canada and Alaska. Summer in these arctic regions—bathed in almost twenty-four-hour sunlight—is bountiful and lush. Swans feed and raise young on new shoots and aquatic plants. But when the weather turns cold, they move in huge flocks to "staging areas" along river deltas or marshes where the water is still free of ice. Here they rest and eat until the time is right for the 2,000-mile journey to warmer coastal areas such as New Jersey or California. During migration, tundra swans fly in V formations at up to 5,000 feet, and keep track of one another with a high, warbling call.

myNotes 

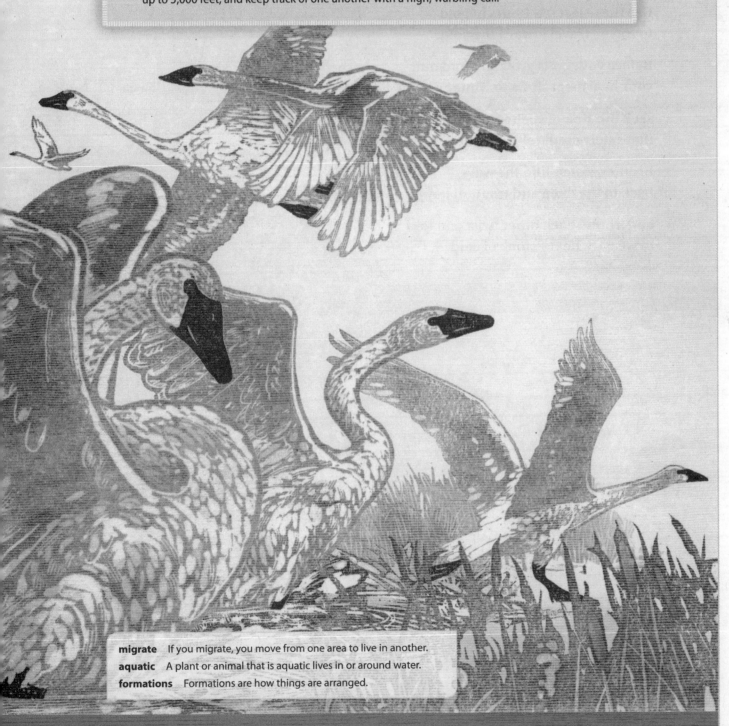

migrate If you migrate, you move from one area to live in another.
aquatic A plant or animal that is aquatic lives in or around water.
formations Formations are how things are arranged.

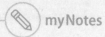

SNAKE'S LULLABY

5 **Brother, sister, flick your tongue
and taste the flakes of autumn sun.**

6 **Use these last few hours of gold
to travel, travel toward the cold.**

7 **Before your coils grow stiff and dull,
your heartbeat slows to winter's lull,**

8 **seek the sink of sheltered stones
that safely cradle sleeping bones.**

9 **Brother, sister, find the ways
back to the deep and tranquil bays,**

10 **and 'round each other twist and fold
to weave a heavy cloak of cold.**

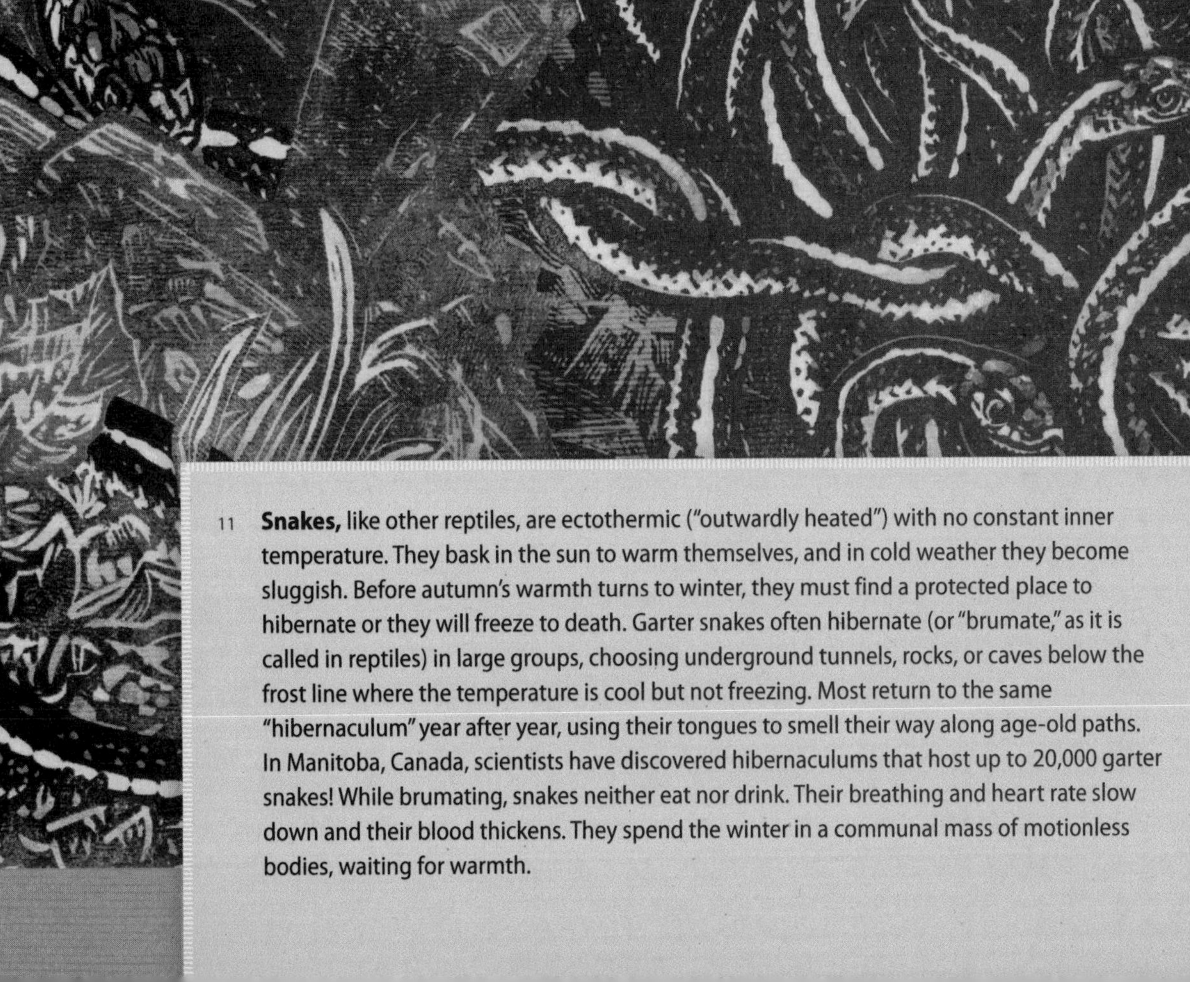

11 **Snakes,** like other reptiles, are ectothermic ("outwardly heated") with no constant inner temperature. They bask in the sun to warm themselves, and in cold weather they become sluggish. Before autumn's warmth turns to winter, they must find a protected place to hibernate or they will freeze to death. Garter snakes often hibernate (or "brumate," as it is called in reptiles) in large groups, choosing underground tunnels, rocks, or caves below the frost line where the temperature is cool but not freezing. Most return to the same "hibernaculum" year after year, using their tongues to smell their way along age-old paths. In Manitoba, Canada, scientists have discovered hibernaculums that host up to 20,000 garter snakes! While brumating, snakes neither eat nor drink. Their breathing and heart rate slow down and their blood thickens. They spend the winter in a communal mass of motionless bodies, waiting for warmth.

myNotes

SNOWFLAKE WAKES

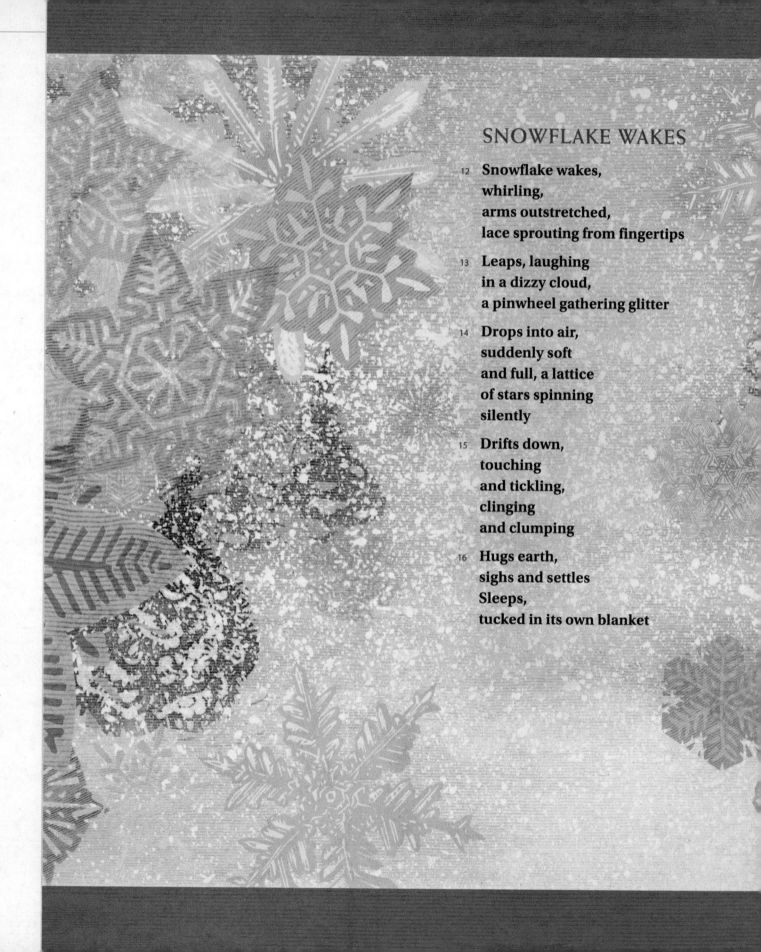

12 **Snowflake wakes,**
whirling,
arms outstretched,
lace sprouting from fingertips

13 **Leaps, laughing**
in a dizzy cloud,
a pinwheel gathering glitter

14 **Drops into air,**
suddenly soft
and full, a lattice
of stars spinning
silently

15 **Drifts down,**
touching
and tickling,
clinging
and clumping

16 **Hugs earth,**
sighs and settles
Sleeps,
tucked in its own blanket

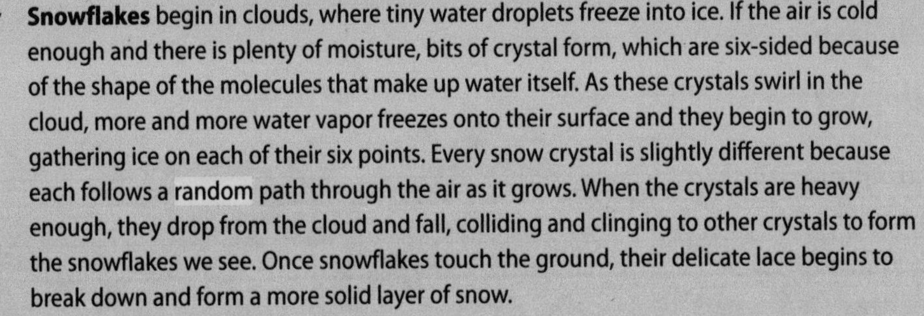

17 **Snowflakes** begin in clouds, where tiny water droplets freeze into ice. If the air is cold enough and there is plenty of moisture, bits of crystal form, which are six-sided because of the shape of the molecules that make up water itself. As these crystals swirl in the cloud, more and more water vapor freezes onto their surface and they begin to grow, gathering ice on each of their six points. Every snow crystal is slightly different because each follows a random path through the air as it grows. When the crystals are heavy enough, they drop from the cloud and fall, colliding and clinging to other crystals to form the snowflakes we see. Once snowflakes touch the ground, their delicate lace begins to break down and form a more solid layer of snow.

random If something is random, it happens without a reason or pattern.

myNotes

WINTER BEES

18 We are an ancient tribe,
a hardy scrum.
Born with eyelash legs
and tinsel wings,
we are nothing on our own.
Together, we are One.

19 We **scaled** a million blooms
to reap the summer's glow.
Now, in the merciless cold,
we share each morsel of heat,
each honeyed crumb.
We cram to a sizzling ball
to warm our queen, our heart, our home.

20 Alone, we would falter and drop,
a dot on the canvas of snow.
Together, we boil, we teem, we hum.

21 Deep in the winter hive,
we burn like a golden sun.

scaled If you scaled something, you climbed over it.

22 **Honeybees** hang together at all times, but especially in winter. They are one of the few insects in the Northern Hemisphere that remain active in freezing weather, and they do it in typical bee fashion: by gathering, sharing, and communicating. All summer they collect nectar, which they transform into honey in wax-covered cells. As the air turns colder, bees begin to cluster around their queen, who represents the future of the hive. The colder it gets, the tighter they huddle, shrinking to a football-size mass that slowly eats its way through the carefully stored honey. Hungry hive-mates farther from the honeycomb will "beg" for food, which is then passed down from bee to bee. When hive temperatures drop to dangerous levels, the outer-rim bees sound the alarm and the cluster begins to "shiver"—flex their flight muscles—to generate heat. While worker bees cycle in and out of the cluster's warm center, the queen remains at its heart, ready to resume her egg-laying at the first sign of spring.

resume If you resume something, you start again after a break or pause.

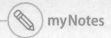

WHAT DO THE TREES KNOW?

23 ***What do the trees know?***

24 **To bend when all the wild winds blow.**
Roots are deep and time is slow.
All we grasp we must let go.

25 ***What do the trees know?***

26 **Buds can weather ice and snow.**
Dark gives way to sunlight's glow.
Strength and stillness help us grow.

27 **Trees,** the giants of the plant world, survive winter in two very different ways. Coniferous (evergreen) trees have thin, wax-covered needles that tolerate freezing temperatures and remain on the tree all year round. Deciduous (leafy) trees, on the other hand, sprout large, flat leaves every spring that are perfect for gathering sunlight to produce energy. Deciduous trees grow like mad while the weather is warm, but in winter they essentially shut down. They shed their luxuriant leaves, which would freeze anyway and suck much-needed water from the tree. The tiny buds, which will hold next year's leaves, develop a tough, scaly coating to protect them all winter. As the temperatures drop, the living tissue in the tree's trunk undergoes a process called hardening, in which cells lose water and become more resistant to freezing. An early cold snap—before a tree has hardened—will damage its branches. But after hardening, the tree will spend the winter months dry, cold, and protected—waiting for spring to swell those hardy buds.

grasp If you grasp something, you hold it very firmly.
resistant If someone is resistant, they fight against something or someone.

Respond to the Text

Collaborative Discussion

Look back at your response on page 342 and talk with a partner about what you learned during reading. Then work with a group to discuss the questions below. Support your answers with ideas and details from *Winter Bees*. Listen to and watch others closely as they share their ideas.

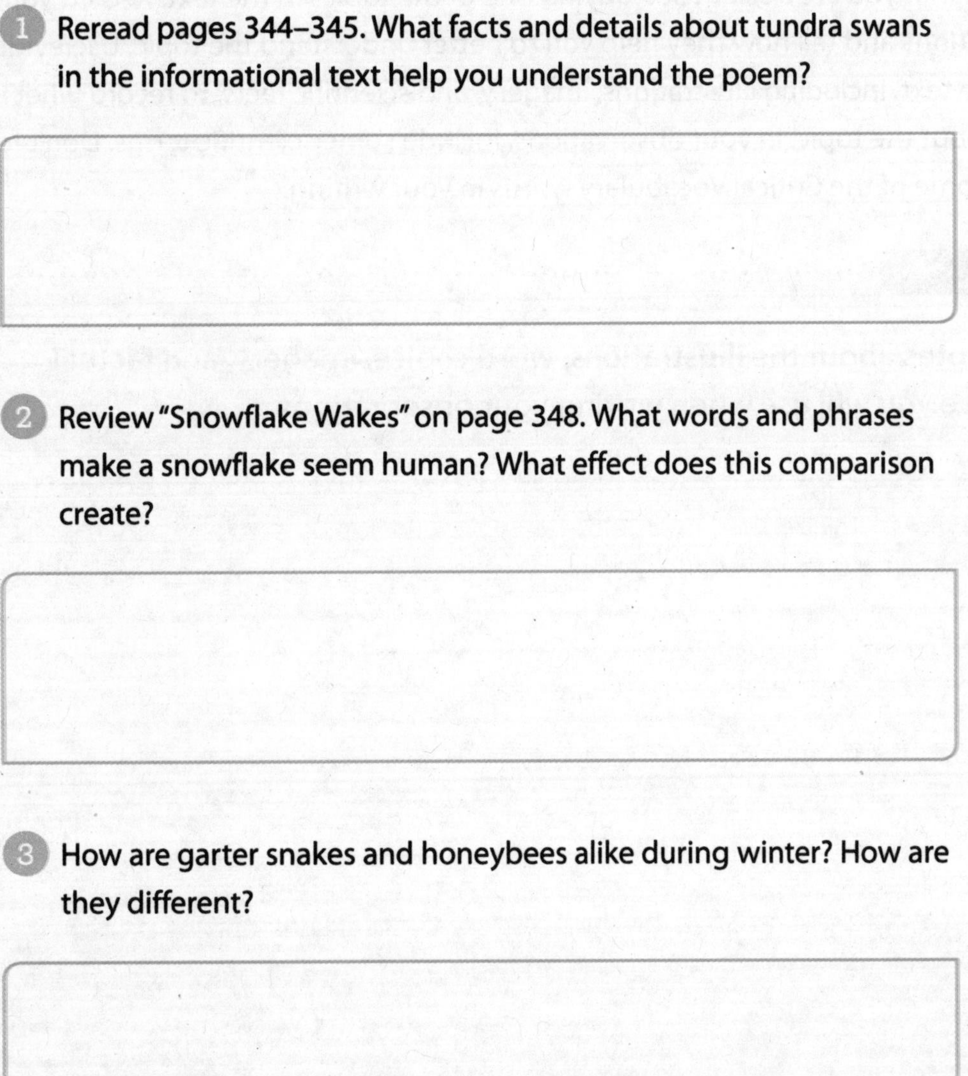

1. Reread pages 344–345. What facts and details about tundra swans in the informational text help you understand the poem?

2. Review "Snowflake Wakes" on page 348. What words and phrases make a snowflake seem human? What effect does this comparison create?

3. How are garter snakes and honeybees alike during winter? How are they different?

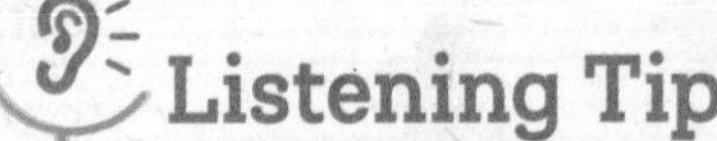

Listening Tip

As you listen, notice the facial expressions and gestures a speaker makes to support main ideas or share details.

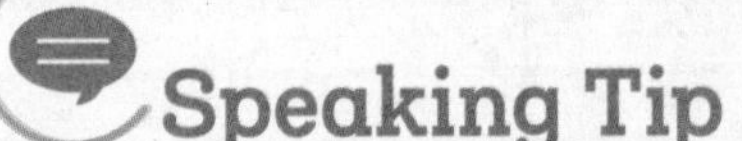

Speaking Tip

When you share ideas, use gestures and facial expressions that will help listeners understand your points.

Cite Text Evidence

Write Observations

PROMPT

Winter Bees and Other Poems of the Cold features poems paired with factual information about animals, trees, and weather in winter. Discovering the detailed information included in the text took careful study and observation.

Imagine that you are a scientist studying one of the topics in the text. Record your observations and tell how they help you to better understand the topic. Use evidence from the text, including illustrations, imagery, and scientific facts, to record what you learn about the topic. In your observations, include some scientific terms. Don't forget to use some of the Critical Vocabulary words in your writing.

PLAN

Make notes about the illustrations, word choice, imagery, and factual evidence you will use when writing your observations.

WRITE

Now write your observations of one of the topics.

Make sure your observations

- ☐ begin by identifying the topic.
- ☐ describe in detail the behaviors or changes you observe.
- ☐ use scientific terms in your descriptions.
- ☐ are based on evidence from the text, including illustrations.

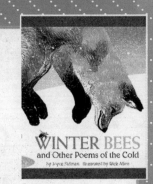

WINTER BEES
and Other Poems of the Cold
by Joyce Sidman Illustrated by Rick Allen

Performance Task

Essential Question

What can we learn about ourselves by observing and interacting with animals?

Write an Informational Essay

PROMPT Think about the animals and relationships you read about in this module.

Imagine that a local zoo or aquarium has invited students to write for its online newsletter. The newsletter's topic is What We Can Learn From Animals. Use evidence from the texts and video to write an informational essay for the newsletter.

I will write about ____________________________________.

Make sure your informational essay

- ☐ introduces the topic clearly.
- ☐ presents ideas in a logical order.
- ☐ supports ideas with evidence from the texts or video.
- ☐ uses linking words and phrases to connect ideas.
- ☐ contains a concluding statement about what we can learn from animals.

PLAN .... **Gather Information.**

What lessons do animals teach us? Look back at your notes and revisit the texts and video to spark your memory.

Plan your essay in the chart below. Write your topic and main idea. Then add supporting details and evidence from the texts and video in the boxes. Use Critical Vocabulary words where appropriate.

My Topic: ______________________________

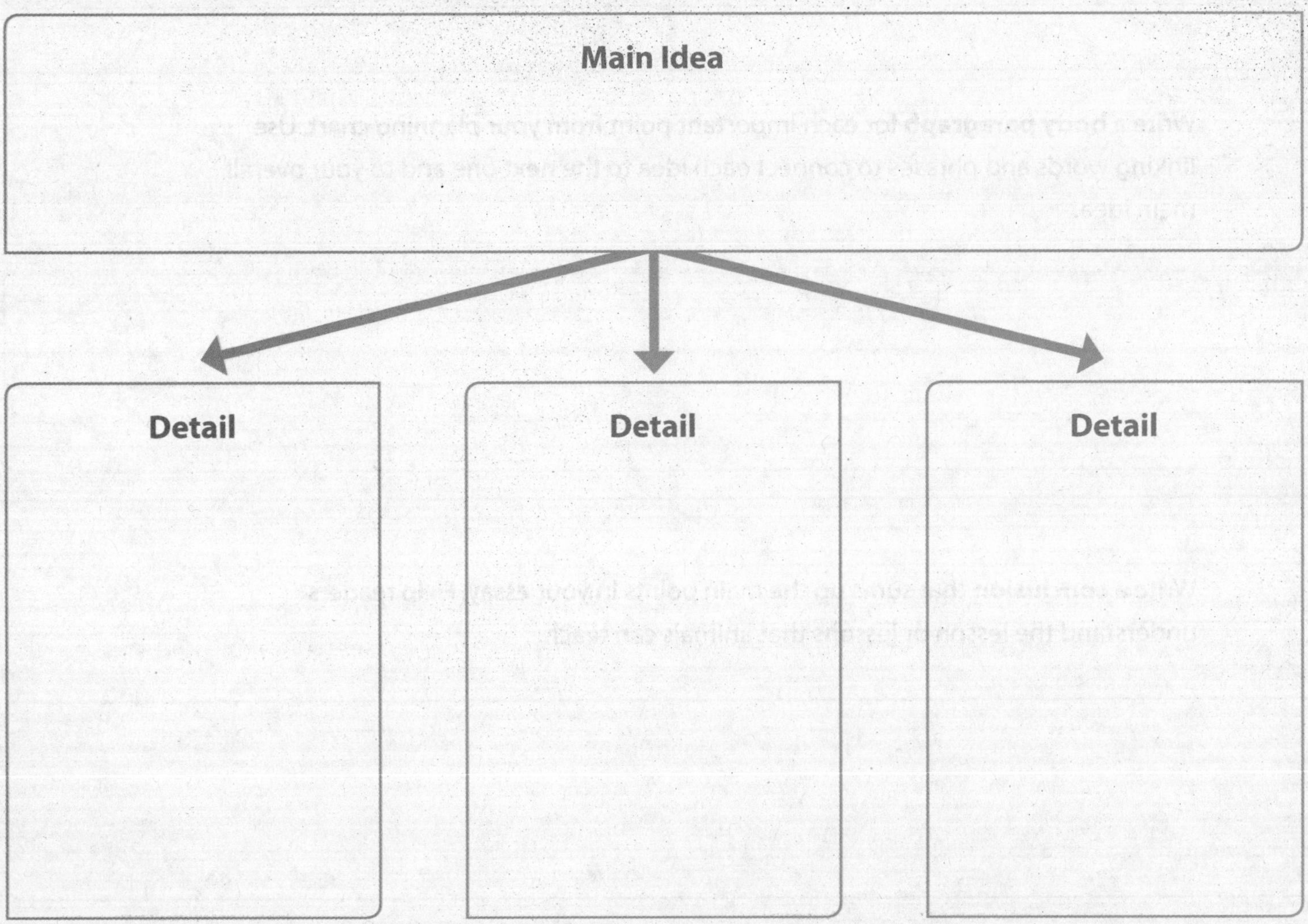

Main Idea

Detail	Detail	Detail

Performance Task

DRAFT ········ Write your essay.

Write an **introduction** that clearly states your topic and focus. Help readers connect the topic to their own lives.

Write a **body paragraph** for each important point from your planning chart. Use linking words and phrases to connect each idea to the next one and to your overall main idea.

Write a **conclusion** that sums up the main points in your essay. Help readers understand the lesson or lessons that animals can teach.

REVISE AND EDIT ······ Review your draft.

Work with a partner to revise and edit your drafts. Read each other's essay and suggest ways to make it stronger. Ask each other questions about anything that isn't clear. Use these questions to help you evaluate and improve your work.

PURPOSE/ FOCUS	ORGANIZATION	EVIDENCE	LANGUAGE/ VOCABULARY	CONVENTIONS
☐ Will my introduction get readers interested in my topic? ☐ Does each paragraph contribute to my overall main idea about learning from animals?	☐ Are my ideas presented in a logical order? ☐ Does my conclusion sum up what humans can learn from animals?	☐ Is each of my main points supported by evidence from the texts? ☐ Is all of my evidence connected to the topic?	☐ Did I define any technical or scientific terms? ☐ Did I use linking words and phrases to connect ideas?	☐ Have I spelled all words correctly? ☐ Did I use a variety of sentence types?

PUBLISH ······ Share your work.

Create a Finished Copy. Make a final copy of your essay. You may want to include photos or illustrations. Consider these options for sharing your essay:

1. Share your essay with another class as you display photos or drawings of the animals you discuss. Practice reading your essay accurately beforehand, noticing when you mispronounce a word and stopping to correct yourself. Be prepared to answer questions and respond to comments.
2. Get together with several classmates for a panel discussion about what humans can learn from animals. After you share your essays with the class or a small group, discuss ideas from the essays that are similar.
3. With guidance from your teacher, post your essay online to a science blog or web site for students.

Glossary

This glossary contains meanings and pronunciations for some of the words in this book. The Full Pronunciation Key shows how to pronounce each consonant and vowel in a special spelling. At the bottom of the glossary pages is a shortened form of the full key.

Full Pronunciation Key

CONSONANT SOUNDS

b	**bib**, ca**bb**age
ch	**church**, sti**tch**
d	**deed**, mail**ed**, pu**dd**le
f	**fast**, **fife**, o**ff**, **ph**rase, rou**gh**
g	**gag**, **g**et, fin**g**er
h	**h**at, **wh**o
hw	**wh**ich, **wh**ere
j	**j**u**dg**e, **g**em
k	**c**at, **kick**, s**ch**ool
kw	**ch**oir, **qu**ick
l	**l**id, needl**e**, ta**ll**
m	a**m**, **m**an, du**mb**
n	**n**o, sudd**en**
ng	thi**ng**, i**n**k
p	**pop**, ha**pp**y
r	**r**oar, **rh**yme
s	mi**ss**, **s**au**c**e, **sc**ene, **s**ee
sh	di**sh**, **sh**ip, **s**ugar, ti**ss**ue
t	**t**igh**t**, stopp**ed**
th	ba**th**, **th**in
th	ba**th**e, **th**is
v	ca**v**e, **v**al**v**e, **v**ine
w	**w**ith, **w**olf
y	**y**es, **y**olk, oni**o**n
z	ro**s**e, si**z**e, **x**ylophone, **z**ebra
zh	gara**g**e, plea**s**ure, vi**s**ion

VOWEL SOUNDS

ă	p**a**t, l**au**gh
ā	**a**pe, **ai**d, p**ay**
â	**air**, c**ar**e, w**ear**
ä	f**a**ther, ko**a**la, y**ar**d
ĕ	p**e**t, pl**ea**sure, **a**ny
ē	b**e**, b**ee**, **ea**s**y**, pi**a**no
ĭ	**i**f, p**i**t, b**u**sy
ī	r**i**de, b**y**, p**ie**, h**igh**
î	d**ear**, d**eer**, f**ier**ce, m**ere**
ŏ	d**o**t, **o**n
ō	g**o**, r**ow**, t**oe**, th**ough**
ô	**a**ll, c**augh**t, p**aw**
ô	c**or**e, f**or**, r**oar**
oi	b**oy**, n**oi**se, **oi**l
ou	c**ow**, **ou**t
o͝o	f**u**ll, b**oo**k, w**o**lf
o͞o	b**oo**t, r**u**de, fr**ui**t, fl**ew**
ŭ	c**u**t, fl**oo**d, r**ou**gh, s**o**me
û	c**ir**cle, f**ur**, h**ear**d, t**er**m, w**or**d
yo͝o	c**ure**, p**ure**
yo͞o	c**u**be, m**u**sic, f**ew**, c**ue**
ə	**a**go, sil**e**nt, penc**i**l, lem**o**n, circ**u**s

STRESS MARKS

Primary Stress ˊ: biology [bī•**ŏl**ˊ•ə•jē]

Secondary Stress ˊ: biological [bīˊ•ə•**lŏj**ˊ•ĭ•kəl]

A

advised (ăd•**vīzd′**) *v.* If you advised someone, you told your ideas about what he or she should do. The teacher advised her students to read the assignment carefully.

ailing (ā•lĭng) *adj.* Something that is ailing is not doing well or is getting weak. The doctor told the ailing child that he would get better soon.

ambitious (ăm•**bĭsh′**•əs) *adj.* If a project is ambitious, it is large and requires a lot of work. The ambitious project will be long and hard to do, but we believe that we can do it.

anticipation (ăn•tĭs′•ə•**pā′**•shən) *n.* If you are in anticipation of something, you are expecting it to happen and are excited or anxious about it. We waited in anticipation to play the game.

antisocial (ăn′•tī•**sō′**•shəl) *adj.* If you're feeling antisocial, you don't feel like being around other people. Usually my cat is friendly, but today he is being a little antisocial.

aquatic (ə•**kwăt′**•ĭk) *adj.* A plant or animal that is aquatic lives in or around water. Our zoo has an aquatic tank for the sea lions.

aquatic

ascend (ə•**sĕnd′**) *v.* To ascend is to go up. The hot air balloons ascend slowly into the sky.

audible (**ô′**•də•bəl) *adj.* If a sound is audible, it is loud enough to hear. The cheerleader uses a megaphone to make sure her words are audible.

authentic (ô•**thĕn′**•tĭk) *adj.* A person who is authentic is real and true to himself or herself, not fake or phony. Each of us has our own authentic smile and hairstyle.

Word Origins

authentic The word *authentic* comes from the Greek word *authentikos*, which means "genuine."

authorities (ə•**thôr′**•ĭ•tēz) *n.* Authorities are the people in charge, who have the power to make decisions or give orders. She reported what happened to the authorities.

B

bars (bärz) *n.* Bars are short sections of a longer piece of music. The musician practiced the more difficult bars of music before his performance.

ă **rat** / ā **pay** / â **care** / ä **father** / ĕ **pet** / ē **be** / ĭ **pit** / ī **pie** / î **fierce** / ŏ **pot** / ō **go** / ô **paw** / ôr **for** / oi **oil** / ŏŏ **book** /

beckoned (**bĕk'**•ənd) *v.* If someone beckoned you, she made a gesture for you to come near or follow. The crossing guard beckoned the children to cross the street.

benefit (**bĕn'**•ə•fĭt) *v.* If you benefit from something, it makes your life better in some way. I will benefit from camping with my dad because I will learn many outdoor skills.

bond (bŏnd) *n.* People who feel friendship or love toward each other have a bond that unites them. The dog and the cat grew up together and formed a close bond of friendship.

bond

C

casual (**kăzh'**•o͞o•əl) *adj.* Casual clothing is not dressy and is meant for everyday use. We like to wear casual clothes when playing outside.

chastised (chăs•**tīzd'**) *v.* If you are chastised, you are scolded severely. He was chastised for his poor behavior.

chronology (krə•**nŏl'**•ə•jē) *n.* A chronology records the time and order of a series of events. The researcher wrote a chronology of the expedition in her digital journal.

civil (**sĭv'**•əl) *adj.* A civil war is one that happens among groups of people living within a country. One of our civil rights is the right to vote, which women had to fight for.

clan (klăn) *n.* A clan is a group of people or animals who are usually members of the same family. The clan of meerkats stays close together for protection.

classic (**klăs'**•ĭk) *adj.* A classic piece of art, music, or literature is one that people appreciate for many years. Its popularity is not just temporary. Mona Lisa is a classic painting that people have been admiring for hundreds of years.

coaxing (**kōks'**•ĭng) *v.* If you were coaxing someone, you were gently trying to convince that person to do something. Dad is coaxing Tim to eat the pasta.

comprehended (kŏm'•prĭ•**hĕn'**•dĭd) *v.* If you comprehended something, you understood it. We comprehended what the author was saying as we discussed the book.

Word Origins

comprehended The base word of *comprehended* is the verb *comprehend.* It comes from the Latin word *comprehendere*, which means "together; to grasp."

consented (kən•**sĕn'**•tĭd) *v.* **If you consented to something, you agreed to it.** My dad consented by agreeing to take our dog along on our family vacation.

contagious (kən•**tā'**•jəs) *adj.* **If a feeling is contagious, it spreads quickly among people.** The excitement of the crowd was contagious as they waited for the singer to arrive.

content (kən•**tĕnt'**) *adj.* **If you are content with something, you accept it or agree with it.** Melanie was content to play with the toys the babysitter gave her.

controversy (**kŏn'**•trə•vûr'•sē) *n.* **If something is a controversy, people have strong feelings and disagreements about it.** The teenagers discussed the recent controversy about the school dress code.

conviction (kən•**vĭk'**•shən) *n.* **A conviction is a strong belief or certainty.** His conviction to climb to the top of the mountain causes him to help his friend make it to the top.

convinced (kən•**vĭnsd'**) *v.* **If you are convinced of something, you are certain that it happened.** Gretchen was convinced that she spotted a monkey during her hike in the woods.

cosmic (**kŏz'**•mĭk) *adj.* **Something that is cosmic is beyond Earth and its atmosphere.** Our vast cosmic universe contains planets and billions of stars.

cosmic

cowered (**kou'**•ərd) *v.* **If an animal cowered, it crouched or bent down in fear.** The dog cowered in the corner when he heard the thunder.

D

dedicate (**dĕd'**•ĭ•kāt') *v.* **Writers often dedicate their work to someone, usually in the first pages of the book, to show admiration or affection.** The author will dedicate his book to his sister.

deploy (dĭ•**ploi'**) *v.* **If you deploy something, you move it into position so it can be used.** The troops will deploy from the helicopter once they arrive.

desperately (**dĕs'**•pər•ĭt•lē) *adv.* **If you are trying desperately, you are trying as hard as you can.** She tried desperately to fulfill her goal of climbing to the top of the mountain.

ă **rat** / ā **pay** / â **care** / ä **father** / ĕ **pet** / ē **be** / ĭ **pit** / ī **pie** / î **fierce** / ŏ **pot** / ō **go** / ô **paw** / ôr **for** / oi **oil** / ŏŏ **book** /

diary (**dī′**•ə•rē) *n.* A diary is a daily record of someone's experiences and feelings. Charlotte writes in her diary every night.

discarded (dĭs•**kär′**•dĭd) *adj.* A discarded object is one that has been thrown away. Some of the discarded items will go to the landfill, but many will be recycled.

discriminatory (dĭ•**skrĭm′**•ə•nə•tôr′•ē) *adj.* Rules, laws, or practices are discriminatory if they leave out a group of people or treat that group unfairly. It is discriminatory for a public place to not have wheelchair access.

dominated (**dŏm′**•ə•nā′•təd) *v.* If someone dominated another, he or she was more powerful and controlled what the other did. She dominated the conversation and did not give us a chance to talk.

duets (do͞o•**ĕts′**) *n.* Duets are pieces of music that two people sing or play together. Laney and Clara prefer to sing duets instead of singing alone.

Word Origins

duets The word *duets* comes from the Italian word *duetto*. The abbreviation for *duetto* is *duo*, which means "two." Thus *duets* means "two singers or two players."

E

earnest (**ûr′**•nĭst) *adj.* If you say something in earnest, you are very serious and believe it to be true. She told the story in earnest, and her friends believed what she said.

effect (ĭ•**fĕkt′**) *n.* An effect in a piece of writing or other art is a deliberately created feeling or impression. In the mystery movie, the director used lighting to create a spooky effect.

elusive (ĭ•**lo͞o′**•sĭv) *adj.* Something that is elusive is hard to find or understand. Because gorillas are elusive animals, the species was not discovered until the mid-1800s.

enabled (ĕn•**ā′**•bəld) *v.* If a situation enabled people or animals, it gave them what they needed in order to do something. Working hard in college enabled Carmen to graduate early.

enclosure (ĕn•**klō′**•zhər) *n.* An enclosure is an area that is surrounded by a fence or walls. The rabbits looked over the yard from their enclosure.

encounters (ĕn•**koun′**•tərz) *n.* Encounters are meetings, especially those that are unplanned. During the safari, we had many encounters with elephants.

engulfed (ĕn•**gŭlfd′**) *v.* If one thing is engulfed by another, it is surrounded or completely covered by it. The old house was engulfed by flames.

o͞o **boot** / ou **out** / ŭ **cut** / û **fur** / hw **wh**ich / th **th**in / *th* **th**is / zh vi**s**ion / ə **a**go, sil**e**nt, penc**i**l, lem**o**n, circ**u**s

exception (ĭk•**sĕp'**•shən) *n.* If something is an exception, it is left out of a group or list because it doesn't fit well. The airline will not make an exception to board a late passenger.

exhaust (ĭg•**zôst'**) *n.* Exhaust is the gas that comes out of an engine as a waste product. The exhaust from the jet's engines could be seen as the plane streaked across the sky.

expanse (ĭk•**spăns'**) *n.* An expanse is a very large area of land, sea, or sky. The Great Plains is a large expanse of flat prairie land.

expedition (ĕk'•spĭ•**dĭsh'**•ən) *n.* An expedition is a trip that has a purpose, such as exploration or research. The goal of the expedition was to reach the South Pole.

exposure (ĭk•**spō'**•zhər) *n.* If someone gets a lot of exposure, he or she becomes well known by performing in many places. My sister has received a lot of exposure since she started singing on stage.

extinguished (ĭk•**stĭng'**•gwĭshd) *v.* A light that has been extinguished has stopped shining. We extinguished the campfire before we went on our hike.

F

factor (**făk'**•tər) *n.* A factor is something that affects a situation. Exercise is one important factor in staying healthy, and eating healthy is another.

falsify (**fôl'**•sə•fī') *v.* To falsify is to change a statement or document in order to make it untrue. My brother tried to falsify my parent's signature on a note to his teacher.

faltering (**fôl'**•tər•ĭng) *adj.* Something that is faltering is hesitant and not confident. She walks with faltering steps since her injury.

feeble (**fē'**•bəl) *adj.* Something that is feeble is weak. We took the feeble kitten that we found in our yard to the vet.

fend (fĕnd) *v.* People and animals that fend for themselves survive without help. The young bear cub is able to fend for himself by finding food.

fever (**fē'**•vər) *n.* A fever is a feeling of great excitement. There was a fever in the crowd before the start of the game.

flourishing (**flûr'**•ish•ĭng) *v.* If something is flourishing, it is growing and successful. The plant is flourishing under grandfather's care.

forged (fôrjd) *v.* A metal object that was forged was heated in a special furnace and hammered into shape. The blacksmith forged new shoes for the horse.

forged

formations (fôr•**mā'**•shənz) *n.* Formations are how things are arranged. Bryce Canyon National Park has many unusual rock formations.

formidable (**fôr'**•mĭ•də•bəl) *adj.* If something is formidable, it is a bit frightening but also impressive because of its size or another special quality. With his height and size, the football player was a formidable opponent.

fortunate (**fôr'**•chə•nĭt) *adj.* Someone who is fortunate is lucky. She is fortunate to have won all four games.

Word Origins

fortunate The base word of *fortunate* is the noun *fortune*. It comes from the Roman goddess, *Fortuna*. This was the goddess of good luck and fate. She was often depicted as holding a horn of plenty. Good things flowed from the horn as *Fortuna* gave prosperity to those she favored.

G

gaping (**gā'**•pĭng) *v.* If you are gaping at something, you are staring at it. The girls are gaping at the bird in the tree.

generation (jĕn'•ə•**rā'**•shən) *n.* A generation is a group of people or animals that are about the same age. The younger generation always seems to be on their cell phones or tablets.

generosity (jĕn'•ə•**rŏs'**•ĭ•tē) *n.* When people show generosity, they give something valuable or meaningful to someone. David shows generosity by sharing his tablet with his sister.

goodwill (**gŏŏd'**•**wĭl'**) *n.* When people show goodwill, they show kindness toward others and a willingness to help. She shows goodwill by helping her little sister tie her shoe.

goodwill

gracing (**grās'**•ĭng) *v.* If a photo is gracing the cover of a magazine, it is making the cover attractive. The first place winner of the dance contest is gracing the cover of the program.

grasp (grăsp) *v.* If you grasp something, you hold it very firmly. In gym class, our teacher told us to grasp the rope tightly.

grateful (**grāt'**•fəl) *adj.* When people are grateful, they are happy and satisfied with what they have. Lisa is grateful that Jack came along with an umbrella.

H

hastily (**hāst'**•ə•lē) *adv.* If something happens hastily, it happens with great speed. The children hastily left the room for recess.

hoaxes (**hōks'**•əz) *n.* Hoaxes are acts that involve tricking and lying to people. The story in the newspaper explains two hoaxes that criminals used to cheat people.

homeland (**hōm'**•lănd') *n.* Someone's homeland is the place where he or she was born. The children dressed in clothes from their homeland for the school assembly.

hybrid (**hī'**•brĭd) *adj.* Something can be described as hybrid if it is made up of two or more different things. This zebroid is a hybrid of two species, a zebra and a donkey.

hybrid

I

ignited (ĭg•**nī'**•tĭd) *v.* Something that ignited caught fire or exploded. A careless camper forgot to put out a campfire and accidentally ignited a fire in the forest.

incorporated (ĭn•**kôr'**•pə•rā'•tĭd) *v.* If items are incorporated into something bigger, they are included in it. The cook incorporated water into the flour to make dough.

incredible (ĭn•**krĕd'**•ə•bəl) *adj.* Something that is incredible is so amazing that it's hard to believe. The hikers were amazed by the incredible lost city that they saw in the jungle.

ingenious (ĭn•**jēn'**•yəs) *adj.* If an idea is ingenious, it is very clever or has not been tried before. Hannah, Carlos, and Linda had an ingenious idea to create a new electronic toy.

ă rat / ā pay / â care / ä father / ĕ pet / ē be / ĭ pit / ī pie / î fierce / ŏ pot / ō go / ô paw / ôr for / oi oil / ŏŏ book /

inhumane (ĭn•hyo͞o•**mān′**) *adj.* To be inhumane is to be cruel and unfeeling. It is inhumane to lock an animal in a cage for a long period of time.

institution (ĭn′•stĭ•**to͞o′**•shən) *n.* An institution is an organization that has a particular focus or goal. The Supreme Court of the United States is an institution made up of nine justices who have the final decision on court cases.

international (ĭn′•tər•**năsh′**•ə•nəl) *adj.* Something that is international is shared or worked on by multiple countries. The Rio Grande River is an international border between the United States and Mexico.

K

keepsake (**kēp′**•sāk′) *n.* A keepsake is something you save to remember a person or an event. This fan is a keepsake that my mother saved for many years.

M

manufactured (măn′•yə•**făk′**•chərd) *adj.* Something that is manufactured was made in a factory. Cars are manufactured in a factory.

mariners (**măr′**•ə•nərz) *n.* Mariners are people who navigate ships, such as sailors. One of the mariners guided the boat through rough waters.

master (**măs′**•tər) *v.* To master an activity is to learn to do it well. Clara is working hard to master the game of chess.

migrate (**mī′**•grāt′) *v.* If you migrate, you move from one area to live in another. Wildebeests migrate every year in Tanzania and Kenya, Africa.

migrate

misperception (mĭs′•pər•**sĕp′**•shən) *n.* A misperception is a misunderstanding. There was a misperception that the shadow was from a very tall man.

monologue (**mŏn′**•ə•lôg′) *n.* A monologue is a long, uninterrupted speech. The audience cheered at the end of the speaker's monologue about immigration.

Word Origins

monologue The prefix of *monologue*, *mono-* means "alone." The word *monologue* comes from the Greek word *monologos*, which means "speaking alone."

muffled (**mŭf′**•əld) *adj.* A muffled sound is quiet and hard to hear. Her hands block her muffled voice.

o͞o b**oo**t / ou **ou**t / ŭ c**u**t / û f**u**r / hw **wh**ich / th **th**in / *th* **th**is / zh vi**s**ion / ə **a**go, sil**e**nt, penc**i**l, lem**o**n, circ**u**s

musings (**myōō'**•zĭngz) *n.* A person's musings are his or her thoughts. Janie's musings took her back to the time when she first learned how to ski.

N

nomadic (nō•**măd'**•ĭk) *adj.* A nomadic person moves frequently and might not have a permanent home. My aunt loves the nomadic life, so she moves to a new place every few months.

nudged (nŭjd) *v.* If you nudged something, you gave it a little push. The mother elephant nudged her calf toward the watering hole.

O

obvious (**ŏb'**•vē•əs) *adj.* Something that is obvious is easy to see or understand. With her hand behind her back, it is obvious she is trying to hide what happened to her phone.

officially (ə•**fĭsh'**•ə•lē) *adv.* If something is done officially, it is approved by the government or someone in charge. After looking at the photo, the judges officially announced which horse won the race.

opinion (ə•**pĭn'**•yən) *n.* Your opinion is what you think or believe about something. In my opinion, this shirt is the best.

outcome (**out'**•kŭm') *n.* An outcome is the way something turns out or what happens at the end of it. The outcome of the storm was flooding in large areas.

outskirts (**out'**•skûrts') *n.* The outskirts of a city or town are its outer edges, farthest away from the center. The lighthouse is located on the outskirts of a big city.

P

persistence (pər•**sĭs'**•təns) *n.* A person who has persistence keeps doing something even when it is hard and takes a long time. The rock climber showed persistence as she tried to reach the top.

physics (**fĭz'**•ĭks) *n.* Physics is the scientific study of matter and energy. In physics, we studied how energy is transferred from one steel ball to another using Newton's cradle.

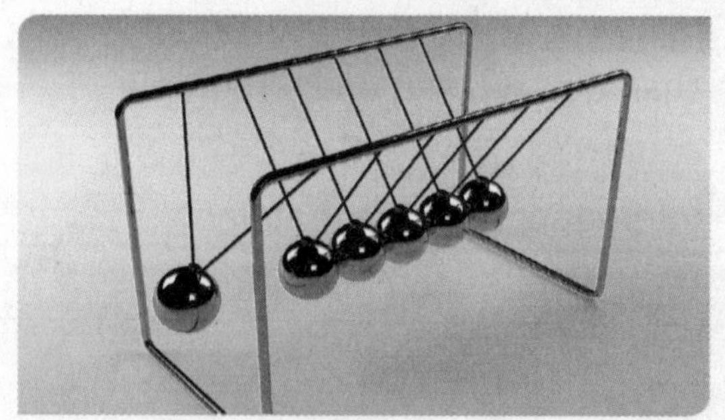

physics

possession (pə•**zĕsh'**•ən) *n.* A possession is something you own. Billy's most prized possession is his collection of toy cars.

ă **rat** / ā **pay** / â **care** / ä **father** / ĕ **pet** / ē **be** / ĭ **pit** / ī **pie** / î **fierce** / ŏ **pot** / ō **go** / ô **paw** / ôr **for** / oi **oil** / ŏŏ **book** /

posture (pŏs′•chər) *n.* **Posture is the position of a person or animal's body.** My sister has excellent posture when she is sitting at her computer.

Word Origins

posture **The word *posture* comes from the Latin word *positus*, which means "to place." Thus the meaning of the word *posture* is "to place your body in a position."**

precious (prĕsh′•əs) *adj.* **Something that is precious has value and should be treated with care.** My aunt considers the necklace to be one of the most precious items she owns.

prefer (prĭ•**fûr′**) *v.* **If you prefer something, you like it better than something else.** If Mikey had his choice, he would prefer to read an action or adventure novel.

preliminary (prĭ•**lĭm′**•ə•nĕr′•ē) *adj.* **Something that is preliminary happens at the very beginning of an event, or just before a main event.** Before the game, Camilla does some preliminary warm-up exercises.

principle (prĭn′•sə•pəl) *n.* **A scientific principle is a rule that explains how something in the natural world works.** The rotation of Earth is a scientific principle explaining day and night.

progress (prŏg′•rĕs′) *n.* **To make progress is to improve or to complete steps toward reaching a goal.** Today, the climbers made great progress toward reaching the top of the mountain.

promptly (prŏmpt′•lē) *adv.* **When you do something promptly, you do it right away.** The children left the school building promptly after the bell rang.

provoking (prə•**vō′**•kĭng) *adj.* **Something that is provoking causes a reaction, such as a thought-provoking book.** The thought-provoking story made me wonder how it feels to be an immigrant.

R

random (răn′•dəm) *adj.* **If something is random, it happens without a reason or pattern.** I performed a random act of kindness by helping my mom unload the groceries.

ransacked (răn′•săkd′) *v.* **If someone ransacked a place, he or she damaged it while looking for something.** She ransacked her room looking for her bracelet.

reconcile (rĕk′•ən•sīl′) *v.* **If you reconcile with someone, you make up after a disagreement.** Jennifer wants to reconcile with her mother after their argument.

relationship (rĭ•**lā'**•shən•shĭp') *n.* The way people feel and act toward each other is their relationship. The relationship between people and their pets can be very affectionate.

relatives (**rĕl'**•ə•tĭvz) *n.* Relatives are the people in your family. My relatives gather together for our family reunion.

relentlessly (ri•**lĕnt'**•lĭs•lē) *adv.* If something happens relentlessly, it never stops. This spring, the rain has been falling relentlessly.

reluctantly (rĭ•**lŭk'**•tənt•lē) *adv.* If you do something reluctantly, you do it without wanting to. Jodie reluctantly drank the green smoothie her mom gave her.

resembled (rĭ•**zĕm'**•bəld) *v.* If two things or people resembled each other, they looked like each other. The sisters resembled each other, but did not look exactly alike.

reserve (rĭ•**zûrv'**) *n.* Reserve is a quiet, sometimes shy, way of behaving. The shy girl shows reserve with her classmates on the first day of school.

resistant (rĭ•**zĭs'**•tənt) *adj.* If someone is resistant, they fight against something or someone. Shots or immunizations can make people resistant to many diseases.

restore (rĭ•**stôr'**) *v.* To restore something is to change it back to the way it used to be. Mr. Jones is going to restore an old house in our neighborhood.

resume (rĭ•**zo͞om'**) *v.* If you resume something, you start again after a break or pause. He fell hard, but knew he had to resume skiing until he reached the bottom of the hill.

ruthless (**ro͞oth'**•lĭs) *adj.* Someone who is ruthless shows no concern for other people and is very cruel. He dressed up as a ruthless pirate for the school play.

S

scaled (skāld) *v.* If you scaled something, you climbed over it. Serious climbers have scaled some of the world's highest mountains.

semidarkness (sĕm'•ĭ•**därk'**•nĭs) *n.* A place that is in semidarkness is partially dark. When the movie is about to start, the theater is in semidarkness.

semidarkness

sensible (**sĕn'**•sə•bəl) *adj.* A sensible rule is one that is simple and shows good judgment. It is a sensible idea to wear warm clothing when you are outside in the snow.

sentimental (sĕn′•tə•**mĕn′**•tl) *adj.* If something is sentimental, it has to do with feelings, often about the past. My mother gets sentimental when she looks through her photo albums.

sheaf (shēf) *n.* A sheaf of papers is a bundle of sheets held together. Kelly misplaced the sheaf of papers that was held together with a large black clip.

shudder (**shŭd′**•ər) *n.* A shudder is a shiver or trembling caused by fear. Sometimes strange noises at night send a shudder through me.

sightings (**sī′**•tĭngz) *n.* If there are sightings of something, people have seen it with their own eyes. Peter has experienced many sightings of the rare birds.

skeptical (**skĕp′**•tĭ•kəl) *adj.* If you are skeptical about something, you have doubts about it. Jackson was skeptical that the tower would stand.

solitary (**sŏl′**•ĭ•tĕr′•ē) *adj.* Someone who is solitary is alone. The library is empty except for the solitary girl at one of the tables.

solos (**sō′**•lōz) *n.* Solos are pieces of music that one person sings or plays alone. Theodore has performed many piano solos at his school.

solos

sponsor (**spŏn′**•sər) *n.* A sponsor helps an immigrant settle into his or her new country. Sal is the sponsor for an immigrant family.

status (**stăt′**•əs) *n.* Status is the level of importance a person or animal has within its social group. The lion had the highest status within his pride.

stereotypical (**stĕr′**•ē•ə•tĭp′•ĭ•kəl) *adj.* A stereotypical idea is one that is false about a particular group, even though many people believe it. It is stereotypical to believe that all mechanics are men.

striking (**strī′**•kĭng) *adj.* If you describe something as striking you mean it's very impressive or noticeable. The huge, colorful mural on the side of the school building is very striking.

suspense (sə•**spĕns′**) *n.* Suspense is excitement or anxiety due to an uncertain situation. The suspense of not knowing what happened made me feel nervous.

Word Origins

suspense The word *suspense* comes from the Latin word *suspensus*, which means "hovering" or "doubtful."

synthetic (sĭn•**thĕt'**•ĭk) *adj.* A synthetic item is artificial rather than natural. The nylon tent is made from a synthetic fabric.

synthetic

T

technique (tĕk•**nēk'**) *n.* A technique is way of making or doing something. The chef has an amazing technique for decorating cookies.

temporary (**tĕm'**•pə•rĕr'•ē) *adj.* Something temporary lasts for a limited time. This tent is our temporary home while we are camping.

tension (**tĕn'**•shən) *n.* A difficult situation can produce a feeling of tension, or stress. There was a feeling of tension and fear when we heard a noise outside our tent.

terrain (tə•**rān'**) *n.* The terrain of an area is what the surface of the land looks like. The terrain had some shrubs, but it was mostly rugged and rocky.

terrain

territory (**tĕr'**•ĭ•tôr'•ē) *n.* Territory is an area of land. The United States can be broken into a western, midwestern, southern, and eastern territory.

testifying (**tĕs'**•tə•fī'•ĭng) *v.* If you are testifying, you promise that what you say is true. The witness in court was testifying that the defendant was innocent, not guilty.

theoretical (thē'•ə•**rĕt'**•ĭ•kəl) *adj.* Something that is theoretical is based on a guess rather than proof. He spent many hours trying to write his theoretical idea so that his peers would believe him.

transition (trăn•**zĭsh'**•ən) *n.* In a transition, one thing changes to something else. With the transition from summer to fall, the leaves turn vibrant colors.

transmitted (trăns•**mĭ'**•tĭd) *v.* When an electronic message is transmitted, it is sent from one place to another. The office manager transmitted the document electronically.

traversed (trə•**vûrsd'**) *v.* A gate that traversed a path extended across it. A bridge traversed the small river.

traversed

tribute (**trĭb'**•yōōt') *n.* A tribute is something that is said or done to show respect for someone's work or actions. The ceremony included a tribute to the respected woman.

U

utilize (**yōōt'**l•īz') *v.* To utilize something is to use it. He likes to utilize the treadmill when he exercises at the gym.

V

vast (văst) *adj.* Something vast is very large. We looked out upon a vast field of wheat.

> **Word Origins**
>
> **vast** The word *vast* comes from the Latin word *vastus*, which means "immense."

voice (vois) *n.* An author's voice is that writer's style of expression. This author writes about moving to a new country in a voice that is very humorous.

W

will (wĭl) *n.* A will is a legal document that tells what someone wants done with his or her belongings after that person dies. The newly married couple meet with an attorney to create a will.

willful (**wĭl'**•fəl) *adj.* A person who is willful is very determined to get what he or she wants. The willful boy refused to eat the apple.

Y

yearning (**yûr'**•nĭng) *v.* If you are yearning for something, you want it very much and feel sad not to have it. Peter was yearning to go outside and enjoy the fresh snowfall.

yearning

ōō b**oo**t / ou **ou**t / ŭ c**u**t / û f**u**r / hw **wh**ich / th **th**in / *th* **th**is / zh vi**s**ion / ə **a**go, sil**e**nt, penc**i**l, lem**o**n, circ**u**s

Index of Titles and Authors

Acknowledgments

Excerpt from *Autumn Leaves* by André Gide. English translation by Elsie Pell. Text copyright © 1950 by Philosophical Library, Inc. Reprinted by permission of Philosophical Library.

"Can We Be Friends?" by Ellen R. Braaf from *ASK Magazine,* Nov. /Dec. 2005. Text copyright © 2005 by Carus Publishing Company. Reprinted by permission of Cricket Media. All Cricket Media material is copyrighted by Carus Publishing d/b/a Cricket Media, and/or various authors and illustrators. Any commercial use or distribution of material without permission is strictly prohibited. Please visit http://www.cricketmedia.com/info/licensing2 for licensing and http://www.cricketmedia.com for subscriptions.

Excerpt from *Christo and Jeanne-Claude: Through the Gates and Beyond* by Jan Greenberg and Sandra Jordan. Copyright © 2008 by Jan Greenberg and Sandra Jordan. Reprinted by permission of Roaring Book Press, a division of Holtzbrinck Publishing Holdings Limited Partnership and Sterling Lord Literistic, Inc.

Elisa's Diary by Doris Luisa Oronoz, illustrated by Byron Gin. Text copyright © Doris Luisa Oronoz. Published by Houghton Mifflin Harcourt Publishing Company. Reprinted by permission of Doris Luisa Oronoz.

Excerpt from *Finding Bigfoot: Everything You Need to Know* by Martha Brockenbrough. Copyright © 2013 by Animal Planet. Reprinted by permission of Feiwel & Friends, an imprint of MacMillan Publishing Group, LLC and Folio Literary Management.

"From Scratch" by Susie Castellano from *Cricket Magazine,* April 2006. Text copyright © 2006 by Carus Publishing Company. Reprinted by permission of Cricket Media. All Cricket Media material is copyrighted by Carus Publishing d/b/a Cricket Media, and/or various authors and illustrators. Any commercial use or distribution of material without permission is strictly prohibited. Please visit http://www.cricketmedia.com/info/licensing2 for licensing and http://www.cricketmedia.com for subscriptions.

"A Hidden City in the Andes", "Ancient Pictures in Hidden Cave", and "Silent Warriors Guard a Tomb" from *Great Discoveries and Amazing Adventures: The Stories of Hidden Marvels and Lost Treasures* by Claire Llewellyn. Text copyright © Macmillan Publishers International Limited, 2004. First published 2004 by Kingfisher, an imprint of Macmillan Children's Books, a division of Macmillan Publishers International Limited. Reprinted by permission of Macmillan Publishers International Limited.

Excerpt from *Inside Out and Back Again* by Thanha Lai. Text copyright © 2011 by Thanha Lai. Reprinted by permission of HarperCollins Publishers and Stimola Literary Agency.

"Into the Unknown: Above and Below" (excerpted and titled from *Into the Unknown: How Great Explorers Found Their Way by Land, Sea, and Air)* by Stewart Ross, illustrated by Stephen Biesty. Text copyright © 2011 by Stewart Ross. Illustrations copyright © 2011 by Stephen Biesty. Reprinted by permission of Candlewick Press, on behalf of Walker Books, London.

Excerpt from *A Movie in My Pillow* by Jorge Argueta, illustrated by Elizabeth Gómez. Text copyright © 2001 by Jorge Argueta. Illustrations copyright © 2001 by Elizabeth Gómez. Reprinted by permission of Children's Book Press, an imprint of Lee & Low Books Inc.

Excerpt from The Mighty Mars Rovers: The Incredible Adventures of Spirit and Opportunity by Elizabeth Rusch. Text copyright © 2012 by Elizabeth Rusch. Reprinted by permission of Houghton Mifflin Harcourt Publishing Company.

"Mr. Linden's Library" by Walter Dean Myers from *The Chronicles of Harris Burdick: Fourteen Amazing Authors Tell the Tales* by Chris Van Allsburg. Text copyright © 2011 by Walter Dean Myers. Illustrations copyright © 1984 by Chris Van Allsburg. Reprinted by permission of Houghton Mifflin Harcourt Publishing Company.

Phillis's Big Test by Catherine Clinton, illustrated by Sean Qualls. Text copyright © 2008 by Catherine Clinton. Illustrations copyright © 2008 by Sean Qualls. Reprinted by permission of Houghton Mifflin Harcourt Publishing Company.

Excerpt from *Play, Louis, Play: The True Story of a Boy and His Horn* by Muriel Harris Weinstein, illustrated by Frank Morrison. Text copyright © 2010 by Muriel Harris Weinstein. Illustrations copyright © 2010 by Frank Morrison. Reprinted by permission of Bloomsburg Publishing, Inc.

"Rita Moreno" from *Portraits of Hispanic American Heroes* by Juan Felipe Herrera. Text copyright © 2014 by Juan Felipe Herrera. Reprinted by permission of Dial Books for Young Readers, an imprint of Penguin Young Readers Group, a division of Penguin Random House LLC, and BookStop Literary Agency.

Excerpt from *The Secret Keepers* by Trenton Lee Stewart. Copyright © 2016 by Trenton Lee Stewart. Reprinted by permission of Little, Brown and Company, William Morris Endeavor Entertainment, LLC, and Chicken House Ltd.

"SpaceShipOne" by Matthew Stinemetze as told to Naomi Wallace from *Cricket* Magazine, January 2007. Text copyright © 2007 by Carus Publishing Company. Reprinted by permission of Cricket Media. All Cricket Media material is copyrighted by Carus Publishing d/b/a Cricket Media, and/or various authors and illustrators. Any commercial use or distribution of material without permission is strictly prohibited. Please visit http://www.cricketmedia.com/info/licensing2 for licensing and http://www.cricketmedia.com for subscriptions.

Excerpt from "Willie B.: A Story of Hope" from *The Heart of the Beast* by Nancy Roe Pimm. Text copyright © 2007 by Nancy Roe Pimm. Published by Lerner Publishing Group, Inc. Reprinted by permission of Nancy Roe Pimm.

Excerpt from *Winter Bees and Other Poems* by Joyce Sidman, illustrated by Rick Allen. Text copyright © 2014 by Joyce Sidman. Illustrations copyright © 2014 by Rick Allen. Reprinted by permission of Houghton Mifflin Harcourt Publishing Company.

Credits

6 (b) Courtesy NASA/JPL-Caltech; 9 (br) ©Perry McKenna Photography/Getty Images; 12 ©MindStorm/Shutterstock; 18 (bg) ©Wolfgang Volz/laif/Redux; 18 (bl) ©Dilip Vishwanat/Houghton Mifflin Harcourt; 19 ©Wolfgang Volz/laif/Redux; 21 (tl) ©Christo and Jeanne-Claude/Roaring Brook Press; 21 (b) ©Christo and Jeanne-Claude/Roaring Brook Press; 22 (tl) ©Christo and Jeanne-Claude/Roaring Brook Press; 22 (tc) ©Christo and Jeanne-Claude/Roaring Brook Press; 22 (tr) ©Christo and Jeanne-Claude/Roaring Brook Press; 23 (br) ©Wolfgang Volz/laif/Redux; 24 (t) ©Christo and Jeanne-Claude/Macmillan Publishing Company; 25 (br) ©Wolfgang Volz/laif/Redux; 26 ©Christo and Jeanne-Claude/Roaring Brook Press; 28 (t) ©Christo and Jeanne-Claude/Roaring Brook Press; 31 (tr) ©Christo and Jeanne-Claude/Roaring Brook Press; 32 (l) ©Christo and Jeanne-Claude/Roaring Brook Press; 33 (tr) ©Christo and Jeanne-Claude/Roaring Brook Press; 33 (cr) ©Wolfgang Volz/laif/Redux; 34 (bg) ©flas100/Fotolia; 34 (bl) ©Silvia Flores/Houghton Mifflin Harcourt; 35 (c) ©Raúl Colón; 35 (inset) ©binik/Fotolia; 36 (inset) ©Silver Screen Collection/Moviepix/Getty Images; 36 (b) ©slobo/E+/Getty Images; 37 (bg) ©flas100/Fotolia; 38 (bg) ©flas100/Fotolia; 40 ©Tibrina Hobson/Getty Images Entertainment/Getty Images; 41 (c) ©Ciao Hollywood/Splash News/Alamy; 56 (bl) ©Michael Stewart/WireImage/Getty Images; 72 ©Houghton Mifflin Harcourt; 75 ©Blend Images/Shutterstock; 76 (bg) ©Willyam Bradberry/Shutterstock; 77 (c) ©Miguel Angelo Silva/iStock/Getty Images Plus/Getty Images; 78 ©Daniel Prudek/Shutterstock; 82 (r) ©Corbis; 82 (tr) ©Fotolia; 82 (br) ©Bettmann/Getty Images; 82 (bl) ©Bettmann/Getty Images; 82 (cr) ©Bettmann/Getty Images; 82 (l) ©Andrey Kuzmin/Fotolia; 83 (l) ©Luigi Masella/Flickr/Getty Images; 83 (r) ©Datacraft Co Ltd/Getty Images; 83 (br) NASA Marshall Space Flight Center; 83 (tr) NASA Johnson Space Center; 83 (bl) ©Marka/UIG via Getty Images; 84 (bl) ©Brendan Corr/Houghton Mifflin Harcourt; 98 (bg) ©Reyaz Limalia/Moment/Getty Images; 100 ©Hiram Bingham/National Geographic Image Collection; 101 ©Kelly Cheng Travel Photography/Moment/Getty Images; 102 ©Eric Kaljo Roos/EyeEm/Getty Images; 103 ©Bertrand Gardel/Hemis/Alamy; 104 ©Bertrand Gardel/Hemis/Alamy; 105 (b) ©Sisse Brimberg/National Geographic Images/Getty Images; 105 (inset) ©Pierre Vauthey/Sygma/Sygma via Getty Images; 106 ©Keren Su/Corbis Documentary/Getty Images; 107 ©Fine Art Images/Heritage Images/Getty Images; 108 (b) ©PhotoStock-Israel/Cultura/Getty Images; 108 (t) ©Asian Art & Archaeology, Inc./CORBIS/Corbis via Getty Images; 110 ©Asian Art & Archaeology, Inc./CORBIS/Corbis via Getty Images; 112 (bg) ©Vipre77/iStock /Getty Images Plus/Getty Images; 113 (inset) ©ZUMA Press, Inc./Alamy; 114 (bg) ©Wachana Puchai/EyeEm/Getty Images; 115 (inset) ©Michele Wassell/age fotostock/Alamy; 116 (inset) ©Reed Saxon/AP Images; 116 (bg) ©Wachana Puchai/EyeEm/Getty Images; 117 (inset) ©Michele Wassell/age fotostock/Alamy; 118 (bg) ©Wachana Puchai/EyeEm/Getty Images; 119 (inset) ©Reed Saxon/AP Images; 120 (inset) ©HARAZ N. GHANBARI/AP Images; 120 (bg) ©Wachana Puchai/EyeEm/Getty Images; 122 (bg) ©Wachana Puchai/EyeEm/Getty Images; 124 (bg) Coutesy JPL/Cornell/NASA; 124 (t) ©enjoynz/Getty Images; 124 (c) ©enjoynz/Getty Images; 124 (b) Courtesy NASA/JPL-Caltech/MSSS; 125 (c) Courtesy NASA/JPL-Caltech; 126 (t) Courtesy NASA/JPL-Caltech; 126 (c) ©enjoynz/Getty Images; 126 (b) ©enjoynz/Getty Images; 127 (cl) Courtesy NASA/JPL-Caltech; 127 (cr) Courtesy NASA/JPL-Caltech; 128 (bg) Courtesy NASA/JPL-Caltech/MSSS; 128 (b) ©enjoynz/Getty Images; 129 (inset) ©AFP/Getty Images; 130 (bg) Courtesy NASA/JPL-Caltech; 130 (inset) Courtesy NASA/Handout/Getty Images; 130 (c) ©enjoynz/Getty Images; 130 (b) ©enjoynz/Getty Images; 131 (inset) Courtesy NASA/JPL-Caltech; 132 (bg) Courtesy NASA/JPL-Caltech/MSSS; 132 (inset) ©Francis Specker/Alamy; 132 (t) ©enjoynz/Getty Images; 132 (c) ©enjoynz/Getty Images; 133 (inset) ©AFP/Getty Images; 134 (tr) Courtesy NASA/JPL; 134 (b) ©enjoynz/Getty Images; 134 (bg) Courtesy NASA/JPL-Caltech/MSSS; 134 (c) ©enjoynz/Getty Images; 134 (tl) Courtesy NASA/JPL-Caltech; 135 (inset) ©AFP/Getty Images; 136 (c) Courtesy NASA/JPL/US Geological Survey; 136 (t) ©enjoynz/Getty Images; 136 (b) ©enjoynz/Getty Images; 136 (bg) Coutesy JPL/Cornell/NASA; 137 (cr) Coutesy NASA/JPL-Caltech/MSSS; 137 (cl) Coutesy NASA/JPL-Caltech/MSSS; 138 (t) ©Bill Ingalls/NASA via Getty Images; 138 (c) ©enjoynz/Getty Images; 138 (b) ©enjoynz/Getty Images; 140 (t) ©enjoynz/Getty Images; 140 (t) ©enjoynz/Getty Images; 142 ©Houghton Mifflin Harcourt; 145 ©Hero Images/Corbis; 146 (bg) ©John Lund/Blend Images/Getty Images; 146 (tl) ©Zurijeta/iStockphoto.com/Getty Images; 146 (tc) ©Houghton Mifflin Harcourt 146 (c) ©Houghton Mifflin Harcourt; 146 (bl) ©Ariel Skelley/Blend Images/Corbis Images; 146 (tr) ©Brand New Images/Digital Vision/Getty Images; 146 (bc) ©Brand

New Images/Digital Vision/Getty Images; 146 (cr) ©Brand New Images/Digital Vision/Getty Images; 147 (fg) ©Houghton Mifflin Harcourt; 147 (tr) ©ImageDJ/Alamy; 147 (tl) ©Comstock/Getty Images; 147 (cl) ©Hiya Images/Corbis; 147 (c) ©Monkey Business Images/The Agency Collection/Getty Images; 147 (bl) ©Getty Images; 147 (r) ©Monkey Business Images/Shutterstock; 147 (c) ©Brand New Images/ Digital Vision/Getty Images; 148 ©bo1982/ Shutterstock; 152 (c) ©LonelySnailDesign/DigitalVision Vectors/Getty Images; 152 (b) ©Tempura/iStock/Getty Images Plus ; 152 (t) ©Joachim Wendler/Shutterstock; 152 (bg) ©Houghton Mifflin Harcourt; 153 (tl) ©Donald Pye/Alamy; 153 (br) ©Monkey Business Images/ Shutterstock; 153 (cr) ©Jim West/Alamy; 153 (bl) ©dlerick/E+/Getty Images; 154 ©Josh Edelson/ Houghton Mifflin Harcourt; 154 ©Teresa Kennett Photography; 226 ©Jose Luis Pelaez Inc/Blend Images/ Getty Images; 229 ©AVAVA/iStockphoto.com/Getty Images; 230 ©andipantz/Vetta/Getty Images; 232 ©jgolby/Shutterstock; 236 (t) ©Keystone/Getty Images; 236 (l) ©Headhunters/Getty Images; 236 (b) ©Circumnavigation/Shutterstock; 237 (r) ©maxpro/ Shutterstock; 238 Courtesy Ivan Kravitz; 238 (bl) ©Charles Sykes/AP Images; 258 ©GeorgePeters/ DigitalVision Vectors/Getty Images; 260 (t) ©Keystone/ Getty Images; 260 (b) ©GeorgePeters/DigitalVision Vectors/Getty Images; 262 ©GeorgePeters/DigitalVision Vectors/Getty Images; 264 (bg) ©Hero Images/Getty Images; 265 (t) ©RapidEye/E+/Getty Images; 265 (b) ©Bettmann/Getty Images; 266 ©Hero Images/Getty Images; 267 (tl) ©l i g h t p o e t/Shutterstock; 267 (tr) ©picturelibrary/Alamy; 267 (bl) ©Belozorova Elena/ Shutterstock; 267 (br) ©kazoka/Shutterstock; 268 (t) ©Victor Habbick Visions/Science Photo Library/Getty Images; 268 (b) ©Martin Hospach/Getty Images; 269 ©Derek Bacon/Ikon Images/Getty Images; 270 (bg) ©kyoshino/E+/Getty Images; 270 (inset) ©Yuriy Seleznev/Shutterstock; 271 (l) ©Allkindza/E+/Getty Images; 271 (r) ©James Doss/Shutterstock; 272 (bg) ©Ralph Lee Hopkins/National Geographic/Getty Images; 272 (b) ©Martin Hospach/Getty Images; 273 ©Getty Images/Photo Disc; 274 (c) ©Savchenko Liudmyla/Shutterstock; 274 (bg) ©Hero Images/Getty Images; 274 (tl) ©RapidEye/E+/Getty Images; 276 ©kyoshino/E+/Getty Images; 278 ©Karen Seagrave/Houghton Mifflin Harcourt; 296 ©Stockdisc/ Getty Images; 299 ©Comstock/Getty Images; 300 (bg) ©Viesinsh/iStock/Getty Images Plus; ; 302 ©Nick Starichenko/Shutterstock; 306 (c) ©Eric Gevaert/ Shutterstock; 306 (bl) ©David Dirga/Shutterstock; 306 (tl) ©Lou Linwei/Alamy; 306 (r) ©United Archives GmbH/Alamy; 307 (l) ©BMJ/Shutterstock; 307 (r) ©kali9/iStock/Getty Images Plus; 308 ©Michael Nichols/National Geographic Creative; 308 (bl) ©Jay LaPrete/Houghton Mifflin Harcourt; 310 (c) ©Tolga TEZCAN/E+/Getty Images; 310 (inset) ©Wiley Perry/ Atlanta Journal-Constitution/AP Photo; 311 (inset) ©George A. Clark/Atlanta Journal-Constitution via AP; 311 (bg) ©Tolga TEZCAN/E+/Getty Images; 312 (r) ©Kimberly Smith/Atlanta Journal-Constitution via AP; 312 (bg) ©Tolga TEZCAN/E+/Getty Images; 312 (bg) ©Tolga TEZCAN/E+/Getty Images; 312 (bg) ©Tolga TEZCAN/E+/Getty Images; 313 ©Corbis Royalty Free; 312 (l) ©Houghton Mifflin Harcourt; 314 (l) ©DNY59/E+/ Getty Images; 314 (inset) ©Valsa/Stockimo/Alamy; 314 (bg) ©Tolga TEZCAN/E+/Getty Images; 315 (tr) ©Getty Images/Photodisc; 315 (inset) ©Isabelle Plasschaert/Alamy; 315 (tl) ©Tolga TEZCAN/E+/Getty Images; 316 (t) ©Zocha_K/E+/Getty Images; 316 (inset) ©BLOOMimage/Getty Images; 316 (b) ©Tolga TEZCAN/ E+/Getty Images; 317 (inset) ©Michael Nichols/ National Geographic Stock; 317 (b) ©Tolga TEZCAN/E+/ Getty Images; 318 ©sbayram/E+/Getty Images; 319 (inset) ©Rich Mahan/Atlanta Journal-Constitution via AP; 319 (bg) ©Tolga TEZCAN/E+/Getty Images; 320 (inset) ©AP Photo/John Bazemore; 320 (bg) ©Tolga TEZCAN/E+/Getty Images; 324 ©ultramarinfoto/iStock/ Getty Images Plus; 326 (t) ©Ricardo Canino/ Shutterstock; 326 (b) ©ultramarinfoto/iStock/Getty Images Plus; 328 (bg) ©ultramarinfoto/iStock/Getty Images Plus; 330 ©Fuse/Getty Images; 332 ©PETER GRESTE/AFP/Getty Images; 333 ©PETER GRESTE/AFP/ Getty Images; 334 ©Robert Muckley/Moment/Getty Images; 335 ©Perry McKenna Photography/Getty Images; 336 (bg) ©PHOTO 24/Stockbyte/Getty Images; 336 (bl) ©Arno Meintjes Wildlife/Moment Open/Getty Images; 338 ©PeopleImages/DigitalVision/Getty Images; 342 ©Andy Clayton King/Houghton Mifflin Harcourt; 356 ©Getty Images; 359 ©Pressmaster/ Shutterstock; 362 ©Brandon Alms/iStockphoto.com/ Getty Images; 363 ©Chendongshan/Shutterstock; 364 ©NikoNomad/Shutterstock; 367 (l) ©Alexey Tkachenko/iStockphoto; 368 ©Images of Africa Photobank/Alamy; 369 ©GUDKOV ANDREY/ Shutterstock; 370 ©Dotted Yeti/Shutterstock; 372 ©Khakimullin Aleksandr/Shutterstock; 373 ©Piti Tan/Shutterstock; 374 (r) ©Lynn Y/Shutterstock; 374 (l) ©Adventure Photo/Getty Images; 375 (l) ©Bplanet/ Shutterstock; 375 (r) ©Igor Marusichenko/Shutterstock